Low Rent

LoW Rent

a decade of prose and photographs from
the portable lower east side

edited and with an introduction
by kurt hollander

grove press
new york

Printed in the United States of America

Library of Congress Cataloging-in-Publication Data
Low rent: a decade of prose and photographs from the Portable Lower East Side / edited and
with an introduction by Kurt Hollander
ISBN 0-8021-3408-4
1. Lower East Side (New York, N.Y.) 2. Lower East Side (New York, N.Y.)—Literary
collections. 3. Lower East Side (New York, N.Y.)—Pictorial works. 4. New York (N.Y.)—
Literary collections. 5. New York (N.Y.)—Pictorial works. I. Hollander, Kurt.
F128.68.L6L67 1994 974.7'1—dc20 94-13395

Design: Rocío Mireles
Cover photographs: Margaret Morton, "Ivan's House, The Hill, NYC"

Grove Press
841 Broadway
New York, NY 10003

10 9 8 7 6 5 4 3 2 1

acknowledgments

Thanks go out to all those who worked on the *Portable Lower East Side* over its more than ten years of existence, including: Arthur Nersesian, Managing Editor; Allison Prete, Associate Editor; Don Kennison, Ira Silverberg, Gregory Kolovakos, Lynne Tillman and other Contributing and Guest Editors; as well as Susan Willmarth and Jon Glazer.

To Rocío Mireles and Kim Spurlock, for the look, size and feel of the mag.

To all the contributors, whether or not their work appears in these pages.

To all the subscribers and readers.

To my family, whose work appeared in almost all issues, whether as texts, artwork or manual labor. Special thanks to Mark and Luisa for their creation of a K. H. room in their Brooklyn apartment.

To Francisco Goldman for his good words.

To Morgan Entrekin, Colin Dickerman and others at Grove Press.

To the foundations and institutions who supported PLES, including the NEA, NYSCA, the Jerome Foundation, and CCNY, Humanities Division.

And, lastly, to the Lower East Side. May it some day give me back my $500-a-month, two-bedroom apartment.

LoW Rent

prose

photographs

introduction
k u r t   h o l l a n d e r

There is a genre I call Slumming Realism which appears throughout the history of literature, and whose plot structure, a U-shaped curve, is one of the most common. In works of this genre, the hero falls from grace with good society, wallows in the depths of existence in a lowly hell-hole, and then eventually finds his way back up to moral redemption and a change of clothes. This simple narrative formula can be found in its clearest form in Dante's _Inferno_, but it also crops up surprisingly often within writing about New York City. The fact that Manhattan happens to be divided between uptown and downtown (with the Upper East Side being one of the wealthiest, WASP neighborhoods, and the Lower East Side being one of the poorest, most ethnically-mixed, immigrant neighborhoods) has led many a writer to employ a heaven and hell structure in their work, with all its moral implications.

In the classic turn-of-the-century work of the Lower East Side, Jacob Riis's _How the Other Half Lives_, an upper-class European descends into the lower depths of the city to record, with photographs and text, the sins and sufferings of a people, and then goes back uptown to publish the results.

What is of special interest in this work by Jacob Riis is the convergence of literary and anthropological elements. Classical anthropology was developed primarily by white European males, like Riis himself, who descended into Africa, Australia, Latin America, and other southern (that is, downtown on a global scale) cultures, recounting, often with great narrative flourishes, the "primitive" and "exotic" qualities of the "natives." These anthropologists' moral baggage, their Eurocentrism, their crude caricatures of the "natives" have been revealed for what they are, but Riis's lurid casting of the "primitive" and "exotic" setting of the "other half" of New York City still lives on in much of contemporary culture.

The novel *Bright Lights Big City* and the film *After Hours* are just two of the many Slumming Realism products from the mid-eighties to the early nineties, a time when the City's economic "success" gave birth to gentrification and displacement, yuppies and the homeless (the sets and casts of these works), as well as big money to convert these works into American blockbusters. *Bright Lights Big City* and *After Hours* both have recourse to the U-shaped curve, the uptown/downtown moral structure, and the tourist in hell narrative, and both sensationalize beyond recognition the neighborhoods they portray. Uptown is synonymous with stability, morality, and civilization, while downtown is cast as an immoral, decadent, crime- and drug-ridden, primitive, ethnic swamp. For "uptown" ideology, what is beneath it geographically is beneath it in every other sense. On the other hand, the recent collection of downtown writing published in France entitled *The American Jungle,* and *Low Life*, the history of downtown as written by a Belgian author, both reveal how downtown New York City continues to be the happy hunting grounds of European cliches, too.

• • •

The first few issues of the *Portable Lower East Side* were typed, xeroxed, collated and stapled by hand—a self-published magazine much in the tradition of Eastern European and Soviet *samizdats*. It came from a similar history of the literary/social journals published in several languages on the

Lower East Side over the past century which focused on local concerns and reached a local readership. (The magazine was first distributed by hand to a few neighborhood bookstores, and local ads—from a Dominican restaurant, a Polish travel agency, a Kosher winery, and a Ukrainian diner—were included to help defray paper costs.)

The Lower East Side was chosen as the focus of the magazine for both personal and political reasons. It was home to my parents when they first got married, home to my father when he first got divorced, and home to me when I first left home. It was where I started writing, and what I started writing about. The Lower East Side was also home to a succession of immigrants from all over the world, who began their stay in the New World in opposition to the mainstream, politically informed by the forces that drove them from their home countries.

The use of the word "portable" in the magazine's title (a reference to the almost-fit-in-your-pocket format) proved prophetic later on as the increasing gentrification of the Lower East Side and the consequent displacement of the working-class, nonwhite community impelled the magazine to expand its focus to encompass a much greater, more diverse area of New York City. Just as the Lower East Side ceased to be the point of entry of the majority of immigrants, its role for over a century, and the new immigration began to cluster more around the City's airports (that is, Queens and Brooklyn, and parts of New Jersey), so too the magazine no longer focused solely on the increasingly homogenous (and no longer low-rent) neighborhood of its origin, but expanded to the more truly international areas of the city.

The writing published in *Low Rent* comes from a common social context (that is, low rent) rather than a social cliche (low life). In addition, the City isn't reduced and split into two opposing, color-coded, morally branded areas to serve as an esthetic backdrop. Besides a much more subtle understanding of the City's geography and ethnography, whether it is of the Lower East Side, Harlem, the South Bronx, Jackson Heights or Coney Island, there is also a pride of place within this writing, an understanding of the neighborhood's contested history. There is, therefore, no need for the writer to caricature their surroundings, no need to sensationalize something that is already quite meaningful, and no need to distort local reality beyond recognition so that it conforms to a "universal" narrative (such as Slumming Realism).

Within New York City, there are dozens of self-contained, local cultures, each large enough and aware enough to partake of its own culture, to be its own public. These publics (whether they be the Haitians, Harlem drag queens or Hasidim) have their own magazines, radio programs, and dance halls, and are well-enough informed about their own culture to reject all force-feeding of the tired old cliches spewed out by the mainstream media. Way before the term multicultural was coined (a term that is ridiculously obvious when talking about New York City, a city that has never been anything but), the *Portable Lower East Side* was publishing writers and artists from communities excluded from the mainstream culture, translating works of writers never before published in English, and revealing just how international New York City culture is.

"International" in mainstream culture usually means European. The truly international New Yorkers, that is, the Asians, Caribbeans and Latin Americans of long-standing, are seen as belonging more to minority, rather than international, culture. There is a cultural Monroe Doctrine that welcomes foreign writers and artists as part of our "backyard" culture, while refusing to recognize those on our "front stoop" (Nuyoricans can't be published as foreign writers, but they're also not gringo enough to be considered "American" writers).

For these reasons, an international series focusing on specific, local cultures was begun. The first issue of this series, published in 1986, focused on Eastern Europeans, chosen because of their long-standing presence and influence in New York City, especially on the Lower East Side. In 1988, the issue Latin Americans in New York City was published. Instead of merely tapping into the Latin American "Boom Boys" from the far end of South

America, however, this issue featured writing (published bilingually) from the most vital communities of Latinos in New York City, especially Puerto Ricans, Dominicans and Colombians. _The Portable Lower East Side_ then began a series of guest-edited issues (New Asia, New Africa and Queer City) which utilized editors from each of these communities, directing the writing toward the specific communities as much as toward the larger reading public.

From the beginning, the _Portable Lower East Side_ mixed fiction, short stories, poems, essays, photographs and artwork of the most diverse styles and from the most diverse cultures, all within the context of New York City. By focusing on the city from as many different perspectives as possible, by publishing theme issues (Songs of the City, Crimes of the City, Live Sex Acts, Chemical City and Sampling the City), the _Portable Lower East Side_ attempted to create lasting documents of an extra-literary nature. Unlike most literary journals, instead of including exclusively "literary" writing by professional writers, the _Portable Lower East Side_ sought out writing that added to the understanding of the city and its inhabitants, writing that was actually involved in what it represented, whether it be sex, drugs or crime. To accomplish this, the _Portable Lower East Side_ included work by those who are more than just writers; that is, cop killers, geographers, porno stars, musicians, political dissidents, AIDS activists, transvestites and junkies. If this is "outsider" writing, then it is "outsider" writing from an insider's perspective.

Although the _Portable Lower East Side_ concentrated on exploring the local experience, it did manage to get caught up in a national scandal. In February 1992, Representative Dick Armey, a conservative Texas Republican, and Donald Wildmon of the American Family Association in Tupelo, Miss., sent excerpts from two issues (including copies of Nan Goldin's photographs and a couple of lines of phone sex recordings from the Live Sex Acts issue, and four lines of poetry from the Queer City issue—in plain violation of copyright restrictions) to all members of Congress and to then President George Bush, claiming that they contained obscene and blasphemous material. Immediately after, amidst Patrick Buchanan's attacks on the NEA for funding such trash, John E. Frohnmayer was forced out of his position as director of the National Endowment for the Arts, and the *Portable Lower East Side* had its funding for the Live Sex Acts issue retroactively nullified, losing the possibility of receiving future funding due to nonfulfillment of the grant.

This fifteen minutes of mini-scandal resulted not only in the loss of funding from the NEA, but proved to be a quick education in how the US mainstream media works. The sensationalist soundbite dominated, with attention being focused on a few lines of poetry, while any mention of the specific contents of the issues, or the magazine itself for that matter, seemed superfluous, even though the U.S. Supreme Court's definition of obscenity stated that the work must be judged *in its full context*. In the end, I gave up trying to fight against the pinhead perspective of the press which seemed to serve perfectly the interests of the conservative watch-dog groups, and went on with the magazine. Then, as soon as Clinton appointed an interim director to replace Anne-Imelda Radice, the *Portable Lower East Side* received one year of back support, a grant for the following year, and went on to finish more than a decade of publication.

Low Rent is a selection of prose and photographs from the fourteen issues of the *Portable Lower East Side*, a document of a decade in the life of a city, and proof of how great culture tends to follow low rent.

Brooklyn/Mexico City 1994

the point-blank page
m a n u e l   r a m o s   o t e r o

> *Love is a punishment. We are condemned*
> *for not having resigned ourselves to solitude.*
> Marguerite Yourcenar

I met Sam Fat in a bar on the Lower East Side, Saturday night, December 31, 1983. I had never seen him before and I would never see him again after arguing long and loud over the reason of our meeting. I had made an appointment with him after stumbling upon his ad in the New York Telephone Hispanic Yellow Pages (1983-84):

> Sam Fat
> *Private Investigator*
> Specialist in:
> *Missing Persons*
> *Custody and Recovery of Children*
> *Lost Valuables*

I won't deny that his name impressed me, that it conjured up Chinatown's crowded streets, forever drenched in mystery, fog trapped beneath lampposts

manuel ramos otero was born in Puerto Rico in 1948 and died in 1990 of AIDS. His published work includes *Pagina blanco y staccato*, a collection of short stories from which this story is taken, and the novel *Invitaciones al polvo*.

transformed into dragons and telephone booths into colored pagodas. I confess that I could almost smell the fetid fumes of sewers clogged with rotting shrimp and fish when I repeated his name, and perhaps I even imagined that a private investigator might know of an opium den where my lame Chinese stereotypes, derived from Charlie Chan and other black and white Hollywood films, would go unnoticed. His name had passed in front of my eyes like a black butterfly alighting on a postcard from overseas, completing its tragic destiny.

I recognized Sam Fat (or he recognized me) in the preciseness of punctuality. Accustomed as I am to arriving late for all appointments and never carrying a watch, I got out of the subway at Canal Street (the main strip of Chinese businesses) and walked leisurely, as in the cliche that Chinese take their time at every crosswalk because they enjoy the pleasure of arriving more than the finality of arrival. I wanted to make sure that the address of Sam Fat given in the Yellow Pages actually existed—a simple shingle with his name would be proof enough. The address turned out to be real, but in place of a private investigator's cramped office there was a Greek pizzeria. The number of the public phone inside coincided with the number at which I had called Sam Fat. No one likes to be made a fool of. I was about to ask the blond cashier if she knew this Sam Fat, but then I pictured him sitting at the formica table closest to the telephone, day in and day out, reading the same Chinese porn magazine, resembling Buddha in his roundness and in the mystical patience of someone out of work who from time to time is thrown a dollar. Sam Fat had to change my life: a Dominican had told me in the course of a Tarot reading, "I see a Chinese man in your future" and, even worse, a Chinese man dressed in white and seated atop a mountain of mist had pursued me in my dreams. What bothered me most was the New Year's Eve celebration outside and the urge people had to burn it alive with fireworks. There was one possibility; although Sam Fat was an impostor, he might still keep our appointment. I turned left on Mott Street, crossed Little Italy, and made my way to a bar on Avenue A called Aguas Buenas Social Club.

I entered beneath a surge of blue neon light. The bar was almost empty. I looked at the clock: two minutes to eight. Two men were drinking at the bar and a third, leaning against the juke box, had just put on a Carmen Delia Depiní song: "... *es mi corazón ... una nave en el turbulento mar ... desafiando la fuerte tempestad ... de eso que llaman amor. ...*" I asked the bartender for a rum and anis on the rocks, trying to forget the *bolero* and counteract the bad habit Puerto Rico has, every time the word *mar* is mentioned, of hounding those who've left the island. At eight exactly, the bathroom door gently slid open and a man walked up to me.

If it wasn't for the fact that I'm a person given to forebodings, I would've continued drinking like someone resigned to his fate. The man stood next to me, almost brushing against my knee with his body, lit a Marlboro and offered me one. Addicted as I am to Benson and Hedges Menthol, I said no, nor did I let him light my cigarette, for in that very instant I remembered that a *santero*, son of Changó, had told me that it wasn't safe to share fire with anyone, but he insisted, making me his accomplice and forcing me to buy him a drink. I believe he asked for Chivas Regal straight up, which reminded me of my dead father playing dominoes on Sundays at my distant town's beach. We looked at each other's face. He wasn't what I had expected him to be—a man with a black felt hat, a half-moon shadow drawn across his face—quite the opposite. He had shoulder-length, jet black hair, like a porcupine; black oblique eyes that hinted at the possibility of a Mongol nomad; a small, round nose, flecked with beads of sweat which kept him from looking too serious; meaty lips too humid for the New York winter; and, even worse, teeth so white and perfect they overpowered a smile that was sensual but lacked intimacy. He was stout, maybe 5'7", and flexible despite his large, fat hands, but most impressive was the color of his skin, too tan to be Tartar and too yellow to be African. His faded jeans accentuated the tightness of his muscles, and the plaid shirt hugged his torso. He was attractive and timid, nervous and casual, curious. He treated me like an old friend (or enemy) and only his voice lightened the imperial roughness of a Chinese in exile: "Glad you came. I'm Sam Fat."

That line was enough for Sam Fat's history and my own to become confused in the night with its bond of millennia. The key to every mystery has always been in hidden details that lead to the final solution, and in being more diabolical than the devil in order to reinvent Hell. When the case under examination is a crime, it's worth doubting from the start all that can be doubted. A murderer is discovered in the corpse as much as the future corpse anticipates the deadly maneuvers of the murderer. The victim always designs the way in which they will become the victim. This moment shared with Sam Fat exchanging drinks and the dispersing of the grey curtain of nicotine had situated our time together in the fatal crossing of characters who meet each other on the same blank page. Four centuries of not having seen each other was insufficient to deny us this meeting whose common ground had been a dream, a phone call and a bar. Every human being has a different scent. I imagine that he smelled danger in me, as I smelled in Sam Fat the suspicion that he was now to be the Inquisitor and I the persecuted witch. He had already begun the chase in an unexpected way: his breath coiled around my neck like a lethal brew of Siete Amarres, his right arm climbed up my back like a Seme Constante potion, his crotch perched on my left thigh like the Great Beast's Claw... and yet, nevertheless, Sam Fat had seen in me a stone for his Oyá altar. Outside, in the frozen night streets, rainy lightning roused his spirit; I remember having seen the lightning bolt like a glass pointer on the blank page of his story, scratching in regular intervals.

It's quite possible that I imagined all this. When I looked at the bar's clock, I corroborated that barely a minute had passed. An electrical reading of Sam Fat's fingertips would have been needed to determine exactly what his emotional state had been during the moment we shook hands. The other men at the bar had seen us, if at all, as a dark mass of solitude recovering from old hates and resentments, establishing our love (or friendship) in the nostalgia of the year that was ending and packing its suitcases to disappear off the face of the earth. But all maps distort the historical geography of man. The proof was that our story, and the course of that night, could only take place on the face of New York. Faces, just like snowflakes or fingerprints, are infinite. Therefore, where on the map were we really standing? In North American maps, the Southern Hemisphere slowly dips beneath the translucent icebergs of Antarctica while the Northern Hemisphere soars like a bald eagle, with China split between East and West. All Chinese understand that the word _China_ means "central country." Sam Fat neither knew nor cared. But he knew other things, things which made me see him as a yellow cat watching over his prey in a dead-end alley. "You're a writer . . . or worse: a dark poet born in the Year of the Rat. You're almost dead. How much time do you have left to fill in your blank page?"

A single blank page wasn't evidence enough that I was dying. The most persistent evidence was (and continues to be) the momentary sensation of a physical dislocation of time, a molecular displacement of body and memory, the other's face as tattooed by hate as one's own, making the synthesis of what one was and what one no longer is impossible; the twin brother of Christ, forgotten by all later accounts, who robbed Christ's decomposed corpse and went from town to town, telling the apocryphal story of his resurrection and ascent to heaven; the castrated youth that so often knew the delirium of being suckled by Pontius Pilate; the first employer of Christ, destined to be called by future centuries a perfect Christian servant; he who lent his face and body so that Michelangelo could eternalize my story in the Sistine Chapel cupola; Manuel, the loyal Jewish convert initiated in the horrors of the Holy Mother Catholic Apostalic and Roman church of Spain; soldier in the Christianization of the copper-colored savages and black slaves of the New World. For many years I had been keeping everything in readiness for this encounter, but never did I imagine that I would need a cabalistic spell to avoid the pain, to repress memory and imagination. To write about it would be easy: the little machine was ready like a compass that traces onto paper its imitation of death; the university had left me without work until the sharp chills of a feverish night ended and my blood was no longer contaminated, until the tumors in my lungs dissolved like pus-filled blisters and the purple sores of Karposi Sarcoma were no longer lethal forecasts of a new death; and, in the end, four bottles of Liquid Paper were still left to erase the words that weren't relevant. I needed only to transfer to the page the restless monologue that, with the luck of suddenly becoming the hunted, had changed into dialogue. At times, it seemed as if the words had been used up and that I was going round and round without end, and each time the blank page looked at me from its other side I was invaded by the challenge of a distant dialogue, as if all the unknown dead had come together to invade my world and take me into their ranks before I could document another funeral. Wearied by reincarnation, I had been embraced by my own death several times; a long-planned suicide with Tuinales ended with me waking up hallucinating in a Harlem hospital that had bars on the windows, tied to my bed while the hospital television set broadcast, step by step, the invasion of the moon by Americans, July 20, 1969, the very day of my birthday, my memory repressing the smell of blood, serum, ammonia disinfectant and stained sheets; a fatal fall from a balcony in Old San Juan, too moth-eaten and worn-away by the sea air to be able to stand anything other than the sea's eternal vigil, later translated into a cast on my leg, into crutches, into poems dug up from an old cemetery where the sea would invade from time to time until the names on the stones were eaten away, into an eternal limp and a pain in my spine where hardly any blood circulates, knowing with scientific certainty that it had all been necessary to continue feeding my total enslavement to words, and that only in words could I realize my life's work. I remembered that exactly 15 years and 4 days before, I had come to a blizzardy New York without knowing a soul. I found a job as an assistant social worker at the Bronx Lebanon Hospital, on streets that had been Jewish but by then were inhabited by Puerto Rican immigrants and Southern blacks of whom I didn't understand a single word. But with words everything is a matter of time, and in this way people recognize themselves in others. And then there's New York, an essential part of the continent, heart of an empire that doesn't seem like one, where the commonplace of exile predominates, men and women transplanted as fugitives from distant lands that are never mentioned in the local papers, men and women who still believe that they are living in New York on borrowed time (a pact with the devil) so they can later return to the home port of a collective memory: Puerto Rico, Jamaica, Guyana, Grenada, Dominican Republic, Colombia, Panama, St. Thomas, Haiti, the South.

I wasn't far from the truth of Sam Fat. His eagerness for the unknown gave him away. His first name seemed an imitation of Sam Spade, the infallible hero of Dashiel Hammet's detective stories, while his last name gave the exotic touch of a genuine unemployed resident of the Promised Land. I managed to cut him off a little, speaking to him of our complicity with logic, psychoanalysis and history, hoping the story would unite us, for better or worse. I attacked him with his own words, overly literary and poetic, worried by the magic symbols in which strangers set the rules, only to disappear later into the veiled delirium of dried poppies. I convinced him (I believe) that the perfect crime was the most remote, where the executioner arrives, without knowing it, to face a victim that has been waiting for him in order to pay him back in kind. But Sam Fat had much better aim than I: "A man doesn't drink vodka because he wants to be Russian, but because he wants to get drunk."

Sam Fat was not drunk, nor was he Chinese. The story I'm about to relate might have another version, although I doubt it would be significantly different. In 1948, when the United States invaded Shanghai under the pretext of saving democracy, a Chinese cook named Ting Yao Fat escaped to the States, buying his passage and exit visa with a shipment of opium which the Marines accepted as payment. It seems that, trying to protect his own life, he only gave them part of the shipment, assuring them that as soon as he was safe and sound in San Francisco he would hand over the rest. Ting Yao Fat didn't keep his promise. As soon as his feet touched shore, he disappeared off the face of California. A few days later he arrived in New York and easily lost himself among the Chinese of Chinatown. He found work as a cook in the Foo Kai Tea Parlor where the kitchen served the dual purpose of a hideout and as a base to establish contacts and sell the opium he had brought from Shanghai. Ting Yao was a young man and, unlike the majority of Chinese in exile, he didn't want to remain stuck in the streets, hangouts and neighborhoods of his people. He had learned English in the British Embassy in Shanghai, working as assistant chef in the kitchen. He was an adventurer, and his immediate goal was to get to Cuba where his uncles' family had been living for several years and ran a business of prostitutes and drug trafficking in Havana. A few weeks after his arrival he met Milagros Candelas, a Puerto Rican who worked as a seamstress in a brassiere factory in the Garment District. I doubt Ting Yao was unaware, from the time he first met her, that Milagro's U.S. citizenship would guarantee him residency and thus facilitate his trip to Cuba; the speed with which they married says as much. But the possibility can't be ruled out that they loved each other, especially when it's understood that neither had any relatives in the city and that the need of a family is fundamental, as much for the Chinese culture as for the Puerto Rican. They moved to a small apartment on Suffolk Street, on a block in which Chinese and Puerto Ricans predominated. It might be that the very act of marriage did him in, thanks to the false documents he produced for the wedding. In any case, one morning Milagros had a visit from two Americans in military uniform who demanded to be told the whereabouts of Ting Yao Fat. Unaware of the opium trafficking of her husband, Milagros identified him as her husband and added that their marriage was legal and that she was pregnant. The next morning, the police found the mutilated corpse of Ting Yao beneath the Brooklyn Bridge; among his few possessions they found a plane ticket with the destination New York-Miami-Havana. Milagros would not have been able to identify the dead man if it were not for the map of China tattooed in the very center of the corpse's chest.

Due to the murder of Ting Yao, Milagros moved to the Lower East Side (or Loisaida, as the Puerto Rican's in the neighborhood call it); in a short while a baby was born in Bellevue Hospital and she had him baptized

Samuel Fat. She lost her job at the factory but, even more, the difficult task of raising her son and knowing that she was on her own in New York compelled her to depend, for subsistence, on Welfare. From the moment she saw the newborn, she knew the boy would suffer the agony of rejection. Sam Fat had inherited from his mother her dark skin; the Mongolian features and self-absorbed nature were from his father. The Chinese would never accept him as one of their own (not only because his mother wasn't, but because no one was there to teach him either the language or the traditions); the Puerto Ricans tried to be more tolerant, but the nickname they gave the boy before he learned to talk, *Chino*, indicated the abusive tone of rejection. Milagros was able to buy an ancient, rusty Singer on installment and began to sew for the women of the neighborhood. She didn't want to go back to the factory right away, for her greatest pleasure was being witness to every second in the growth of her son. Between stitches she taught him Spanish, the only language she really knew, and told him stories of the country she came from and to which they would one day return.

Milagros had been born on San Sebastian Street in Old San Juan, near the Colegio de Párrulos. Her mother made her living washing and ironing clothes, but like all women on her side of the family, she had spiritual powers and was devoted to working the ouija board for those who asked for her disinterested help. In the sacred altar of her home, locked behind latches and hooks, the spirits of the light lived in harmony with their African deities, the elder *orishas* disguised as Catholic saints to avoid persecution and death for practicing witchcraft. The mother of Milagros was named Madama Candelas and her name openly acknowledged a distant offense. Milagros' grandmother had been Milagros Candelas Humphreys Johannes, a daughter of Yemayá, as had been her mother, the mother of her mother, and so on down to the first woman who had been initiated in the Valle de Ifé, before a Dutch slave ship had uprooted them to the Caribbean and she wound up being born on the island of Curaçao and then, in nineteenth century Puerto Rico, ended up being a slave of the sugar machine of Vieques. With joy and white handkerchiefs flapping in the breeze she had said good bye to the Spanish who left with their tail between their legs in 1898, only to welcome with the same handkerchiefs and the same joy the Americans who arrived in Vieques that same year. She went to Vieques to cut cane, but she didn't forget revenge, either; she knew that only a stretch of water separated her from the island where one of the daughters of Yemayá had been burnt at the stake on Mondongo Street in the sixteenth century, on the nefarious islet of San Juan Bautista, where the bishop Nicolás Ramos de los Santos, supreme representative of God and Spain in the dirt-poor military colony of Puerto Rico, had condemned the prisoner to flames. Madama Candelas Humphreys Johannes, who could curse in Creole without anyone understanding a word, was concocting her fate, little by little; in a white handkerchief she kept the pebbles of an African river, passed down from woman to woman, from century to century, and she didn't untie the handkerchief or touch the river pebbles until the day she was able to live in peace in a home of her own. From that time on, in the house of Madama Candelas Humphreys Johannes on San Barbara Street in Vieques, forecasts for the townspeople were conjured up by Spanish tarot cards already marked with the spilt blood of Gypsies. The house was (and perhaps still is) in El Cañón, the prostitute district: made of wood, it had a ceiling of zinc sheets, four doors, was mounted on stilts, and in the back had a cemetery watching over it. She married one of the Spaniards who decided to stay in Puerto Rico after 1898, but after she gave birth to a daughter her husband left to join the ranks of General Franco in the Spanish Civil War. She called her daughter Madama, and gave her the name Candelas so she would never forget the murder of one of her mothers who had been sacrificed at the stake. Everything had already been written in the Chart of Ifá when Madama, barely turned 13, was bartered in marriage to a certain Benzol, constable of Central Iqualidad. Benzol offered Madama Candelas Humphreys Johannes a cement house and assured her that he would take care of Madama's education. He kept his word, but he never understood Madama's silence. He took her to San Juan, not realizing that he had accomplished her goal, living on San Sebastian Street without knowing that for Madama it was still called Mondongo Street. There Milagros was born. Two years later Benzol died of uremia, leaving as inheritance a collection of useless accounting books. But they remained protected by other, greater forces: the shells had revealed that Milagros was also a daughter of Yemayá. From her childhood, Milagros worked as a servant for Señora Albanese of San Justo Street, who was dedicated to providing charity to the poor and teaching them the righteous life. They sent Milagros to the Lincoln School, erected in the exact location where the Bishop Nicolás Ramos de los Santos had condemned so many blacks to death at the stake. Even after so many centuries, Milagros could still smell the burnt flesh. She was around 15 when Madama Candelas died of gangrene, having lost a hand in the cylinder of a washing machine. It was the last years of World War II, the Puerto Rican emigration was at its height, and Milagros went off to look for work in New York. She came to the city with a suitcase of her belongings and seven African necklaces which Madama Candelas had made before her death. When she arrived she found the home of one of her mother's god-children and there she lived until she finished her _yabó_ and became initiated in _Santería_. From then on she officiated over ceremonies and was protectress of several devotees. Through _Santería_ she returned to the roots of her spirit and the history of her body. Her people had begun the pilgrimage from Nigeria and had lost their shadows when the European slave ships sacked the Yoruban villages, chained their bodies to the sea's tide and brought them to the islands. On these islands they had to come to grips with eternal night and they learned to survive on yucca and water, and to cross themselves with holy water while dreaming of Olodumare. Thanks to Yemayá, who would speak through her mouth, she conjured up the memory of a Caribbean where blacks were tortured by starvation and the branding iron to make them cut sugar from the earth, where black slaves were forced into baptism and marked forever with a Christian name that bore witness only to their wretchedness and struggle for survival. The day she found out she was pregnant, Milagros untied the knot from an old white handkerchief she had inherited, caressed the grey pebbles of an African river and knew that she would give birth to a boy, a son of Orunla, destined to be a *babalao*.

• • •

I gave him the necessary information to find the other; after all, in the Yellow Pages he was advertised as a 'specialist in missing persons.' We were born exactly one month apart, though Sam Fat wasn't in the New Year of 1983, but in the lunar New Year of 4681, before the Year of the Rat began. I told him all I knew of the other because in that way he would doubt me and there'd be nothing left to do but feel hunted. I told him that the first time I saw the other, we were both 7 years old. I had climbed onto the local bus in San Juan to go to the Celebration of the Cross on San Sebastian Street. The bus stopped, trapped in a traffic jam, stuck like a prehistoric dinosaur at the cross streets of Diego and Vallejo in Río Piedras. I looked through the window and the other was standing on the corner, staring at me. I fell in love with him because I had never seen anyone so similar to me (it might be that we didn't look at all alike, but his staring eyes were exactly the same as mine, between black and amber; his way of not laughing, or of laughing to himself, was mine; his way of parting his hair on the left was mine; his joy at having finally seen me was mine); when I tried to get off the bus it was too late, he had either vanished into the realm of the spirits or else the earth had swallowed him whole. Sam Fat seemed to me, all of a sudden, a giant smoke-breathing paper dragon; on a paper napkin he had written: "Play it again for me, that same old jukebox tune about a man that never comes to say good bye."

If the other had said good bye I would have had to forget him or to cry nostalgically over José Angel Buesa's *Poema del renunciamiento*. But it wasn't like that. I couldn't go through life without knowing what happened. His absence (or his unbelievable presence) caused me to sleep with his shadow night after night, recounting to myself the story of my solitude. Seven years later I wrote a story entitled Milk for Angels, whose epigraph, *Guardian Angel, sweet company, forsake me neither night nor day*, recaptured the presence of the other. At the very moment Dr. Margot Arce de Vázquez read the praise of the jury that had awarded me a gold medal inscribed with the image of Aladdin's Lamp, the other smiled at me from the last row of the auditorium. He knew that the angels were he and I, and that, what's more, the revolving fan turning above the two naked bodies on the cot represented the crucifixion of our separation. When I stepped down from the stage and managed to get through the wall of hugs and congratulations, the other had vanished, confident that he was already inserted in the written word, like an astronaut. Sam Fat looked to me then like a black angel with thorns on his back, perched atop the Great Wall of China: "We weren't talking about astronauts, we were talking about space."

Who can speak of the never-ending torture of infinite space on a blank page? I promised that I was never going to write another story about illicit love, but the person who made the promise and the person who now breaks the promise are not the same. I told him not to come off so intellectual and serious, that everything about me, everything about him, everything about us was a great melodrama. Who could assure us that everything that happened between one New Year's Eve and another, there on the Lower East Side, wasn't just a perfect lie? I told him that we seemed like two gossipy spiders and the only thing that mattered was that one didn't swallow the other before the story (or the gossiping) could justify our meeting. I suspected that from the first Sam Fat and I coincided off the page. We understood that it was necessary to perfect our ritual and love each other a little; in the end, everything that had been written was nothing but a desire to take revenge on reality, just as all men wanted to take revenge for not being able to have children.

But in Loisaida, things always happen different. The origin of the word Loisaida could be traced by any interested literary critic (or demographer); I will limit myself to saying that it is not a bastardization of the words Lower East Side. Mythologically, I can assert that there is a relation between Loisaida and Rio Grande de Loíza. I believe that, at a certain point of our conversation, Sam Fat and I mentioned it between drinks, between cigarettes, between remembrances, between vengeance. And I repeat it now, aware of the little time I can count on to free myself from all those blank pages that have followed me throughout my life. Those interested will understand that the fear of every storyteller is that they'll never again be able to tell a story, forcing them to alter reality and characters in the hope that they'll never have to be alone. Why did my meeting with Sam Fat take place in Loisaida? Why did it have to be there, in the Aguas Buenas Social Club, where it was set as if the place didn't matter at all? Why had Loisaida always been the neighborhood to which so many immigrants came looking for a communal existence? I'm not sure. Maybe I should try to summon it all up, describe the buildings crumbling in sheets of rotten bricks, the urge Puerto Rican immigrants have to build gardens so grass and sunflowers could grow in every abandoned lot, the Czech stores with their wonderful fur stoles, the crowded counters of eat-and-run Ukrainian diners, the police every now and again busting the kids that sell $5 bags of weed. All this, which might seem to be nostalgia but is not, makes it reasonable that Sam Fat and I would meet each other, as fate would have it, in Loisaida.

It's best to relate a few pertinent facts about Sam Fat. Sam Fat wasn't a son of Yemayá, as the line of women who preceded him, but a son of Orunla, expert in the Chart of Ifá and master of the past, present and future; being a son of Orunla he was destined to be a *babalao*, a priest of *Santería*, and to be one of the horses that Orunla would mount to embody himself and to speak through his mouth. The most probable is that he rejected this rendezvous with his destiny and the history of all those women who had waited centuries for the moment of his birth. He had been born in Loisaida; his mother had told him that in Puerto Rico there was a village of blacks in which the slave prison of a sugar cane refinery had been, that the village was named Loíza and the Rio Grande flowed nearby, its crystal waters becoming like mulch each time Ochún bathed in the waters of his love. His mother had told him what at first seemed to be an African fairy tale, that the first Puerto

Rican emigrant who arrived in Loisaida had been born in Loíza Aldea and that he, only he, had baptized this impoverished neighborhood with the sacred name of Loisaida. Sam Fat believed this, as much as he believed in the tale of Aladdin and the magic lantern, but when he looked out of his apartment window he saw neither rivers, copper rain, nor invisible temples, only garbage jungles, packs of fat rats and skeletal cats. It's very likely that because of the ill-fated visions of his childhood, he had thought his mother was crazy and that Puerto Rico didn't exist, that his mother invented these stories with the same skill with which her hands created women's dresses with the rusted Singer whose wheels and pedals fluttered like butterflies. But he knew that his mother's insanity had made it possible for him to feel at home in this world and to know his real name to be Sam Fat Candelas. In the neighborhood, they made him see himself as a monster, an accident, as someone from another age. His adolescence made him Sam Fat. Once, walking through Chinatown, he stood terrified in front of a window: the red and yellow mask of a dragon with a rat's snout was his own face. At that very moment he felt the heat of his own sensuality and realized that between that mask and him there existed a distant relationship. In the same window, a few feet away, he saw the reflection of a man with a brown felt hat and a raincoat which looked more like a silk kimona. The man had an opened black umbrella and was leaning slightly on a crooked cane, waiting out patiently the sudden downpour. He was much taller than Sam Fat, brunette, with a moustache so large it hid most of his mouth. Behind the man a wet street of wounded buildings transformed by neon lights into cathedrals and cabarets extended to the edge of a pier full of barges. Sam Fat kept his eyes fixed on the window, knowing that behind him the other man stood still, looking at him from his own shadow. He saw the man with the umbrella turn around and then begin to disappear down the street. Sam Fat followed him until he passed through a black gate and stopped in the middle of an inner courtyard encircled by a seven-story building shaped like a horseshoe. A crisscross of shadows and clotheslines hung with sheets kept him from seeing clearly the face of the man. The night was dark and the man didn't say a word, and then, suddenly, a gust of wind lashed them with the scent of a wisteria-covered grave. The man climbed the stairs and Sam Fat followed. They didn't look at each other, though both were anticipating trouble. They arrived at the top floor, climbed a narrow spiral staircase, the man opened a door, and they went in. Sam Fat found himself below a dirty skylight, lit up by the neon signs from the street that soaked the garret in color. Sam Fat spoke: "Colors do not exist if you are not there. You want the other Sam Fat. I am the wrong Sam Fat. I just came in through the translucent plastic jewels of the doorway."

But it wasn't true; he was the Sam Fat the man was looking for. Chance doesn't exist. Sam Fat himself understood this when he decided to stay and get undressed, his body painted by the magenta neon light, and to crawl like a rat through a sea of pillows. Things fall into place on their own, even with eyes closed. Sam Fat's eyes stayed open, watching the man's raincoat drop, looking forward to the moment the man's body was completely nude, the moment he came close; his breath would make him shiver, and then his flesh, as damp as a crab's shell, would envelope him. For the first time Sam Fat got a taste of the sea and knew what it was like to be an island. The sun was shining through the skylight when the man said to him: "I tell tales and I've been waiting a long time for Sam Fat just to invent him. Whatever happens, I'll tell your tale." Afterwards, the man fell asleep and Sam Fat left.

He was on the street, freed from the apartment, and he tried to reproduce the sensation of having been created. He understood, though, that his youth and beauty had no limits and that hustling on 42nd Street or at Port Authority, waiting for someone who would pay what he asked, was the only thing that would give him control over the situation. The situation, at that moment, was life. His reputation as a hustler would soon set the boundaries of his territory; he had the required flesh and a prick bigger than the dreams of a beggar. He quickly learned that a hustler only gave his body, while a faggot gave his body and his soul. His soul belonged, if to anyone, to the other, the man of that night. But an important event changed everything: Milagros Candelas, his mother, having returned to work as a seamstress in the Garment District, was accused of robbery after she complained about making less than minimum wage. Charges were trumped up, her employer, Malave Fashions, took her to court, and Milagros Candelas wound up unjustly in Bedford Hill Prison. It was a short sentence, two years, but it was jail nonetheless, and Milagros Candelas never got over the humiliation, though she never lost touch with reality, either. When she got out she realized that Sam Fat was already a man, but that she hadn't lost him completely. He reciprocated with timeless love and took care of her. Milagros Candelas wanted to return to Puerto Rico and Sam Fat obliged; they would return together. He was prepared to return to a place where he had never been except in stories. In addition, he knew that everything had a purpose and that he was about to fly over the sea carrying an empty coffin, as the corpse was still alive. When they arrived on the island, they found a room with a balcony on San Sebastian Street, close to where she had been born; later, they rented an old Ford. They travelled all over the island; he drove, staring at the surroundings, while she told a tale for him to memorize. Milagros was looking for something else, though. She was looking for a promising site so that, when the hour arrived, she wouldn't have to be put into a tomb that didn't belong to her. She found one in a cemetery in a northern village; it wasn't by the water but neither was it invaded by seasalt. Dusk found them on a beach with cliffs of black rock one afternoon; they sat on the sand and on a small mat Milagros threw her sixteen shells and read them to Sam Fat. "Son of Orunla," she read, "master of the past, present and future: this is your duty, if you so choose." Sam Fat saw the vengeful force of her words. But this world of *orishas* wasn't his world, nor these tropical ruins, nor the history of the Mandarin Chinese. His time on earth was given to him to become a Chinese-Puerto Rican detective of *noir*, Hollywood films that would be shot too late; he only wanted to be that which he had already been, an actor in a cheap melodrama where treason, passion and fatal love were the rules of the game. He had dreams of living on the black and white wall of a movie screen: the man with the black umbrella haunted his dreams, thinking he recognized him on the street only to be mistaken. He had awoken one night, covered in sweat, having dreamt that he was one of the witches dressed as a Chinese courtesan in a travelling production of Macbeth. All this, in short, had predicted his fate better than any blood-inherited myth. His mother was reading the shells to him in the Chart of Ifá, but Sam Fat only heard a man with a cane drawing a map on the sand with his piss. She didn't understand him when he said to her: "Urine on dust. You just transpose it. These are the saints. These are the altars on the side of the road. It's a pity… these are the martyrs. And all I know is that wallpaper was made for fire, mirrors were made for light, and we were made for remembering a time that doesn't exist, a light that doesn't remember, and dreams of silk that the seamstress cannot unravel."

With those words he had killed his mother and the eternal shadow of the mother he had always carried within himself. Milagros Candelas wanted to revenge that mother of the mother of her mother who a certain Nicolás Ramos de los Santos had condemned to the public pyre on Mondongo Street back in the sixteenth century, a century that only exists in stories and history books. For that, Sam Fat needed the necessary protections: the white and red necklace of Changó, spirit of virility, fire and thunder; the honey necklace of Ochún, spirit of love and rivers; the blue and white necklace of Yemayá, spirit of fertility, life and the seas; the red and black necklace of Eleguá, the messenger who shows you the way; the multicolored necklace of Babalú Ayé who protects against sickness; the necklace of Ifá, spirit of the impossible. But, for Sam Fat, the *Santería* necklaces were only snakes in the sand of his neck. Nonetheless, he took the necklaces and put them on one moonlit night after being bathed in shredded coconut and coconut milk. He knew that Milagros Candelas wanted a *babalao* to cross the curtain of time and return to the past centuries in order to find himself in the ashes of a burnt corpse. Once he could touch the ashes, he would understand that the origin of his history was a murder. There were too many coincidences: sixteen shells had predicted his destiny, the sixteenth century lay claim to his past, and now he knew that the sixteen letters in the name of the man with the black umbrella fixed his place in the present. Sam Fat buried Milagros Candelas where she herself had arranged; after the burial he returned to New York.

There are secrets which a writer never reveals. As is natural, Sam Fat studied to be a private investigator in a school. His calling can't be doubted, a government licence attests to it. It was a way to make a living and to be the cliche he had already become. His life was a film and he was producer, director, writer and principal actor—a role that can only be achieved when the page is completely blank. He was, naturally, the point of the story, the lost dagger. He began waiting for a telephone call that would put everything into perspective. He placed an ad in the Hispanic Yellow Pages: Sam Fat/ Private Investigator/etc. He waited like a Buddha for the call of his victim to come. The victim would have to be a writer, a constant deformer of history. He was already well-informed and knew the odds. A writer, white, a crazed mythologizer of the outcasts and druggies of Puerto Rican society, or maybe the other mythologizer of faggot outcasts, promoter of the sexual passions of a people lost since Sodom. Both mythologizers were related by their self-involvement and even, perhaps, both sons of a single father, as they had the same last name and had been born in 1948, which was also the Year of the Rat, the year in which Sam Fat was born. Even worse, the full name of each of the two writers had 16 letters, a product of fours, too clear to be mistaken.

Sitting at a formica table in a Greek pizzeria in Chinatown, he waited, organizing the available elements of his life in the same way a storyteller organizes the indispensable elements of his story. In the air there was a distant love, a window, a street that conjured up doors, a foggy night, lampposts like dragons, a skylight, a faceless man (a bit old), a hatred in love that condemns us. The call came on a Christian New Year's Eve that, for the Chinese, for the slightly Chinese like he, wasn't very important. He recognized the voice of the man with the raincoat on the telephone. It had to be one of the writers, surely. But it didn't matter. One had seen the image of the other from a bus, one had seen the other from a stage, they had read of each other, without doubt, in one book after another, neither daring to write the necessary history of the other, the unlived part, for one the urban life amidst broken clumps of dirt, for the other the metropolis among abandoned buildings, where the druggies of the other would have tried to cast an exorcist spell on drugs and literature. They loved each other, nevertheless, although one was more enthralled than the other, having identified each other in the torture of a blank page. Either one might call under the pretext of telling a tale. With a sharp knife Sam Fat carved onto the formica table the name of the other two: *Ramos*. The phone rang immediately.

Perhaps it was the black umbrella
Perhaps it was the obscenity of his gnarled cane
But we never really did invite him here
He was never announced
But would suddenly be there.

Telling another story
And about love never curing our diseases
Thinking that we were
Willing to receive him
Another boring Angel of the night
Reduced to solitude and tears.

We began to wonder
When he arrived
Dressed in a black kimono and a black umbrella
He danced of the wisteria that grew
By the grave of another
Uninvited one.

We've never been accustomed
To count the colors of our guests or our invaders
We have always respected our ghosts
And our enemies have shared
Food and poison at our table
We feel no fear
We always fill our empty graves.

He no longer had the face of an out-of-work *babalao* when he wrote these verses on another paper napkin in the Aguas Buenas Social Club. Without doubt, Orunla had mounted him and it had been he who wrote through the hands of Sam Fat. The New Year's fireworks transported him as if by magic back to another body and another time and all of a sudden he was a black man condemned to the stake for practicing his African witchcraft against God's empire; in his flesh he felt the fire so near that he ran, like a spooked war horse, into the bathroom to give himself up to the water and to calm down. He looked at himself in the mirror and saw his face completely painted by the red bulb. Now he had only to imagine what would happen to him; from the man with the black umbrella he had learned that chance doesn't exist when things are anticipated. He had arrived early for the meeting with the man, he had imagined and waited for him; aware of it, the hunted managed to transform himself, with patience, into the hunter. He was no longer the black witch hounded by the false history and the reinvented story, he was a simple private investigator, born and raised on the Lower East Side, and more than just a weak person he was an infallible character that, with his presence, had filled a mediocre writer's blank pages, at least of a character more mediocre than he, a literary suicide whose only possibility for reincarnation consisted in killing off as many characters as he felt like. What he expected when he opened the bathroom door and the wall clock read 8, was much more complicated. Between blank pages, the man with the umbrella as much as he, had loved each other. And now the passion of meeting the person he was always looking for had become the biggest obstacle.

When he left the bathroom, the other was seated on a stool in front of the bar and his raincoat lay on the floor like a slimy puddle. At first sight, Sam Fat had the impression that the man with the black umbrella didn't recognize him, or at least he wasn't playing his part. He walked right over to the man and stood so close that he knew the other couldn't help but smell his sweaty armpits. He lit a cigarette, but he couldn't see the face of the other because of the shadow cast by his felt hat. But the other, in the end, revealed his image of the Inquisitor; Sam Fat determined in the silence that he was an enemy. When the other took a drink, Sam Fat recognized the large moustache and imagined his mouth. Sam Fat breathed onto the neck of the other, put his right hand on the other's shoulder and lowered his crotch onto the other's thigh before introducing himself, saying: "Glad to meet you. I'm Sam Fat." But then in his hands he felt the trembling bones of a dying man and caught a whiff of rotting flesh, and when the other finally took off his hat and was lit up by a neon sign, Sam Fat discovered a skull bald and pale, whose skin stained with cancerous blotches no longer had any relation to flesh and blood. The man was still attractive, like someone who knows they're going to die and has just met the person who'll push them into their grave and, happen what might, has told their tale as promised, creating with their life a tragedy based on an ethnic anachronism. But what Sam Fat resented most was that the other had robbed him of all the aura of reality he once had since, having become aware of his past, he could no longer live tranquilly in the present, and having loved him so much he was obliged to forever suspect love. And now, even worse, the other had made him a murderer.

translated by kurt hollander

go now

r i c h a r d   h e l l

It was 1980. The sun came up. My eyes opened. Uh oh. I've woken up again. The bed didn't smell good, but it smelled like home. It smelled like a refuge. It was the way the bedclothes seemed to crumble and disperse into particles against my skin that was irritating. And then there was the morning light: strictly on schedule, empty and smug, like a prison guard, and so fucking ugly. It was infuriating, and that made me tired all over again. But here I was, waking up. I know what the problem is: I've gotten so skinny there's no distance between my nerve ends and my brain and everything has too much impact. All that flooding light out there that people seemed to flourish in. The morning was like a big ocean pressing its moronic face against the windows and walls of my lost apartment, and there I was alone. I was sunk.

richard hell has recorded 4 CD's (*Blank, Destiny Street, R.I.P.* and *Dim Stars*), is the author of *Artifact* (notebooks), *Across the Years* (poems), *Wanna Go Out* (a novel written with Tom Verlaine), *Untitled* and *Big Show* (two poem karaokes), and *Meet Theresa Stern* (a short movie). This piece is from a novel-in-progress of the same name.

Still I was handsome and young...

I smelled my armpits. Oh no. I knew it anyway, I'd known it all along, but there it was, that smell. It had come up like a fragment of a dream suddenly recalled, just a little haunted feeling, like the snap realization that what's different in the house is that something's burning. It wasn't the normal smell of sweat. It was the sharp chemical-metallic smell sweat glands make when they're deprived of heroin.

I'd made the mistake of waking up again. Terrible to start the day with a mistake. I was starting every day a little bit *behind* and it was mounting up until pretty soon I'd be dead without really ever having been born. It was a burden. It was preoccupying me more and more.

I threw the covers off. I couldn't stop thinking. It was spring. Spring had a smell to it too, even in New York. It smelled like just-cooked heroin. It was the exhaust fumes mixed with the wet air that still carried subtle hinted promises of voyage and growth. Sea air and foliage. The hot spoon of clear brown liquid had replaced all that. I thought of the crowds out there swarming over the streets with their minds clicking and buzzing and yawning with schedules and breakfast table slights and anticipations of the boss's reactions and big hopes and my mind went blank the way it does when a mathematical problem gets too complicated. I didn't get it. I couldn't reach the strands.

I was alone and I thought, that's one good thing about heroin, it keeps you conscious that you're alone. Still, I didn't want to die before I was born. My faith in myself was going. It had actually started years before but everything happens glacially, in geological time, with dope. You fall behind. It had just recently gotten serious enough that I had to notice it. I needed something to believe in.

I got up naked and in the same motion lifted my thick biker's belt from the doorknob beside the bed and slipped along the wall into the livingroom to avoid being seen through the livingroom window. I pulled loose the loop of string that held a roll of tattered bamboo halfway up the window and the shade fell with a sharp clatter like a pang of guilt gone in a second. I hung the belt over the back of a wooden chair I used as a footrest and went into the kitchen where I filled a glass with water and grabbed a handful of toilet paper. Back in the livingroom I put the paper and glass on the chair. There was a small hidden drawer in the table beside the window opposite the couch. I opened it, reached in and pulled out a spoon and syringe. The spot where I sat on the couch was permanently dented by my weight and radiated a broken fringe of cigarette burns. The spoon, which was black with carbon on the underside, held a crusty piece of cotton in the middle of a brown stain. This was the residue of my last shot of the night before. I sucked up some water from the glass with the syringe and squirted it into the spoon. Using the tip of the needle I loosened the cotton and swirled it in the murky liquid to dissolve every last encrusted grain. Then I lit a cluster of five or six paper matches and held it under the spoon. Get it sterile, make sure it all dissolves. It bubbled, a wisp of steam arose. It clarified. Everything was focused there. I pulled the fluid into the syringe through the filtering cotton, pressed the syringe free of air bubbles, tightened the belt around my bicep and slid the needle into the main vein of my forearm. I pushed the plunger out with my thumbnail and a thread of blood appeared in the liquid. A hit. I loosened the belt. I pressed the plunger in and yanked the needle out. Fuck. Hardly feel a thing.

Still, I'd usefully killed five minutes. Now what?

I erased with the tissue the indifferent bulblet of black-red blood from my badly scarred forearm.

• • •

I liked my apartment. I thought of it as a cave. When I was a kid in Kentucky we used to go cave hunting. There are lots of caves in Kentucky. In the open fields and pastures around the suburb where I grew up you could spot their likely positions by the isolated clumps of trees that rose from steep depressions where the farmers couldn't plow. We'd take candles and sandwiches and flashlights and go exploring. Get really muddy. Find tiny animal skulls and salamanders. We would make a fire and cook up plans to run away and hide in the caves, live there, and only appear to civilization as guerrilla marauders, like Jesse James, popping up like hallucinations in supermarkets and raiding unlocked kitchens to pocket some bread and baloney and batteries, running through backyards, caught only for a flash in peripheral vision, escaping back to our hidden caves.

There was nothing worse than getting stuck though. The main object of every new cave exploration was to find a cavern as big as a room. We never did. But you never knew what a tunnel might lead to. That was the excitement. You'd push yourself inch by inch, crawling, timeless inch-diving through rock on your belly, squirming and squeezing in the chilly darkness, sweat and cave-water dripping in your eyes, sharp stone scraping the back of your head, in hopes that the passage would open up like a castle. And then you'd find you'd pushed yourself in so far that you not only couldn't go further but you couldn't go back. You were wrapped in rock and trapped. Claustrophobic panic would rise like gigantic internal missiles and then either explode or fall down dead. Sometimes the muscle-rockets would blow you far enough backwards to get free. Sometimes you gave up and that was great for a minute or two, dreaming of rot and revenge with your face in the tiny rivulets. Lovelorn jewels inside your eyelids. Then the fear and desperation would kick in again.

Never thought of that. I reached for a notebook to note the similarities between past and present. Couldn't see making a song out of it but someday these notes would pay off. If I kept track of what seemed interesting or revealing or beautiful long enough to find out what was worth writing down I'd be able to look at it and know who I am, or was. Then make some serious revisions. Maybe I could even make something beautiful. I knew I was all out of focus. There was the me who was still pure and acted truly and knew what mattered and there was the me all battered and impulsive and torn by the bombardment of cheap shiny foreign ideas and they overlapped and shared loops and capillaries and were shadows of each other that kept me ugly and baffled.

• • •

It was 1980, but it could just as well have been 1880 or 1780. 1780 would be good. I'd be some cadaverous, over-refined ("Oh my God, it's spring again. I can't abide the din of those atrocious budlets"), end-of-the-line aristocrat, locked away in his decaying manse, miles of Spanish moss from the nearest Devil Dog or Ding-a-Ling. And then the impertinent sun comes up. Ugh. Brush a cobweb from my elbow. The vulgar sun: oppressive, tasteless, indiscriminately pushing itself upon the landscape again, uninvited, intruding upon my dusty bedchamber. Another day. I'd made the mistake of waking up again. "Again" is the codeword, the password, the ubiquitous secret marking: take something, turn it over, pull it open, press deeper, look closely, and there it is: "again..." and again opens into again. Again and again and again. But the patient died. Maniacal laughter.

"Morning. I get out of bed. 'Time to start pretending!' " Boy it would be great to be a cartoon.

I needed to piss. Just got off and I needed to piss. That was bad. Meant I'll be sick again inside of two hours. I only felt normal. I wasn't really straight. I hated feeling normal, it was nerve-wracking. The only thing feeling normal meant was that you'd be sick again soon. It meant you were a little afraid. Impatient. Jumpy and angry.

I put away the works. I went and took a piss and then went into the bedroom and pulled on a pair of jockey shorts and a skin-tight pair of black Levis that had a couple of small brown-rimmed holes in the thighs where I'd hung them too long inside the oven to dry one night when I had to play a gig. I always like clean clothes for gigs. I buttoned on a tight striped shirt with frayed sleeves cut off real high and pulled on a nice thick pair of socks that smelled alright. Then I carried the phone from beside my bed back into the living room and put it down beside my spot on the couch. I sat there.

I sat there. There was my dick inside my pants, really warm and heavy and potent. Maybe I should jerk off. I felt obliged to take advantage of every opportunity for any kind of relief. It would fill up another few minutes with fun. I hadn't come in days—it was like taking a shit, you could only do it between highs. The dust is falling. The skeleton pulls out his dick. Whoa. The pleasure, like piercing shards, like pieces of triangles skimming, banging around in your body. Whoa. God it happens fast when you're straight. Floods of it. And it's practically a convulsion, a little epileptic fit. You almost see stars. But then it's gone and all that's happened is you're a little emptier, too alert and skinned bare to even drift in the sweetness for more than a minute. Satisfied by slightness, as if you'd eaten too much popcorn. I pulled my pants back up. I let the feeling wash through me for its allotted time.

The sun was really up now, all the window coverings in the house were off and I felt overlit. The day was making its demands. Who should I call? Was everybody burnt out? There's always ten dollars somewhere. There's always twenty dollars. Did I have any books worth selling? Should I pawn my guitar again? That was always an option.

It felt a little chilly in here. The spring was the coldest season because the outside temperature hovered around the level where the slumlords were legally required to turn on the heat and they exploited it for all they were worth.

The phone rang. All *right*. My charm was intact. This had to mean at least ten dollars. Anyone who'd call me at this hour must know what they're in for. They're begging to be fleeced.

It's Chrissa. This was a little delicate. Our relationship ran deeper than was convenient at a moment like this. Still I knew she was solvent and wanted me to be her friend.

"Chrissa, I was just thinking about you."

"You were? That's nice."

"It is? It is."

"It is."

"What were you calling about?"

"To remind you we were meeting Jack."

"Oh shit. I totally forgot."

"That's why I'm calling. You don't have anything to worry about. Jack thinks you're great. He has big plans for you."

"Yeah, but I don't feel very good today."

"What's wrong?"

"Well, you know, I don't feel too well and I'm flat broke. My refrigerator's a ghost town. It's fuckin' demoralizing. I just woke up feeling like this, God damn it, and I'm outta ideas."

"You're hungry?"

"Well, I'm a little hungry. There's some oatmeal. I'm not going to starve, but another day like this? I'm outta books to sell. I don't wanna pawn my guitar again. I've got rehearsal later and now that Jay down the hall is on the road it'll be hard to find one to borrow. I'm getting a royalty check from my lawyer next week but he doesn't give advances. Listen, Chrissa, sorry to lay this on you outta nowhere first thing in the morning, but do you think you could lend me twenty bucks till I get that bread from my lawyer?"

I really felt like a clown, teetering. My fate—pathetic loser or lovable poor artist—balanced in the tone of her reply. I hated this, but I was inured to it. It was like a greeting. Hello, how are you, can you lend me ten bucks? But I didn't want to fall.

Fortunately, I knew Chrissa was hoping to benefit from this meeting with Jack herself, and besides, she didn't like to see me embarrassed.

"Alright. But you're going to be good with Jack, right? This is important."

"I will. I'll be in top form. I'm going to make it up to you some day, Chrissa." Suddenly I remembered it would be really nice to have something to eat, too. "But listen, actually, do you think you could make it 25, cuz I have a little debt to pay back, too?"

"Okay, but you have to come over here now because I'm going out."

"I'll be there right away."

I hung up, feeling great and slimy at the same time. But soon enough the brilliant light of my unfailing luck had seared the slime to a thin thin crust, it fell away, and I was innocent again. Another eight hours arranged for.

Dealing with humans was always a drag. They forced me to lie. They always had to be made to feel that either they were going to get something from me or that I cared about them before they would give me any money.

• • •

Off to Chrissa's. I didn't like being outside. I kept feeling like there'd be a loud noise and I'd jump. I thought how I lived here so long nothing looked new and interesting any more. It was hard to find a route where I wouldn't be likely to run into someone I knew and realize that they were worried that I was crazy because of the way I was trying to force myself to look into their eyes in order to show that I wasn't crazy, and then I'd have to make an abrupt excuse that made me seem even crazier and move off fast.

I was a machine that was set to skim, power-walk, to that doorway, collect, and move on to the next. I felt pretty good. It was nice to be seeing Chrissa, too. I could never see enough of her. Someday I would make it all up to her, show her how completely I loved her, outside of time and with no thought of gain. But in the meantime something a little material when I got paid. Like, um, a champagne and caviar dinner. Or better yet, a trip to the country (with me). I bet we could still have a really sweet, very sexy night together. I loved her breasts. I loved her butt. I'd like to ski off it. Or would she laugh me off? Just thinking about it made me feel cute. I hated it when she made me feel cute.

She knew me too well. I'd had to apologize too often. I'd confessed too much. And made the wrong confessions. She'd seen my resolve fail too many times.

Why am I going on like this? Am I a broken man? I laughed, and a passerby glanced at me and looked away instantly.

Springtime: not hot enough for the garbage to smell. These old people with their dogs are ridiculous. How could someone let himself get old and wander around with a fleabitten hound on this vicious battleground? Well, they're just wallpaper to me. But this existence needs some redecoration.

Then again, nothing ever changes. I could just imagine myself a time traveller and it all became interesting again. Where was I? I walked down Tenth Street where proud Puerto Ricans—after all, they'd survived to be teenagers and were making money at a good clip—exchanged little ticket-sized envelopes of marijuana for five dollars. Out in the sun like that, the money always looked like it had a silver patina you could smudge with a thumb. As if it were magic and if everybody would stop pretending the stuff would just disintegrate.

I'd had a little epiphany, a little insight into the timeless state of things once when I was walking alone on 14th Street, the budget bazaar for the area, the most grotesque gallery of souls to be seen this side of the tenth century. I'd seen everyone in the dignity of their fate, their origin, their condition, each one a separate manifestation of the earth's possibilities. And of course humankind itself was just one example of what it was possible for the world to say. The self-determining animal one. But now I'm thinking the race was nearing its death and it's going to realize, like the artist in the Borges story, that its effort to fathom the universe and fulfill itself, the patterns it has created in striving for knowledge, beauty, and harmony all merely add up to a self-portrait, and it was going to be a very ugly, brutal, destructive, selfish face. The more lines that are added to the face of the earth, the more detailed and clear the subject of the portrait becomes as we near our finish, and soon the world will erase us and return to the drawing board. Maybe dinosaurs'll get another chance.

Chrissa lived on the top floor of a building on St. Mark's Place. It shocked me mildly to see how I could resent her for forcing me to climb seven flights of stairs to borrow 25 dollars from her.

I get up there and she's sitting in the middle of the floor thumbing through a single-drawer file cabinet. A glance at her does two things to me: it makes me glad to be alive, and makes me feel left behind and shut out of life altogether. Damn damn damn. I don't like this real life, where actual people with their own desires and intentions can look at me, expect things of me, interpret my behavior, classify me. I like my mental life where Chrissa and I are together forever the moment we locked eyes five years ago.

How did I get to be old enough to say "five years ago"? If I can get to be 30 I can get to be 40. That throws a new light on things. How will taking that into account change the way I act? I'd been thinking about this question.

"Hi Chrissa, whatcha doin'?"

"I'm looking for some pictures for a job I got."

"Oh. You know, I was just thinking about something. I read somewhere recently that the Greeks thought of the past as being ahead of them and the future behind. You know, because the past is what you actually see, it's what your eyes are open to, whereas the future . . . it's wherever your back is turned. And anyway, it's mostly made outta the past. Kind of comforting, don't you think?"

Groan. I was playing the fool because she made me feel at a loss.

"Yes, I know you'd like to put your future behind you."

"Don't be mean now. Don't be cruel."

"There's your money over there. I know you're in a hurry."

Ow. Fuck. Well, she was just mad at me because she knew I was performing and it offended her.

"You know, those Greeks . . . how did they get to be so philosophical? It must be because they made up the word. But, gee, it seems like they saw the big picture all the time. It must have been because of their gods. When all we have are movie stars. See, their gods were like people, while we've degenerated into treating people like gods. Can you imagine if Liza Minelli or Al Green or Clint Eastwood could turn you into a duck? That would make you philosophical."

She started laughing. Wow, that was good luck. I still had a little juice. I could get out of here on a good note. I loved to make her laugh. It made me love her all over again.

But this was just a stop on my dope run and to whatever degree she knew or understood that, it was enough to make her despise me a little, with regret. This flaw in the moment was like a secret vanity of mine she'd discovered, as if she'd caught me posing in the mirror kissing myself, and it only made me want to leave sooner.

"I'd be a duck for Al Green," she said, getting a dig in, "but our god of the moment is named Jack and for some twisted reason of his own he has a special fondness for you, which for all our sakes I hope you appreciate. I don't know how many more chances you're going to get—I admit you always seem to be able to find another one—but I'm wrapped up in this, too."

She sure could get cold. She wasn't giving me an inch. Well, it was only sensible. I picked up the money.

"See you." And then, "I'm going to come through, Chrissa. I know you're right. Whatever this plan Jack has, if you think it's so interesting, it must be worthwhile. I'll be there today and I'll be in good shape."

I made her stand up and hug me before I left.

Back to the street, where I was King. Lord of the Garbage. I went to cop.

Copping was about as interesting as waiting for a subway train. Nothing good could happen—there was never a pleasant surprise—it was just a monotony that always had the potential of turning into something worse.

I went on automatic again, pacing the most efficient route at a steady high speed sufficient to discourage all but the stupidest or craziest passerby from thinking they might be free to detain me. I was on important business. I knew how to walk mean, with an expression of intimidating determination that was by you before you'd recovered enough to jump it, friend or foe.

Once I'd copped the bags, the trip home was a breeze. I was set free, nothing could shake me except for the reflexive anxiety that would push my fingers into the watchpocket of my jeans every couple of blocks to make sure the bags couldn't get dislodged. I felt like school was out. There was nothing else in the world I needed.

I leapt up the stairs to my apartment and had my shirt off before I got to the livingroom. I assembled my paraphernalia with a speed, precision of movement, and conservation of energy the equal of the finest mystic craftsmen of old. A tea ceremony of sorts.

In a moment I was high. The silence and inching shadows in my room were very beautiful when resonant with heroin, all anxiety dissolved. My writhing ceased; I was competent, I was good, I was in tune.

I had my notebook beside me, a 16-ounce bottle of Coke, and a bag of peanuts.

I was a ticker-tape machine of poetry, an acrobat of spiritual language who would even feign slips for the hair-raising grace and hilarity of my recoveries for God alone. God being all the dead poets. All and everything. The watcher who grows and branches and forgave me while hoping for the best. Me dreaming the world in my image where it radiated from my empty room where I was alone and happy.

I picked up a magazine and by total "coincidence"—one sees what one is alert to— read "There is no I... there is only God. It is He who glistens on the ocean's surface amid the orange groves; the heady fragrance is also He, and so is the wind, the snake, the shark, the wine. Do not see yourself as yet another dream; go on dreaming yourself." The guy must be Mediterranean, somewhat over-Biblical, plus he's a little short in the shark department, but that last line has a good twist. I set to dreaming.

• • •

I shook my head and the tiny acrobats fell like spangles, like the cool rain on another planet, down to the inside of my feet.

romans 12:19

kelvin christopher james

When we first set up this arrangement, it worked great. Operations went smoothly as two eels swimming in a barrel of oil. In this cushy system, Rusky and I were the slipperies, the psychiatric emergency department was the easy employment that kept us keeping on as we worked that sleepiest third of the day—the midnight to eight shift—and the arrangement was that we parceled the dullness of this graveyard duty, and bore it equally, albeit singly. I was the early half, Rusky the late.

We also shared a suspicion that the boss was aware of the deal but let the split ride because it worked so well. We managed every situation, and he never had to be called in. Or maybe he figured it from our point of view: that one physician's assistant, rested and alert for any eventuality—be it sleepiness or roving supervisors—was ever more efficient than two bored men keeping awake by learning each other's uglier personal habits. For the twelve-to-eight is less hard than awkward timewise, and although we're there for

kelvin christopher james is a born-Trinidadian living in Harlem. His most recent collection of short stories is *Jumping Ship* (Villard Books).

emergencies, the workload is normally light. Then again, when we split the shift, I know I worked harder than ten men, and Rusky probably did his best also. And for further failsafe, whenever the necessity showed up, he and I had wherever phone numbers to recall each other in.

So matters were running chilly and smooth as a soft breeze on ice. Then Rusky, like a too-happy bird, began shitting in this comfortable nest; all because he's weak to his own flattery that he is a charmer, and he met up with this girl who puffed some hot air into his ego balloon.

About a month or so ago, he rushed in ten after four, saying, "Morning, Jack. Gotta tell you this one."

He put his coffee on the desktop, and took a mirror out of a drawer, and stared fondly into it. He shook his head admiringly. "Jack," he said, "you wouldn't believe this if it wasn't me telling you."

Soon after I got this job and met Rusky, I realized he was devotedly in love with himself. He was always ready with amusing exposition on the affair, but this morning I was tired. "Tell me tomorrow," I said.

"You gotta hear this," he persisted. "Listen up just one single minute. Okay, I'm coming to work, okay? I change to the express at Seventy-second, okay? Maybe three, four people in the car, and then there's this fine, fine fox. She's wearing a sort of, y'know, a western outfit. All white, with silver sequins on the belt and the brim of the hat, and along her legs and down her boots. And y'should see her milkers, man. Plus she's pretty, too. Well, y'know me. I sit down near the door, opposite her, okay? And. . . ."

"Rusky," I said, "you gotta tell me this one tomorrow. I'm dead right now."

That night, I handed over to him and escaped home by four-twenty.

It took about a week more—while he went from ten minutes late to fifty—for me to realize that Rusky had seriously fallen, and become a latenight cowpoke to this rodeo queen of west Harlem.

Now, I knew that Rusky had a wife at home. His (always with a leer) pet name for this Trinidadian woman was "Sweet Black Pepper," and one reason he gave for choosing the late part of our split shift was that he could stay home and be a gourmet in hot dishes. Well, lately, to permit him more riding with the cowgirl, the story he gave his wife was that we got busted. There'd be no splitting for a while. So, every night the Missis saw him leave home for "work" at eleven-thirty.

Well, I say Right on! for Rusky. Bravo. But with all his gourmandizing at home and cowpoking on the ranch, Rusky was overworking his range. The worst of it was him making me the suffering sidekick responsible for saving his ass.

I maintained a tight schedule. I was doing a Master's in public health during the day; I had this night job to keep me alive; and, of course, I had my normal social activities to keep me living. The bottom line was, I was always in need of sleep. So, when Rusky, the nightly range-roamer, came in four-thirty or fiveish loaded down with tired smiles and apologies, he's threatening my precise program and disarranging the quality of my life.

Four-thirty this morning things were as usual: the general of love late again. And I was so tired of his dalliance, I had a yen to arrange his Waterloo. My plan was to call his home at four-forty or so and ask Ms. S. B. Pepper if Rusky was coming in soon, since I needed to go home immediately.

Later on when he was seeking explanations to mend the shreds of his blasted marital peace, I'd apologize that, in the excitement of my emergency, I had dialed his home number by mistake. Whether he believed that or not, I figured he'd want to come to work early enough, if just to escape from Missis Pepper's heat.

I decided I'd give him until four forty-five. Then at four thirty-three, the EMS brought in this patient.

They'd restrained him. The paramedic at his head wore an angry scowl as he roughly pushed the stretcher in. His partner, at the guy's feet, was grinning hugely. Curious, I raised an inquiring eyebrow at him. He signaled me to wait as the three of us transferred the patient to a bed in the psych room and buckled him down on it. Then, while the offended one immediately strode out, the amused paramedic paused to give the story.

The patient had been rushing up to passers-by in the street and shouting, "Romans 12:19!" in their faces. Someone had complained to the police. As it wasn't exactly a crime, they called for an ambulance to bring him in to us. For nearly an hour the EMS guys had coaxed and maneuvered to get him inside the ambulance. Then as soon as they did, he had peed all over the floor and on the pants leg of the offended fellow.

Left alone pondering the paramedic's satisfied departing grin, I looked at my restrained crazy and mused ironic about all those off-base others going loose out there. He was older and thin, and being quiet on the bed, so I decided to do his paperwork first. Then I would refocus on spiting Rusky's tardiness. My disinformation plan was still green-lit.

He beat four forty-five by twenty-eight seconds. Breezed in with a chatty "What's happening, Jack?" in a tone irritating as the first rabid car alarm early sleepy-Sunday morning. Still, I was relieved by his presence; sighing, I swallowed my vexation and aborted the countdown. I got up and pointedly went to my locker.

He eyed the guy on the bed. "What's with him?" he asked.

"For observation," I said. "They just brought him in. He was bothering people preaching at them in the street."

"So what's new about that?"

I didn't answer.

He asked, "You talk to him yet?"

"I thought you might want to do some work before you go back home," I said sarcastically.

Rusky grimaced, threw exaggerated eyes at the ceiling and retreated to the desk. "You want me to finish writing him up, too?"

For reply, I glowered hot spikes through the back of his neck.

He turned around. "You smell piss?" he asked.

"The patient pissed himself in the ambulance," I said coldly, and continued getting my carrybag together.

"Pissed up the ambulance, eh? Well, I back him up on that. I say piss on the ambulance, too, for sticking me with this stinking job." And at nearly five o'clock in the morning, he found his stale humour funny enough to burst out cackling like a hen just shit an egg.

My resentment nearly broke on him then: so casual and callous he was; souring my end of our arrangement in his search for early morning sweetness. But I didn't have the energy. Truth was that lack of sleep had battled me down to about half a man, and only anticipation of my warm bed kept that halfman moving. He was far too tired to indulge in routine anger. I put off challenging the charming Rusky for another day.

Five minutes later I was telling him my usual: "Say I'm at lunch and call me if there's a problem."

Then, out of nowhere, a gruff voice chimed in, "Don't miss the lesson, sleepyhead. The more that's known, the better."

Rusky's and my eyes ganged up on the patient. I was suddenly most curious about this guy. For working in the psych emergency teaches one thing. Crazy people may seem funny, but they never try to be. And this guy had just called me "sleepyhead"—a pretty smart crack, considering his situation. So all at once, this guy wasn't so much crazy as he was a suspicious character.

Rusky, fresher from good sleeping or whatever, responded first. "Know what? What's to know?"

The guy never looked at him, but kept his head toward me, while his eyes looked off to a point close left of my face. He addressed the space beyond my ear: "The very truth, my brother. Romans 12 and 19."

Rusky sounded a professional "Hmmnnn." Then, as if wanting one small point cleared up, he continued, "What's true about it?"

The guy remained transfixed by the inquisitor behind my ear. His eyes were steady as if painted onto his face. He said, "This human being," and nodded with the grand authority of special privilege.

Rusky's slow glance sidled over to me as he persisted, "What about him?"

It seemed to me that he also had glanced apprehensively behind my left ear before he looked back at the guy. Now, that got to me. I immediately wanted to know what he had seen behind me to make him avoid my eye. But the guy was asking of his out-of-sight vision, "Is this human tired trying? Isn't this human tired?"

"Why don't you tell me? I'd like to know," said Rusky.

Abruptly, the guy focused on my face, then on Rusky's, then back and forth he switched two or three times before settling on Rusky. Maybe his face was less tired-looking. I seized the moment to make a quick search behind me. Nothing there but room.

Reassured, I looked the fellow over professionally, classifying him. That eyeplay of his declared against psychological normalcy. Such sly avoidance behavior was typical of some disturbed people. Just as I decided this, though, I happened to meet his eyes. They were light brown and soft, and sensible, slow-moving as though weighted with a heavy sufferance, and the appeal in them was so sincere that he didn't seem crazy at all.

Abruptly, I was completely taken by that call in his eye. All madness had slipped away, leaving his face earnest, intriguing, persuasive. And my urgent nagging pull to go home and rest departed sullenly, rebuffed by his call for sympathy.

He said—no, more argued sensibly as in debate, "This here human being, he shouldn't be manacled. He's already imprisoned, and without his heart. He can hurt no one. No need to tie and tame him like a beast."

The voice was calm and reasonable, a little chiding, maybe. With a sense that he'd next recite his patient civil rights, I looked at Rusky for support, and met shoulders shrugging, and an okay-with-me face. I was for it also; the guy was frail, didn't look dangerous. In any case, it was two to one—us against him. Before I could even nod, Rusky reached over and removed the restraints. The guy sat up on the edge of the bed.

Slowly, he studied the wall before him, and the desk, and the lamp above it, and then the ceiling. With his attention caught on something up there, he resumed his flat reasoning tone, "This human lost out to the beasts. Lost his heart to them. Lost it when it rode away with them. It was only nine. But on that cold, cold morning it was long gone."

As he spoke this, dead-toned, gaze hung up on the ceiling, his eyes suddenly filled and trembled on the brink of spilling. The wet in them sparkled reflections of the ceiling bulbs, shining a bleak, electric vitality. This vigor, incongruous against his gaunt dark face, was like jewels gleaming in an open grave. And at this notion, a sinister idea sprang at me, unexpectedly convincing a chill of goose bumps to run up my arms. For I thought: here was a very sad man, raging sane under a guise of madness!

He had continued speaking, pausing a lot but persistent, as if dragging some personal sense out of his story. ". . . big, square, yellow. Typical. It rode this human's heart away. Bussed him out, to get him off the street. Out the jungle with the monsters and their dogs. Those strong, hard monsters out there. Tried to send him away from the rampage. 'Send him off to school,' the mother said. 'We gotta join the struggle.' And this fighting human put his heart in the yellow school bus. Since there was nothing useful he could learn 'round here.

"But the slaves of the Beast are everywhere. There is no escape. The old monsters always win. Safe in the yellow bus, a driver-monster took my heart down near the sea, and ravaged him, and when he was done, tossed him in and left him there. Left him cold and raw, and drove away, because the monsters triumph every time.

"And that monster won each day they searched the streets for my heart. The monster won with each scream that bled the mother's eyes. That monster grinned its crocodile teeth each time it joined the searching, gleeful it had won. Until the ocean would stomach all the nastiness no more, and threw this human's heart up from its belly, and laid it dirty on the beach like vomit.

"Laid it rotten there, carrion for flies and seabirds. Puked it clear, so everyone could see, still screaming on his face, a terror no sea could ever wash away. Laid bare, so all could see the ripped up flesh at his asshole. Plain there, where the monster fucked this human's little heart.

"The police came. 'Identify,' they said. Recall a face forever gone, except for the snarl from his fear, and the torn flesh at his ass. That was all this human could identify."

The guy stopped talking, his brimming eyes screaming for a blink to shed their painful load. He stared at the ceiling, frozen and aloof as quiet swelled in the room like air into a balloon. I glanced at Rusky for some echo of my discomfort. He didn't notice; stock still, mouth hung open as if for better intake, he was gasping for more.

The patient continued, "They caught that monster, though. On the lookout, they caught it dead at the business. A little girl this time. It touched on her, she told her daddy, and they tracked the monster to its den. Found all those babies' clothes there—some of this human's heart's, too. The monster had kept them in its closets.

"And after that was the pictures. Everywhere was its pictures. Big monster pictures. Black and white, and color. Everywhere. High school graduating class pictures. Saluting the flag army pictures. With its ex-fiance pictures. Everywhere was monster pictures. In some it was smiling.

"The lawyers said it was insane, city lawyers working for the Law. The history was nervous breakdowns and anxiety, the city lawyers said. The tenth-grade teacher, grey-haired honest, said it'd always been a problem child. It was totally mental, the city lawyers said. It needed treatment, and it'd be useful to society again. So they put it in a hospital to get well. And they brayed about it in the picture papers. The monster lawyers said it was best for society.

"For this human, sleep scoffed and ran away forever. Trumped by the trials, this human caught a need to go. To be ever-moving. Went into the raging monster streets, and sought to understand those raging ways, while the woman at home complained, and wept. This human was too ever-roaming, she said. This human was a ghostman, never talking, ever walking. Help her try to live, she begged. It was better if he permanently disappeared, the goodly woman fretted. So this human did.

"The Salvation Army, it was, that took the human in. 'Twas there he found the Good Book. 'Twas there he learned to deal with watching outward. Uncle Time is a patient teacher. Remember, Almighty Lord, too, he lost a son."

The guy stopped again. Expressionless in the accumulating silence, he stared fixedly, between Rusky and me. I wanted him to go on, but didn't have the courage to interrupt his pause. As he talked, his eyes had dried out; now their inner rims were raw and smarting, suggesting blood. In involuntary sympathy, I squeezed my eyes tightly shut, but he never even noticed, far less followed suit.

Again, Rusky was stronger than I. He cleared his throat and prodded, "Mm-hmm, so what's that gotta do with Romans? Huh?"

The guy didn't take him on at all; just remained sculpted in his silence.

I found it difficult to guess his age, except that he was older than maybe thirty-five. His hair was foul and matted with knots, but it was plentiful, and vigorously black. He was thin, the skin so taut-smooth over his face bones, no age lines or wrinkles showed. Yet, there was an over-used look to him; like wrapping paper that's been crumpled and smoothed out many times. With him, years seemed an inappropriate measure of age. His life itself was worn.

He startled me out my thoughts by resuming in his abrupt manner, "But this human couldn't fasten to the Word. The wayward goat, he strayed. The burning eye in his mind betrayed him. Led him from verse and chapter of the Holy Book. Pulled him from the strict line to the captions in the papers.

"For the monster's face was there, released and born anew in bold black on white. More hair and fatter, but smiling. The Prodigal was home again. The doctors, city doctors, had tested him. A visit to a clinic once a month, but he was fine. The monster could come home again.

"Drawn and driven, don't know why, this human watchmanned the cure clinic, until one day the monster visited. And that counted one last chance this human got. He might have tamed his wilding eyes. But the vision of his heart was in his mind, ripped and floating in cold brine. And this human's salvation lost out to the sting in the wounds.

"So the wildness braved the train, and trembled as it dared to sit beside the monster. Right next to it; heard it whistling, looked into the sunny face it wore. It was going home, and happy. Bold and frightened the wildness trailed it all the way to its den, and the monster never noticed the shadowing.

"Then the shadow got purpose. It went to the Salvation Army shelter, and washed; but couldn't clean its human's soul. It dressed in their donated suit, and their donated shoes, and still reaching for the Way, took the Holy Book in hand before returning to the monster's den, and rapping on the door.

"From inside, the monster's voice said, 'Who?'

"The shadow gripped the Good Book tightly: said, 'Salvation calls,' then clutched the Book even tighter.

"The peephole rattled. An eye—enlarged—glittered through and was gone. Locks clacked quick and the den's door opened. The monster, from the dim hallway, said, 'Hi, Reverend, come on in.' Its smile was the same as in the tabloids.

"The shadow thrilled with terror as it passed the monster clothes—touching close, and went on in. The same again when the monster led it to a chair, and lightly touched the shadow's shoulder but never felt the scorching flame within it. And trembling, the shadow realized the monster did not recognize its past. It was so at home, at peace.

"In the middle of the room there was a camera mounted on a tripod, klieg lights all angled at a couch near the wall. What was the monster up to? Giggling like a shy person, it explained, 'Self-portraits, he-he-he. Yessir, that's what I'm at, sir. He-he-he. It's my therapy, a sorta self-esteem thing. Y'know. I really enjoy it now. Don't want to brag or nothing, but I'm pretty good, too. The staff at the clinic like my pictures. Without me asking they say so. They think I learned it good. They were really supportive when I told how I converted half the kitchen into a darkroom. They're great people. Every thing's great since I put my life in the hands of the Lord, amen. . . .'

"It went on and on, that monster, while somewhere in the shadow's mind an idea was trying to form. But the monster was such a talker, going on about the staff, and the doctors, and the therapists, and how well things were going, and the new camera, and more and more, and too much more, all of it only frightening the baby idea that was trying to birth in the shadow's mind; all the constant chatter squishing up the baby idea against the sharp corners and twists inside the shadow's head.

"The monster never stopped chatting, '. . . yes, Rev, I'm okay now. Saved by the Blood and proud t'say it. Yessir, I've sinned and fallen on bad times. I know that. But I've done my time, and I've found my Lord. Oh yea! I'm cleansed, washed pure by the Blood of the Lamb. . . .'

"In the mind of the shadow, the idea was starting to breathe a little easier. Was growing close to tell its secret, its purpose and plan. But it was muffled back into hiding when the born-again monster intruded. '. . . y'gotta stay for dinner, Reverend. You just gotta. We could pray afterwards, but first y'gotta share my pot. I don't get much company. Can't afford to let one go after I catch him. Ha-ha-ha. I'm just not gonna let you go this evening. What y'say to that, huh, Rev?'

"There was no way around it, so for answer, the shadow began helping the monster clear photography things off the table.

"The monster remained a-ceaseless talking: 'These fried fish is something else. They's porgies, y'know, inexpensive, but deep-fried. Really good fish. Y'know what I mean. Ha-ha-he-he. They all swim in the same sea, huh? Ha-ha-ha. It's really great you're staying, Rev. Really great. Y'going to like these crispy porgies. When I was inside, used to dream about Fridays, 'cause Fridays was fish-day, and mos' times it was porgies deep-fried.'

"While the monster was talking, it had set down on the table two yellow place mats, then two broad plates on the mats, then two glasses of water. Next, it placed a vase with little white roadside daisies in the center of the table.

"The shadow just stood out of the way, watching and listening as the monster went back and forth, its voice rising and falling in a wavy rhythm, loud near the table, soft from the kitchen. The shadow gripped the Good Book still in hand, and concentrated on trapping the baby idea. But the monster said, 'Rev, come help bring in the food.' So the shadow gave up and trailed the monster into the kitchen.

"The kitchen was a very clean place. It didn't seem the monster had just been cooking there. No dirty spoons or gravy spots, or bits of food about the counters, or anything like that. The place was gleaming. Three iron pots were on the stove burners. The monster took two of the pots and said, 'Rev, you bring this big one with the porgies.' It led off for the table, promising, 'Y'going to like this fish, Rev. Just don't you be bashful now.'

"The shadow followed carrying the fry pot.

"The monster asked, 'And guess what we got for dessert, huh? Guess.'

"From behind it, while the monster shut up for that little bit, the shadow swung the heavy pot of crispy-fried porgies.

"It was a good hit, made a solid *thunk* when pot and skull connected, before the monster sagged down to the floor. Some hot oil spilled on its neck, slowly burning a new color there. Other than the clatter of the smaller pots as it crumpled, the monster was quiet, although it wheezed some. The den seemed roomier with the chatter gone. And slowly, the shadow felt becoming human and hungry, so he picked up a deep-fried porgy and crunched into it. It was okay.

"The monster was groaning, and feeble, trying to get up but unable to hold its balance. The head moved lead heavy. With each scramble forward on its elbows, the monster slipped in the gravy and greens from the two smaller pots. It strained and grunted, gentle noises though, not a bother.

"The monster squiggled its red eyes up to the shadow, its hands covering the monster face. Blood had run down one side of its neck, clotting like jello. The monster tried talking again. But just a mishmash of grunts and groans came out.

"The human returned to the living room and sat on the couch. He felt the heat and glare from the spotlights, and closed his eyes to wonder if the monster had recognized his past as yet.

"When he opened his eyes the camera was looking straight at him. And at last the idea birthed. It flew right out the human's head and into the camera's violet eye. He followed over and examined the camera. He studied it and studied it, and then understood. 'Remember this, remember this,' the idea whispered. Then it explained what was right for the occasion and what the human must do.

"Back on the floor near the kitchen, the monster was slushing and slithering around like a big, slow monster worm. It couldn't even crawl. Patiently, the human had to pull and drag and position it near the couch before taking off its clothes.

"The monster moved without support as if in sleep, blank eyes rolling around in their sockets. It took good effort to make it naked. Then, when positioned on the couch under the lights, the human found the face too bloody and dirty, so he had to clean it with a towel from the kitchen. When all was right, he went behind the camera and took a picture of the monster, just so, rolling eyes and all. Then he returned to the kitchen for the chopping knife he had seen.

"Blood on the couch would mess up the pictures, so the human put the monster back on the floor to cut its dick off. When he put his hand on its balls, the monster jerked up almost to sitting. The human chopped on its face with the big knife to put it back down, slashing its forehead and most of its nose. As the monster tried to keep the blood from coming out, it kept shoving aside the chunk of loose nose. It looked messy, but it was really okay, since the face shots were already taken.

"The mess grew when the monster's dick and balls came off. It was tough to cut the meat with all the bloody slipperiness, and the monster jerking around struggling and kicking about. The human had to get the frypot and bash its head again before it sagged limp like a sack.

"With this slippery dead weight it was even harder to position the monster for the next set of pictures. The balls and dick kept sliding from its mouth...."

"Okay! Sir, okay. All right now! That's enough of that. You've gotta stop this stuff, sir."

As the story went on, I'd vaguely noticed Rusky slowly backing away from the bed's edge where he'd first sat down. Now, as he shouted sternly, I looked closely at him, and saw his strained face trembling and shiny. It was the first time I saw how fear formed on his face. I wasn't sorry for him, though. I remembered my own frustration during the many early-morning minutes I'd spent waiting for him. A smirk in my tone, I said to him, "Take it easy, Rusky. Calm down. This guy needs to talk his thing out. Y'can't let it get to you."

Our side play hadn't mattered one iota to the patient; like a Harlem hydrant in hot summer, his mouth never stopped running its spiel, just slowed in volume. Rusky, in his fret and choosing not to listen anymore, went to the desk and began taking charts from the work drawer. But I wanted to hear the patient's mad story; I still couldn't figure his Romans, whatever the score.

"... and took a portrait of that, too," he was saying. "By now the monster was dead meat. There was enough pictures, though, so the human dragged the corpse to the bathroom. With all the blood and shit, the house was a stink, so he stripped and cleansed himself. But, no sooner he'd stepped out on the bathroom's floor, his feet were in blood again. So he took all the sheets and towels from the closets and spread them on the floor. That way it was cleaner to walk about.

"He got to the rest of the idea right away. With the cleaver from the kitchen, he chopped the monster into smaller bits. It hadn't seemed so big stretched out whole, but in chunks of joint to joint, it almost filled the bathtub; took ten garbage bags to package. By then the human was tired and took another shower and a little nap. The idea was working out fine.

"Later on, he took the camera into the darkroom to process the film, as he well knew how.

"He found in there like a how-to advertisement, every solution labeled and dated, every jar, every soaking tray, cupboard, can, and counter. It was so neat the human felt at loss. But he managed a few prints, contrasty, but good enough.

"Except for the monster stacked and packaged in the bathroom, the human was near done. Several careful trips out the hallway to the garbage compacter took care that the monster garbage safely went down the chute. Then the human pocketed the negatives and prints, and with the Holy Book in hand, went out the door of the monster's den, and was well gone.

"It all went exactly as the idea had said—except that, when this human sent the prints to the papers, they never presented them to the public at all."

"You did *what???*" Rusky shouted, so loud and sudden, he startled me off my chair. He'd been listening all along. His revulsion seemed even to penetrate the patient's aloofness; as the man stopped talking and lay back on the bed. He was still for a moment, then rolled halfway to the wall, hiding his face from us. We could see his shoulders jigging up and down, though, and we could hear his soft, throaty chuckling.

Inexplicably, the sound teased a hesitant smile to my face, and I looked over at Rusky. His consternation was also slowly changing to a doubtful amusement. I think he had my thought—that we'd been at the fool's end of a most elongated talltale. It was funny, how we had been caught up in it. You never can know with displaced streetfolks. Their lives are so improbable that you expect anything, so they can fool you a bit every time.

As the mood of relief and the ridiculous passed over us, Rusky ventured forth his cackle, and I had to smile, too. But when only the memory of our smiles lingered, we realized the patient had never stopped his chuckling, and he had been going on too long.

We became an emergency team then, quick and efficient as one, two, three. Rusky called out, "He's hysterical!" and as I was swift to the medicine cabinet for a syringe, he rushed over and rolled the crazy supine. And again we were surprised. The man had never been laughing. It was sobs that he chuckled, and still was crying out through his dry, skinny face.

Ugly deep grooves bracketed his mouth, mawed downward as if in wait for his guts to heave through. The fine skin around his eyes now showed a million wrinkles, making his face a horrid, haunting mask. Yet still his eyes remained dry and parched, denied the soothing warmth of tears.

Mine, though, were smarting fast. And I wanted somehow to help this poor man. I put a hand against his face, murmuring, "Not to worry," or something, while with the other I made a covert motion to Rusky indicating I was ready to administer the sedative.

In an instant, Rusky had pinned him, and despite his feeble resistance, I pulled his pants down and gave him a shot in the gluteus. I've got to say this for truth's sake: when Rusky and I work in synch, we're just about the finest psych emergency team anywhere.

The guy calmed down gradually, although with his breathing in dry shudders and long sniffles, he still seemed to be straddling the ragged edge of mental sickness. But even as he relaxed into oblivion, he continued a soft protest: "Lend him no aid. It's meet and right that the human suffer. . . ."

I held his frail shoulder and tried to console, "Just let the sleep come, my man. It'll do you good."

He shook his head slowly. "This penance will not be denied. He's got to suffer Hell. This human needs to bleed his sin. . . ."

I didn't want him going off again. I didn't want to hear more. Whatever his story, it'd wait another time; at least until the doctors of the day shift. Right now it was too painful to me, and maybe even unethical to let him continue.

But he fought the sedation to get his say in: "The tabloids, y'see, they never showed a single picture. Made this human's effort never matter, never happen. They never did a thing. And they scorned him so only 'cause he went against the Word. He grievously sinned and strayed from the Way, and is compelled to suffer Hell. For he cannot blame the idea born of his brine-stung heart. He should've denied its whispering and serpentine way: always in his head, hissing over and over, soft as a sigh, ever selling its poisonous song of. . . ."

Then he was asleep.

For a little while, we listened to the emptiness his voice had left. Eventually I said, "Poor guy."

"Madness is a bitch," Rusky agreed.

But our words said but the froth of our thoughts; I know much more was brewing in my mind, at least. Rusky looked at his watch, then at me. "You're looking tired, Jack."

It was almost six o'clock, I saw. I picked up my carrybag again. Rusky said, "Go on, man. It's late. I'll call you if the boss shows. Promise I'll be good tomorrow. Serious."

Day hadn't quite cleaned yet. The streetlights' glare on Lenox seemed contained by the lingering bulk of the tall concrete buildings. The scant folks about seemed grim and huddled close within their own concerns. Above, the sky was a gloomy, silvered grey, unfeatured as the face of God.

As I walked along, my thoughts returned to the tormented sleeper. I remembered his talking face, empty of emotion as the dawn sky. Yet when he cried, he had been so completely taken over by his anguish. If his story was true, it seemed a shame his mad grief had diminished the measure of his justice. This made me think of God and judgment: that maybe His system of justice was too oblique for mortal man. Maybe He didn't realize that people were direct—more conscious about time. So we've got to be busy: probably even busier than He is, just as ants're busier than people. But perhaps that was how He saw us: just a scurry of busy little ant-types!

Down in the subway, waiting, my thoughts persisted around the guy's surrender to his suffering. Somehow, he seemed oddly content with it, devoted to reliving the ordeal that unraveled him. This yearning toward his pain puzzled me. What was the nature of such a hellish ease? I thought of his fearful and never explained Romans 12, whatever.

Back home, I look at the Bible in my bookshelf. Romans 12:19 reads: *Dearly beloved, avenge not yourselves, but rather give place unto wrath: for it is written, vengeance is mine; I will repay, saith the Lord.*

veronica vera at show world sex emporium. photograph: annie sprinkle

a day at the peep show

v e r o n i c a   v e r a

The Walrus carries a brown paper bag into the glass booth. I call him the Walrus because his face is covered with long, shaggy hair, sideburns and a scraggly beard. The Walrus is not very attractive and he shows it by dressing like a slob. But armed with his brown paper bag and a pocket full of tokens, he is about to treat himself to a fantasy fuck.

He takes his jar of Vaseline out of the brown paper bag and drops a coin in the slot. The window shade rises very, very slowly to reveal me grinning at him from the other side of the glass. My body is covered in stretchy black lace that displays every curve.

veronica vera and annie sprinkle, both former porn stars, have for the past ten years documented the sex industry as "high-heeled journalists." Vera, a literary artist and activist, is involved in Sexual Evolution. The above piece will be included in her forthcoming book, *Mary Veronica, A Good Catholic Girl*. Sprinkle has a one-woman show and book, *Annie Sprinkle, Post-Porn Modernist*. Both women are members of P.O.N.Y. (Prostitutes of New York).

The Walrus unzips his baggy pants and pulls his big red cock through his fly. He spreads the Vaseline over his penis and works his hand up and down, up and down, over a familiar path. I lean back in a high chair and plant a shiny stiletto pump on either side of the window. The Walrus extends his left hand to pick up the telephone. "Hello," he purrs, sounding much better than he looks. I cradle the phone under my chin, reach into my blouse and lift out my breasts. He stares at me from behind his thick glasses. I stare at the Walrus from behind my hard, dark nipples.

It's 1985, four years since the publication of my first explicit story, three years since I popped my porn cherry in a fuck film. I enjoy the sex biz but there's been this little gnawing fear that one day I'd wind up a side-show attraction, a girl in a peep show. When I decided to write about the 42nd Street Show World Sex Emporium, I knew that I would put myself inside this cage, a tiny glass booth, where men would drop their tokens and their pants to pay for the pleasure of seeing me naked. I guess what I want more than anything is to jump through this ring of fire, to live out this experience. The story is just an excuse.

The peep show is a seductive, rock & roll, neon cave that promises to all who enter some longed-for satisfaction. The customers look for an end to their frustrations. Most walk around like zombies, their hands in their pockets, while through the disco dazzle, the hawkers promise: "Hard core action upstairs in 10 minutes! Girls, girls, girls. Wall to wall pussy." The people who work here are attracted, at first, by the money. It's a job, a way to pay the rent and put food (sometimes drugs) on the table. But there are other hungers. Yes, each action is determined by the dollar, but there is desire for affection, the need for a basic, one-to-one, human connection that motivates every person who walks through the door.

I learned a lot about the Walrus before he entered my booth. I interviewed him upstairs after we watched a strip show in the Triple Treat Theater. He is a bridge player. He reads a lot—one of those unwashed intellectuals. He even tells me about his preference for Vaseline as an aid in jerking off. When he hears that I plan to spend a few hours working a booth, he runs across the street to Wahlgreen's and buys himself a king-sized jar of petroleum jelly.

The Walrus spends $50 in my booth, pumping in one $2 token after another. He wags his big tongue in circles up near the glass and pretends that we are kissing. His hairy mouth gobbles desperately at the phantom kisses. I am sorry for him for just an instant, but then enjoy a surge of power as I lick my lips and watch his tongue perform tricks in the air. He seems to relish the kisses even more than the creamy explosions he leaves on the glass.

Damian comes to work in a three-piece suit. He could be a cocky young clerk on the floor of the Stock Exchange or a bright guy from a tough neighborhood who has decided to work his way up in a bank. Like any guy just starting out, he doesn't quite have his look all together. A Brooklyn accent, patchy mustache, and the curls that creep over his shirt give him away. What Damian does have plenty of is ambition. His body jumps with it. You might say that he is perfecting his craft, tightening his act while he fucks on stage upstairs in the Triple Treat Theater, for twenty-five minutes, six times a day, sometimes six days a week. Damian wants to be a porno movie star.

His partner is Baby Doll, a slim Haitian girl with a tomboy quality. Her stiff black hair is cropped real short and her body is lithe like a bow. "We have some show-stoppers," Damian tells me. "There's the 69 we do with me standing up eating her and holding her upside down while she sucks my cock. We also have the 'wheelbarrow'—she bends over and puts her hands down on the floor, I stick my cock in her and wheel her around the room."

"Don't call them 'teams,' " warns Ron Martin, the manager of Triple Treat Theater. "You don't hitch them up to a wagon. These are 'performers.' " These performers, these teams, these women and men are engaged in a very unusual and controversial occupation—the Love Act. They do it for money.

Ivory and Major Motion have been working together for two years. Ivory calls herself that because she isn't quite black and she isn't quite white. She is very beautiful, the color of strong coffee with cream. Ivory hopes one day to live on the island of Jamaica. When Ivory met Major Motion, she was a virgin. They went out together for four months before they made love. Major Motion took his time with Ivory. He knew that she would be worth the wait. He was not exactly starved for sex because he followed the family tradition established by his older brother and got a job fucking on stage. Shortly after Major Motion and Ivory became lovers, they began performing the Love Act in public.

The men in the theater sit in quiet anticipation when Ivory enters the room. She dances on stage in a tight black dress. She is very tall, at least 5'10", and most of that is leg—gorgeous long legs that come to perfect points at the tips of her toes. Her arms, legs and back show a hint of muscle from her workouts at the gym. Ivory's perfect body wraps around the shabby black sofa on the stage. Soon, she is completely naked. Her thick, curly hair forms a lush mane around her face. Her eyes are big dark almonds that avoid the hypnotized stares of the audience.

Ivory pours herself like golden rum over the couch. She lifts her ass high in the air and her dark bush becomes the focus of every eye in the house. Her cunt looms up larger than life. It's a gateway to Paradise and Major Motion is about to slide in.

He saunters in from the side of the stage to join his partner. While he casually strips, she lies on her back, twists her long legs toward the ceiling and plays with her nipples. The Major's thick black tool pops out of his shorts. It is swollen with excitement, filled with the Major's spunk and with the horny desire of every man in the house. The Major fucks Ivory gently. He fucks her hard. He kisses her nipples, her belly, her thighs. The Major buries his face between her legs. Ivory, the serpent, coils around her man.

They are careful to make sure the audience can see every move, can watch every inch of cock as it is swallowed by cunt. My pussy muscles twitch as I feel the Major's cock sliding in and out of my hole. A man a few seats to my left masturbates vigorously. "Touch it, please touch it," he begs. Well, you'll never know if you don't ask. I admire his opportunism but ignore his request.

Major Motion and Ivory hold back on the orgasm. They still have four more shows to do today. The Major, like every stage stud, has to conserve some of his strength. Like the nutritionist in the health store up the block told Damian: "You've got to replenish your seminal fluids. If you don't take care now, by the time you are sixty you'll have shot your load."

Ivory knows exactly how much money she can make from a full week of shows. She and the Major each make $10 for every twenty-five minute performance. They work six days a weeks, six shows a day, and sometimes double shifts. It's the money, she says, that keeps her coming back. Her grandmother left her a house and she has to pay off the mortgage. The men in her family have all disappeared. But now there's Major Motion and he's daddy and brother and lover. She tells me of her dream to open a body-building gym in Jamaica. "There's so much I want to do," she says, "but I just don't know how to get started."

For Baby Doll, the money, too, is important. Baby Doll is twenty-one and the mother of a three-year-old daughter whom she raises alone. I ask her if she ever regrets having a child without a husband. "I used to feel bad," she tells me, "when I had nothing to give my little girl. But I don't feel bad anymore because now I earn the money to take care of her." Another dancer passing through the dressing room overhears her and adds, "Right on, sister."

Zoila, also known as "Z," worked for a year in the booths before she was promoted to manager on the first floor, a position she takes pride in. When I tell her that I want to spend a few hours in a booth, she looks at me like I've got glory holes in my head. She has seen me all week, dressed in a conservative skirt and blouse as I interviewed her and all the other people in the three-tiered emporium. She is delighted, dollar signs dancing in her eyeballs, when I come downstairs in my black lace lingerie.

"The split is 60/40," she tells me. Sixty for the house, forty for the booth baby. Each $2 token buys 90 seconds of time. I mentally calculate that in one hour's time, if the booth is never empty, the customers could deposit $90 worth of tokens in the coin slot. That's $36 for every hour of taking off my clothes, playing with myself, talking to the customers, spreading my legs, sticking my fingers inside my pussy, spreading my cheeks. . . .

The men enter in a steady stream. One is a whitebread college boy who wears a Princeton sweatshirt. Another is a young black man who spends twenty minutes dancing with me: by the times he leaves I am ready to collapse. Clink, clink, clink, clink. I love the sound of those deposits. The money inspires a Pavlovian reaction. Up in the chair, out with the tits, hand in the panties, stand up, strip down, start all over again. An eighty-year old regular has a neat gimmick. He carries a big box of flimsy lingerie and offers to sell it to the performers real cheap. I met him upstairs when he sold me a bra and then copped a feel when I tried it on. Now he's in the booth pulling out his nearly hundred-year old dick. It's got a few hairs growing out of it that probably weren't there when he was forty, but the thing still works and he's real happy with it. When he exits, the lingerie salesman presses a buck tip into my palm. It's nice to be appreciated. Another man with a gruff voice and gold chains around his neck barks orders at me through the glass. He is the only one of a dozen men who chooses not to use the two-way telephone. He wants only to see my asshole. "Turn around. Spread your cheeks. Wider. Wider!" He doesn't seem to understand that I'm a fucking goddess. I can't wait for him to get out. "You want to see an asshole, mister, look in the mirror!" Lines like that are made for guys like him. He is one of the few who goes without coming. And he's definitely the one who could use it the most.

I get along well with the other women in the row of cubicles. Only one is pissed because until I showed up, she was the only white woman on the block. The others all work upstairs on the main level. She walks off the floor and for this she will be fined by Z.

Z runs a tight ship. She is protective of the women who work for her, but she believes in nipping trouble in the bud. When she does not have enough women on duty, she has to fill in herself and this manager has no desire to rejoin the labor force.

In the two hours I stay in the booth, I take in $112 out of a possible $180. My end is approximately $45, not bad for a couple of hours of work. But could I do it for six or eight hours a day, five or six days a week? A lip-licking wind-up doll. Not all of the women can. The most reliable workers have well-lighted spots on the main floor in a place called "the hill." The women who show up only when they feel like it work in a dark corner referred to charmingly as "death row."

When I return a few days later to pick up my check, I stop in to see Ron, the boss of the Triple Treat Theater. He tells me that he's sorry he missed me in the booth and offers me ten dollars to show him my tits. He lays a ten on the table and I unbutton my blouse. I give him a look at my naked breasts and scoop up that ten in my greedy little fist. Now I am starting to get the hang of this place. The boss sees the big smile on my face and decides that he's parted with his ten too easily. "Now, how about paying ten bucks to see my cock?"

Is he crazy! Maybe he thinks I'm really cockeyed! I saw enough dicks that week to last me quite awhile and every one of them got whipped out for free. It does not take long to learn that in the game of sex and money, it's the man who comes up with the cash.

But do they really know what to do with their money? It's been several years since my first visit to Show World. I've made it my business to do considerable research in the field. The Love Act is currently forbidden but except for technological changes, the peep shows remain the same. As we approach the new millennium, why not have erotic emporiums reflect a new attitude? I propose the creation of one or more SEC's in cities across the country. This does not stand for the Securities and Exchange Commission which governs Wall Street, though it is an interesting coincidence. No, these SEC's would be Sexual Evolution Centers, conceived in liberty and dedicated to the proposition that sex is a nourishing, life-giving force and that sex work is of benefit to humanity. Let's begin with the practical considerations, how to make the SEC's accessible to both the clients and performers. On-premise child-care facilities are a must. Professionals like Baby Doll would welcome this convenience as would prospective clients, particularly housewives. SEC's would be for the female as well as male clientele.

No one would have to go without sexual nourishment for want of funds. We could issue fuck stamps the way we do food stamps. Or access to sexual nutrition could be incorporated in our desperately needed national health care plan. The government, however, would not be allowed to legislate the libido. For the guiding principle of SEC's would be the concept of sexual evolution. We are all at different stages in our sexual development. In terms of each individual's experience, nothing is bizarre, kinky or perverse. It all makes sense. Or, more succinctly, "different strokes for different folks." The prevalent atmosphere would be one of ecstasy and experimentation.

Working in SEC's would be an enviable position and the sex professionals would be revered for their expertise and the potent sensuality that keeps them strong and vibrant. Wages would reflect a grateful society.

Scientists could develop ways to channel the tremendous energy generated in SEC's so that it could be used to fuel entire communities.

The very first time I entered a Times Square burlesque house, a pretty blonde with a pony tail came dancing out, wearing only a pair of high heels. She bobbed around for a while, then sat on the edge of the stage, leaned back on the floor and spread her legs. The men in the theater left their seats and formed a line, single file, in front of her cunt. Each one of the men clutched a bill in his hand. I looked at that scene through my Catholic girl eyes and I knew this was a form of Holy Cummunion, another ironic coincidence of words. After ten years of explicit research, I see sex more than ever as a sacrament. A powerful and intimate connection with the universal energy, no matter where it is performed, or for how long, or with whom. And I also believe that what you see is what you get.

acid snow

l a r r y   m i t c h e l l

Jake was staring at the frost on the window, thinking about dead friends and longing for love to invade his life when the phone rang.

"Is it still cold there?"

"My windows are frozen over."

"It's not natural."

"It's January."

"It's the Greenhouse Effect."

"That's supposed to make it warmer."

"It makes everything more extreme. The cold is colder and the hot is hotter. Wait 'til this summer. Then you'll cook."

"Is it still cold there?"

larry mitchell has lived and worked in New York City since 1960. He is the author of *My Life as a Mole and Five Other Stories* (1989), *In Heat: A Romance* (1986), *The Terminal Bar* (1982) and *The Faggots and Their Friends Between the Revolutions* (1977).

"Unbelievable. And I have to go out each morning and poke around in the bushes under the bedroom window with my broom to get rid of those FBI agents. The neighbors must think I'm batty."

"He still hears them drilling?"

"He's up all night, stamping on the floor, yelling at them to go spy on Richard Nixon. By morning he's hysterical 'til I go out with my broom and chase them away."

"No wonder he thinks they're real. You shouldn't go out and chase them away since they're not there."

"It calms him down. He's an old man. They did terrible things to him during the reign of terror headed by that man whose name we don't mention. They got him fired and got him expelled from his union. He loved that union, and then they blacklisted him. I had to go to work in that hat shop at the very moment when hats were going out of fashion. Terrible."

"I know about the bad times. I was there."

"You were young."

"I was young, but I was still there. That was thirty-five years ago. They hurt him then. They're not after him now."

"We still read the *Nation*, big deal. I buy the other stuff downtown at the newsstand. You know, the one you worked at that summer. Mr. Daminsky's son has it now. We don't even belong to it anymore." Her voice went higher and louder. "And we haven't belonged to it for years." Her voice returned to its normal shrillness. "That was in case they are listening. I still see some of the old gang here and there. Your Aunt Zelda and I went to a demonstration against those awful antiabortion fanatics outside an abortion clinic. Your aunt brought her usual flask of bourbon, which for once I must say I was grateful, 'cause it was beyond cold out there. She brought some wire coat hangers, you know her flair for the dramatic, and we were waving them in the air and yelling, 'We won't go back to the alleys,' when I spotted Martha Hopwood, that real WASPy one who used to wear a mink coat to party meetings. She remembered Zelda. She was still wearing that same coat, though we thought it looked a little ratty. I guess even mink wears out."

"I got a new bird."

"A bird? You need a boyfriend. A bird is no substitute for a boyfriend."

"I have good friends."

"What about that nice boy you brought to Cleveland? I liked Adam."

"His name was Harry and he moved to L.A."

"I wish you and your sister were closer. Then I wouldn't worry so much about being alone. But she's too rich to care about her family."

"I had dinner there the other night."

"She cooked?"

"Madeline cooked."

"What does she know about cooking. She comes from big oil money."

"They have to eat too."

"They hire people to do that for them. What'd she make?"

"Steak, potatoes and salad."

"Your sister couldn't do that?"

"Kate made the martinis."

"Why is it when people get some money, they start in on the martinis? Did she get drunk?"

"I got drunk."

"I hope you watched your wallet."

"She *is* my sister." Jake looked at the ice crystal spider webs on the window to remind himself that there were worlds other than Sophie's.

"The rich have no scruples. Sam always says they'll send their own loved ones to the poorhouse if it will make them any richer." Jake heard banging. "Oh god, Sam's banging on the wall. You wait right there and I'll get some pills in him and call you back."

Jake put on the answering machine and went to bed.

• • •

The weatherman, close to hysteria, warned of a blizzard. When Jake left the library, a few flakes were floating in the wind. The streets were empty. The cold had finally driven the drug dealers inside.

Sylvester opened the door, holding a long fork with a piece of something stuck on it. He looked awful. "I'm making tuna melts. That's all I can cope with. Coffee?"

"Sure."

Sylvester poured a cup for himself, drank it in one gulp and screamed, "Shit! I burned my mouth!"

"Do I get to burn _my_ mouth?"

"I forgot." He handed a cup to Jake and began to pace.

"What is wrong, Sylvester?"

"Jason didn't come home last night."

"Where was he?"

"If I knew would I be worried?" Sylvester barked.

"Did he show up for work?"

"Yeah, but he left early. That jerk said he arrived plastered, played a few songs, then left in a huff. It's cold and he could be anywhere."

"Or with anyone."

"If he'd just come home, the rest I'll deal with later."

The phone made Sylvester jump. "Hello. . . . No, he's not here. . . . I'm sure he'll be there. . . . If I see him I'll tell him. . . . I know about last night. You told me last night. . . . Yes, I'll tell him, Mr. Pepperoni."

"Mr. Pepperoni?"

"Did I call him that? What's his name? Pepitoni? Oh god, he'll think I'm a racist."

"Jason's not at work, I take it."

"Cocktail hour has started without him and if he doesn't show soon and sober, he doesn't need to show at all."

"A cocktail lounge is probably not the perfect place for Jason to work."

"I thought a job would do him good."

"AA would do him more good."

"You tell him."

"Jason doesn't listen to me. He doesn't even like me."

"Yes he does. He says, of all my friends, you're his favorite."

"That doesn't mean he likes me."

"He's so gloomy and solitary these days. He doesn't seem to be here or there or anywhere. He's wandered away from me."

"Drinking is a gloomy, solitary pleasure."

"It's an addiction."

"Addictions are pleasurable. That's how they get us hooked. I remember your year with Sister Morphine."

"She was a dream. There was pleasure. But I woke up and gave her up. Give me a cigarette, Jake. My nerves are shot." Sylvester inhaled until he coughed. "Now I've got no sex and it looks like even simple affection is over. Jason stopped touching me and stopped hugging me, stopped all hints of tenderness. Maybe I can cope without sex, but living without affection will be a real test of my nerves."

The front door banged open. Jason weaved toward them, smiling. He was covered with snow.

"Looks like a blizzard hit," Sylvester said, masking all emotion.

"It's just acid snow. Lovely acid snow killing everything it lands on." He went to the nearest cabinet and pulled open the doors. "Where's the bottle of gin?"

"You drank that weeks ago."

He noticed Jake. "Jake. Haven't seen you in a long time."

"I saw you at Alexander's party a couple of weeks ago."

"Oh yeah, I don't remember. Must have been a dud of a party. So let's have a drink. It's cold out there."

"There's coffee."

"Fuck coffee." Jason opened cabinets and drawers until he found a pint of rum.

"I didn't know that was there," Sylvester said softly.

"Thank god I did."

"Your boss called. He said if you don't come in tonight, don't come in."

"Good. I can't play fucking *Volare* one more fucking time."

"Where did you stay last night?" Sylvester tried to keep any tone of accusation out of his voice.

"Last night? I don't know. It was warm." A smile appeared. "Some guy tried to suck me off but I don't think I let him."

"Who was the guy?"

"No one important. None of it's important. Just a way to pass the time until. . . ."

"Until what?"

Jason fell onto the floor like a tree that had just been cut down. He began to snore.

• • •

"What's that?"

"A geranium."

"Looks in bad shape."

"It froze to death." Jake plunked the geranium in the garbage and made room on the table for Edgar's two large bags of vegetables. Edgar walked up to the bird and began to say, "Pretty Boy, Pretty Boy," over and over. Jake stuffed vegetables into the crisper drawers until they were full. Then he stacked the rest on the counter. Edgar's "Pretty Boy" began to take on an edge as the bird remained mute.

"This isn't working," he announced.

The phone rang. It was Kate. "Did you get the tests?"

"I went to the doctor yesterday. He says I'm his healthiest patient."

"Did he do a sperm count?"

"I have to go to a fertility clinic for that. It's very embarrassing."

"What about the HIV test?"

"I'll know in a couple of weeks."

"A couple of weeks! Madeline's going to ovulate in three days."

"Another wasted egg down the tubes."

"She thought she'd get the trust fund the moment she conceived, but the lawyer says she doesn't get it 'til she gives birth. She is pissed off. She may sue."

"Could be a landmark case," Jake said with irony, knowing Kate never heard irony.

"Let me know what the results are. Send me the bills. We'll pay for everything. Oh, and can you check out a storefront for Madeline? It's right near you. She may rent it for her art gallery. I think the neighborhood is too slummy for an art gallery, but Madeline says you can sell art anywhere."

"My neighborhood may be a slum, but it's a high rent slum."

"Who wants to step over derelicts and drug addicts to buy art?"

"Drug addicts are people too."

"You know what I mean," Kate said sharply.

"I thought it was art *or* a baby."

"She can't make up her mind, so she's doing both. Let's hope one of them works out. Some success would be good for her."

"To match your own success?"

"If *you* had some success, you wouldn't be so nasty."

"That was my sister," Jake said, hanging up the phone.

"You don't like her very much."

"She's still my sister. I try."

"You still don't like her."

"Every decent thing our parents ever taught us, she dismisses."

"Like what?"

"Like thinking equality is good and justice is worth something. That there's more to life than making money." Saying such things embarrassed Jake and he laughed. "There I go being old-fashioned again. Nobody believes in that stuff anymore."

"I do."

"Well, maybe a couple of us still do."

"But your sister's not one of them."

"If she weren't so damn militant and smug about her greed, I could take more of her." Jake found himself waving a celery stalk in the air and staring at a curl on Edgar's forehead. "Thanks again for the vegetables. What do I owe you?"

"They're a present. They're too old to sell."

"They won't all fit in the fridge. I'll make a soup and you can stay for dinner. Do you want to?" He hoped he didn't sound too eager.

"Dinner? Sure. But not overnight."

"Overnight?"

"And no sex."

"Sex? Who said anything about sex? I just mentioned soup."

"It's in the air."

"Yeah, but who said anything about it." Jake began to furiously chop celery.

"It's nothing personal."

"It's always personal when someone says no."

"It's disease and dying and the idea that sex equals death. It's just turned me off."

"Your letting that filthy government propaganda ruin your sex life." Jake started in on the carrots.

"The erotic is fragile."

"Mine isn't."

"I'm too self-conscious. The city has made me paranoid. I haven't been here that long. I'm not used to rushing into things."

"Not everyone here is in the fast lane. We'll just have vegetable soup." Jake grabbed the phone on the first ring.

"Jake?"

"Edgar's here."

"Who?" Sylvester asked.

"The man I buy eggs from."

"Oh," he said, giving the word more meaning than it could bear.

"For dinner."

This "oh" became a thirty second sentence.

"But not for sex."

The "oh" deflated to normal. Edgar looked dumbfounded.

"He was getting the wrong idea," Jake said, hanging up the phone.

"I'm just here to teach this bird to call you Pretty Boy. Pretty Boy, Pretty Boy," Edgar cooed.

The bird squawked, "Sucker," and they both laughed.

• • •

Walking up the stairs to Paul's, Sylvester asked, "How did it go with the egg man?"

"We ate vegetable soup and then argued about politics. He thinks the organic, new age movement will save the planet. And I think capitalism and greed will destroy it."

"That's why you didn't have sex?"

"The epidemic has lowered his libido."

"You didn't mention safe sex?"

"I'm more interested in love than I am in sex."

"I think sex is safer."

When they walked in, Paul was sitting up in bed, going through his rolodex. Discarded cards lay everywhere.

"Feeling better?" Jake asked, hoping the question was appropriate.

"I pooped. That was better." His words came slowly and his voice sounded like it was hiding high in his head.

"It's great we moved our bowels," Sylvester said cheerfully.

"They are *my* bowels, and I moved them myself to New Jersey and I think I'll leave them there." Pleased with his little joke, he extracted a card from the rolodex. "I won't have this card anymore. I met this slime-ball on the street and he read me."

"He said what?"

"He said I looked better and I said, a damn sight better than you look." Paul giggled. "I won't have him in my life." He tossed the card on the bed. Jake picked it up. It had Sylvester's name on it. He handed it to Sylvester. Sylvester shrugged and dropped it on the floor. "I'm clearing out my life. There's too much crap in it."

"Are you hungry?"

"I'm tired. I went to Mary Beth's party. Everyone was so polite, no, so cautious with me. They smiled and complained about the weather. You get sick and suddenly no one will dish you anymore. Tedious." He lay back exhausted.

"I'll make you some dinner," Sylvester said sadly.

"Hold my hand, Jake. It feels so friendly." Jake got on the bed and took his hand. "It's not about sex. It's just friendly."

"I'm not your type anyway, remember?" Jake said, trying for a light note.

"Mean boys are what I liked, I guess. Anyway, that's what I always got. Not much friendliness there."

His eyes closed. Jake couldn't hear him breathe but he felt the blood moving through the veins in Paul's hand.

"Fish on our favorite blue plate." Paul's eyes opened a slit. "Have some fish, Paul," Sylvester said firmly.

"Is it dead?"

"Of course."

"Poor fishy's gone to heaven. Paul's going to heaven with the fishy." He took the plate and poked the fillet with his finger. "My mother called me."

"That's unusual," Sylvester mused.

"She's snooping around, trying to see if I've got any money to leave her. I told her I had plenty of poop stored up and she was welcome to that." He put a sliver of fish in his mouth and swallowed it. "She's trying to get in some old man's pants. I told her to leave the old men alone or she'll give them heart attacks." The plate slipped out of his hand. Sylvester caught it.

"No more delicious fish?"

"I'm so tired." His voice was far away. "All the tiredness there ever was is inside of me." He moved his hand across the bed. Jake took hold of it. "Rub my feet." Sylvester took a foot and stoked it. "This is no fun, Jake. Not that my life was that fun before, but this is really not fun." Sylvester stroked until Paul slept.

"He's losing his mind," Sylvester announced.

"He seems as evil as ever."

"None of those things happened. He refuses to speak to his mother. There wasn't any party at Mary Beth's, and I never read him on the street."

"But all those things could have happened. So he's not completely nuts."

"Not yet."

• • •

Piles of blackened snow, left over from the brief blizzard, made walking treacherous. Jake had his head down as a wedge to force his body through the wind, when he ran into some who muttered, "Shit." He looked up at Jason in dark glasses and no hat.

"You'll freeze to death."

"Buy me a drink." He took Jake's arm firmly and shoved him into a bar. "A double scotch with a beer chaser," he ordered. "What do you want?"

Jake wanted to go home. "A beer, I guess."

"Give my man here a beer." Jason took off the dark glasses and Jake saw the eyes of a man on a long binge. "I have to leave Sylvester." Jake's heart broke. "But it's hard to do."

"You've been together a while now."

"So what. The problem is it's Sylvester's apartment and he pays all the bills."

"Then get a fucking job." Jake's anger was too hot to conceal.

"I can't keep a job."

"Then sober up."

"It always comes down to that. Sober up. And when I sober up, I get so depressed over what a mess I've made of my life, I want to kill myself."

"Then kill yourself." Jake wanted out of there.

"There would be no one to mourn me but good old loyal Sylvester."

"Why'd you stop loving him?"

"'Cause he wouldn't stop loving me." Jason's hand shook so badly he couldn't light his cigarette. Jake lit it for him and lit one for himself. "No matter what I've done to him, he just keeps loving me. I cut off sex, I stopped touching him, I barely talk to him and he never says a word, never complains. I'd throw me the fuck out, but he just goes on being nice. It's finally made me hate him."

"Leave him. Leave him tonight." Jake's rage was steaming.

"I'm too busy getting drunk." He finished his scotch and ordered another.

Jake fumed. "Tomorrow you won't remember any of this and I'll remember every word and where will that leave me?"

Jason laughed. "You need to drink more. If you don't have to remember what you do, you can have more fun." He leaned closer to Jake. "Why don't you take me home and I'll fuck you."

Jake was horrified. "Do I look that desperate?"

"Sylvester's always saying how lonely you are and how he wishes you'd find someone."

"I don't think it was you he hoped I'd find."

"It was just a thought. You drink enough of this shit and you don't care if you get rejected. Drink enough of this shit and you start to like being rejected. It goes with the territory."

"Have you told Sylvester how you feel?"

"No need for that. He knows. One day I'll just split. Go live with Ma. She's dying in Miami. They give her a lot of morphine."

"You two can die together in Miami."

"At least it's hot there."

"You've been with Sylvester a few years. Doesn't that mean anything to you? Don't you have feelings of friendship or something for him?"

"When it's done, it's done. Someone's got to end it. He won't. He just holds on like there is something left to hold on to. It's pathetic."

"I've heard enough," Jake said and swung on his bar stool. Jason caught his arm.

"Buy me one more drink and I'll tell you funny stories."

"Do you know any?"

"I used to play the piano in this cocktail lounge in North Miami Beach. At five o'clock all the blue-haired ladies would show up, have a couple of drinks and beg me to play romantic songs from World War II. Then they'd stare silently into their drinks and remember when their men went off to war."

"They were sentimental about slaughter?"

"The fear that death was near made romance sweet and passionate."

"This is not a funny story."

"The funny part is that when the danger passed, so did the romance. All that was left was kids and mortgages and hard work. Now the husbands are dead and the blue-haired ladies drink too much and long for the only time there was any passion in their lives."

Jake put a five-dollar bill on the bar and walked out.

on the bowery
j a c k   h e n r y   a b b o t t

It is not my intention to say here that the City commits crimes
against its citizens. There is an ancient piece of wisdom which tells us that
a city is what the people living in it make of it.

Manhattan is a marvelous, fantastic, multi-faceted world of high culture.
There are people there whose talents and genius have no challengers,
people whom only the gods stand beside now. Manhattan is the sun at the
center of all the wealth in the universe. No power on earth, or in the rumored
colonies of the moon and the planet Mars, is greater than the power
emanating from Manhattan. If there was a Golden Age of Babylon, in which
all that made it a name of infamy had not existed, Manhattan is that Babylon.
There are streets of gold in Manhattan.

But there are streets of refuse, too, and for whatever reason, in the cosmic
scheme of things in Manhattan, there are the lowest dregs of humanity as
well. I have been to many cities, cities that have no slum sections, cities that

jack henry abbott is the author of _In the Belly of the Beast_
(New York: Vintage, 1981). His most recent book is _My
Return_ (Buffalo: Prometheus Books, 1987).

are uniformly clean, uniformly middle-class (even their workers), and these cities are what we call "decent."

Manhattan is not a decent city. Salt Lake City is a decent city. There is no mad rush of human beings to go to Salt Lake City, either. Unless we carefully define what we mean by the word culture, we cannot seriously say that there is culture in any "decent" city.

I say all that to say this: No one should be held responsible for Manhattan. Manhattan is not only alive and well because of its wealth and culture, but probably also because of its variety. Because everyone is responsible for himself.

When I first went to Manhattan I was overwhelmed. I had mixed feelings. I saw the worst sides of Manhattan because I lived there. But I was also a visitor to the best sides of Manhattan. From where I lived, in the darkest corners of the City, the brightest promises beckoned me to all the fabulous culture of Manhattan.

I arrived in Manhattan at three o'clock in the morning of June 6, 1981. I had just served nineteen years in prison. I arrived in a taxi at the Salvation Army on Bowery Street, between Second and Third Avenues, located directly across the narrow street from the Men's Shelter. Few people know there is such a thing as Bowery Street. First Street is Bowery Street. But everyone has heard of the Bowery. During the six weeks I spent in Manhattan I lived in a room in the Salvation Army on the Bowery. In all honesty I found nothing pleasing on the Bowery. Not one fond memory—and I have many memories of the Bowery during that summer of 1981. I am fully aware that what does not suit me probably suits someone else. Merely because I did not like the Bowery does not mean it was a bad place. Indeed, I can even imagine how the Bowery could be a wonderful place for others. I am not the judge of the Bowery, nor of anything else that runs against my grain. But, I have no grudges and it is not my intention here to do anything but give a description of only a few of my memories of the Bowery.

One more preliminary remark. I spent as little time as possible on the Bowery. I fled uptown, or to the park on Washington Square, or to the Staten

Island Ferry. The gentle reader might softly retort that had I spent more time on the Bowery getting to know everyone, and what it was all about there, I would have had fond memories. That may be true, but I prefer even now not to find out. This was not the East Village, despite what my critics say.

I cannot recount the succession of things that follow with any certainty. They are memories of random events, random images. They are only samplings and are not a complete list. I do not recall even one dull moment on the Bowery, and I remember every moment.

● ● ●

I was shown to my room and I immediately took off my clothes and got into bed. I could not sleep, due to the effects of jet lag. I tried to force myself to sleep. I did not get out of bed until dawn began to rise. I opened my tired eyes and stared at the ceiling. The grayness of dawn began to filter through the windows, casting its glow on the ceiling. As I lay there staring at the ceiling, I heard the beating of what sounded like a steel drum. It was being beaten by someone's hands, like a tom-tom, and had started with the first rays of dawn. It began to ring monotonously in my mind, so I finally rose and stepped over to the window. I raised the blind and looked out. The window was open. Sitting on the curb at the corner across the street there was a man wearing filthy jeans and a tee-shirt. He needed a shave. He was sitting on the curb with his feet in the gutter. There was a dirty handkerchief tied around his head. His long brown hair fell wildly about his shoulders. He had a steel garbage can turned upside down between his legs. All its contents were in piles around him and he was beating the bottom of the garbage can with a pathetic vengeance. He was using his fists and the palms of his hands, alternately. I stared at him for awhile, then my gaze passed along and took in the immediate environment. Debris was everywhere in the street and sidewalks. Third Avenue traffic had not yet started. The streets were deserted.

Then I noticed a body laying stretched out on the sidewalk against a rundown building. And then another and another and another.

The bodies of sleeping derelicts were scattered liberally around the sidewalks and on the stoops of buildings. It took me by surprise. My mind was blank. I finally thought: "What the hell is this?" I decided I had better find out. I had worn an expensive three-piece suit when I left prison and taken the flight to the City. I had no other clothing. I put on my suit and stepped out into the hall. I went quickly down the stairs and approached the man on duty at the desk. I asked where I could get a cup of coffee. He informed me that feeding time there at the halfway house would not begin for another hour and a half. He suggested I go to a restaurant in the neighborhood. I stepped out onto the sidewalk. As soon as I stepped out the bodies lying in the gutter, all around me, came to life. I glanced around and could see no restaurant as I walked to the corner of Third Avenue. Behind me the hurrying footsteps of at least a half dozen derelicts caught my attention. I stopped and glanced over my shoulder. I was instantly surrounded by demands for money. I looked at the haggard faces of aging middle-aged men, at their desperate eyes, as their requests, repeated over and over again, rose to high whining pitches. I pulled out all the change in my pockets and extended it in my palms. It vanished. There were more pleas, so I reached into my pocket and took out several one dollar bills and passed them out. As they shuffled away one at a time other derelicts rose up and came to me until there was almost a mad rush to me. I stepped backward and almost fell off the curb into the street. I looked around at all of them, and the others who were still coming. I felt sorry for them but at the same time I knew that I could not feed them all. I turned my back to them by way of walking a few steps farther into the street. Miraculously a taxicab appeared. I signalled and it stopped. I climbed in. He drove up Third Avenue as he asked me where I wanted to go. All I replied was: "To any restaurant away from here."

I was later told by a friend uptown that the conditions in the streets of the Bowery were worse than usual because the mental hospitals, in particular Mattawan, had been recently closed down. Thousands of mental hospital inmates had been sent to the City with instructions on how to find the Men's

Shelter for food. They were also instructed that, if they did not want to sleep in the Men's Shelter, they could sleep on the sidewalks and in the doorways of buildings. I was told by several experts that the mortality rate in the mental institutions was too low; they expected a sharp rise in the mortality rate of the inmates if they had to care for themselves. The idea was to let nature take its course. The plan worked.

So I understood that the situation on the Bowery that June and July of 1981 was exceptional. I was told this a few days after I arrived.

These were the last days before the police apprehended a man who was known as *The Slasher*. He was arrested a block away from the halfway house about two weeks after I arrived. He had been terrorizing the streets in that area for a long time by wielding a knife against unsuspecting people.

That first day in the City I bought a new pair of trousers and a shirt at Macy's. The next day I wore my shirt and trousers and left my expensive suit in my room. When I returned to my room the suit was gone. A new lock was installed on my door, at my request.

Rossi, a big Italian a few years younger than I—I was thirty-seven at the time—took me up Third Avenue to a restaurant just on the outskirts of the Bowery. It was nighttime. As we were waiting at the counter for the pizza we had ordered, with the doors of the restaurant wide open to the sidewalk, a drunken woman staggered in and threatened everyone in the restaurant. She was a young woman in a nice-looking beige dress. She was good looking. She was a slim blonde. She was bare-footed and had apparently lost her dentures. She did not have a tooth in her head. As she staggered belligerently into the restaurant she began waving her fists. I pulled my head away and dodged a blow. Rossi shouted: "You fucking whore! Get outta here!" We got up from our stools and I stepped out on the sidewalk to leave. Rossi came behind me. The woman followed us out screaming obscenities, trying to hit us with her fists. A man in his mid-thirties ordered her to stop. She stopped immediately, with a frightened expression on her face. He walked up to me, ignoring Rossi, and told me that this woman was his "whore" and belonged to him. He narrowed his pale blue eyes. He told me, as I stood there amazed, that if I did not leave her alone he was going to have me killed by one of the men he indicated standing in front of the establishment next door to the restaurant we had just left. Before I could say anything, Rossi took me by the arm and pulled me away. We walked away down the sidewalk. Rossi had been raised on the Lower East Side. He had taken a liking to me. He wanted to help me adjust to the area.

It was that night, less than an hour after the incident with the "whore," that I saw a parked car fire-bombed. It was about ten o'clock at night. Rossi was explaining to me, on the sidewalk in front of the Salvation Army, that the Bowery had many strange people living there but that they were basically harmless. Rossi was facing me with his back to Third Avenue. Rossi talks with his hands. As I stood there watching him talk to me, there was a sudden flare of light just over his shoulder. My attention locked on it. Rossi spun around. It was as if a bomb had exploded. Just as the inside of the parked car was engulfed in flames, I saw the furtive figure of a small man run from the car and vanish in the shadows between two buildings. We both stood and watched the car as it was consumed by flames, until the fire engine from the firehouse, only a hundred yards away, arrived. They put out the flames and left. Most of the people on the sidewalk did not bother to watch.

The next morning Rossi was taking me over to Washington Square Park in his effort to help me adjust. The park was a few blocks away. When we were about a block away from the park a frazzled, excited young man ran up to us, stopping us on the sidewalk. He was out of breath from running. He was frightened. He needed help. He had just been beaten and robbed by "a group of black men." He needed money to have his car repaired so he could go home. I reached for my wallet without hesitating, but Rossi grabbed my hand. "Don't give 'im nuttin'!" Rossi shouted. The young man grinned as he started walking cautiously backwards, away from Rossi. "Come 'ere, ya scumbag!" Rossi shouted. The kid spun around, giving Rossi his back, and ran for his life. Rossi chased him up the street. They disappeared around the corner. I must have waited around that area for an hour. Then I went over to the park alone.

That night Rossi explained to me how the kids had been pulling con games by playing on racial sympathies in the streets.

I never saw a child anywhere on the Bowery, which must have been an indication of something. I saw, on different occasions, two dogs off their leashes. One was a black, female Belgian shepherd, who came every evening to eat garbage from the gutter in front of the halfway house. She walked slowly with her head lowered, her gray eyes glowering madly. She had acquired a reputation as dangerous by the men at the halfway house. They said she had a litter of puppies somewhere nearby.

In all the delis I had occasion to try to eat in, all the pastries were moldy and the meat was half rotten. I complained once and the waiter would do no more than take a fork and scrape the mold away on a piece of pie. One evening as I walked to a deli half a block away, I looked up suddenly as a Great Dane brushed past me on the sidewalk. It was the first Great Dane I had ever encountered. It was the first time a dog had ever intimidated me, even though he was friendly. I had never experienced that same feeling of vulnerability before, nor since then.

I remember several times one or another of the inmates pointing and explaining to me that what was taking place a short distance away from where we stood was a mugging. The last one that was pointed out to me was on the sidewalk next door to the Men's Shelter across the street from where we stood. As I looked—and everyone in my group was watching—all I saw was the broad back of a bald-headed male with two ears that resembled door knobs. Then, as he stepped away, a man was sitting on the sidewalk with his back resting against the building as if he were sleeping.

As I was walking alone to the laundry on First Street three or four derelicts, one of whom I used to give money to, stood in my path and confronted me like mobsters in a movie and demanded money. I looked at the one I had befriended. He must have been fifty years old, perpetually needing a shave, haggard, weak, emaciated. They called him Joe the Wino at the halfway house. I grinned at him and he glared at me gangster-style. I laughed at the old farts and asked them how much they wanted. They brokenly explained that they needed enough for at least three bottles of cheap wine. I gave them the money. I told them never to ask me for a handout again. I walked through them and continued on my way.

It must have been a day or two later, in the afternoon, when Joe the Wino and one of his fellow winos were fighting in the gutter in front of the Salvation Army. Two old winos fighting has to be one of the most amusing sights there are. It was impossible for them to hurt each other, they were so weak. Finally, Joe seized an empty wine bottle by its neck and smashed it against the curb. He stumbled toward the other wino, who started stumbling backwards and finally turned and swerved a few feet away, glancing about him on the ground. He too found an empty wine bottle, broke it and turned and faced Joe. They circled each other and moved around in a stumbling way, cursing in the middle of the street. I do not know the outcome, since I did not stay and watch.

Aging transsexuals losing the battle against their male hormones hung out in front of at least three tenements on the Bowery. They all looked like grandfathers in dresses and makeup. I am not aware of them ever bothering anyone.

Two or three derelicts tried to sell me a variety of items, which had clearly been stolen out of cars or apartments. One of the stops along their route selling swag merchandise was the halfway house. I bought a radio for a dollar, just to get rid of them one day. I wondered if they knew anything about my stolen suit.

The purchase of heroin was as easy as buying beer. It is well known among drug addicts that the best heroin is to be purchased on the streets of the Bowery. Real junkies only buy good dope. The neighborhood was rife with addicts. Some of them occasionally imposed upon me to give them urine samples to hand in—the halfway house was also a drug-use screening center.

One day, about a block away, I saw an amusing incident. A tall thin man wearing black shoes, blacks slacks, a long black overcoat, a black hat and beard walked up to a tenement building carrying a black attache case. Two derelicts saw him coming from the landing at the top of the steps to the tenement. Both were around forty years of age. One of them was stocky. The man dressed in black was collecting rent, I was told. As he started up the steps the husky derelict moved like a cat down the steps past him, as part of a plan to encircle him and rob him. I watched this with someone else, from a distance. The man in black stopped midway up the steps. The man at the top of the steps was confronting him as the one behind him started closing in. Without hesitation, with an air of irritation, he placed his attache case on the step in front of him, snapped it open, lifted up the lid with one hand and calmly, without pause, reached in and pulled out a small hatchet. He raised it and turned, frowning impatiently, to the husky one behind him, who backed away in fright. Then he turned and took a step up toward the other. He irritably stood and watched the derelict as he leapt over the railing and landed on the ground. He stepped up to the landing, put his hatchet back in his attache case and opened the door. He walked into the tenement. It looked like a routine procedure. The derelicts crept away down the street.

One morning someone came in half carrying a man in his late twenties. The man being helped was over six feet tall. He helped him sit on the cushion of the naugahyde couch I was sitting on in front of the fan. It was exceptionally hot that summer. The man was filthy, his clothes were torn. His right pants leg was bursting at the seams. They were trying to talk to him to find out what was wrong with him. He had been lying in the gutter down the street for three days before someone decided to help him into the Salvation Army. From what they could get out of him, he had been wandering in the street one night and a car had struck him. He had crawled between two parked cars. His right leg was broken. It had been bleeding. He was wearing a tennis shoe without shoe laces, on his right foot, without socks. His foot was swollen and it too had been bleeding. From the odor he exuded it was clear that he had soiled his pants. He was angrily insisting on a sandwich. At times he balled up his fists threateningly. Shocks of ash blond hair stuck out from his head in all directions. His eyes were crazed. When the ambulance arrived he struggled. They had to subdue him to get him onto the stretcher.

Coming back from the laundry down First Avenue I and two other inmates, as usual, had to step over sleeping bodies in various positions on the sidewalk. About twenty yards from the halfway house, lying on his back in the middle of the sidewalk, someone was masturbating intensely, straight up to the sky. His eyes were squeezed tightly shut. It should have been amusing, but it was not. None of us could laugh although we tried to see humor in it.

There were a few chairs along the wall in front of the halfway house which faced the Men's Shelter across the street. One day I was sitting there with other inmates, most of whom were standing. Directly across the street a huge derelict, who must have weighed close to three hundred pounds, was sleeping on the sidewalk in the slanting shadows of the building. He stood up and, in full view of all of us, walked into the exact middle of the street. He lowered his pants clear to his ankles, pulled up his tee shirt, spread his legs and squatted in almost a standing position. Then he took a bowel movement that must have been two feet long. It was so long it curled on the asphalt. Then he took a step forward, pulled down his shirt, hoisted his pants back up, shambled back to his spot on the sidewalk, lay down and went right back to sleep. Again, everyone found it difficult to laugh. Everyone looked at each other and tried to talk about something else.

There was a large madwoman, a screamer who shouted and talked angrily to hallucinations everywhere she went. She was always coming and going in the area. She was stocky, muscular. She wore loose flesh-colored stockings without shoes; usually an old but expensive-looking dress as well. She wore costume jewelry bracelets and rings on both hands and arms. She wore lavish earrings and usually some kind of bright hat with flowers or feathers. Her fingertips were covered with bright red nail polish smeared on the tips. She wore bright red lipstick smeared on and around her mouth, like a clown. She wore beige powder makeup on her face and thick penciled black eyebrows.

Her hair was naturally brown but it hung down in crazy waves with streaks of peroxide-red on the ends. She looked to be a little over fifty years of age. Everywhere she went she stomped and swung her arms threateningly and aggressively at her sides. The last time I saw her she was standing on the sidewalk on Second Avenue, holding the receiver of a telephone to her ear with one hand. The cord was stretched almost to the breaking point, from the pay telephone about six or seven feet away from her. She was screaming and shouting and thrusting her fist into the air. Of course, no one on the sidewalk seemed to notice her, including me.

It must have been close to ten o'clock at night when I walked over to a neighborhood grocery store on the corner of Fourth Street and Second Avenue. I bought a beer, open in a paper bag. There were no customers except me. The only employee, a young woman, was working behind the counter. It was a family business. She knew me. We exchanged pleasantries and I walked to the door with the beer. The door opened outward onto the street. I pushed it open and stepped out just as a man was charging toward the door with three other men directly behind him, chasing him. The pounding of their feet and the angry curses, shouted at him by the men chasing him, startled me. The door closed as I stepped away from the entrance and began walking quickly away. I had taken only a few steps when the man being pursued made it to the door. He pushed on the door, throwing his weight into it, thinking that it opened inward. That miscalculation, which cost him a few moments of time, brought his pursuers down on him. I was still walking away, glancing quickly over my shoulder as I went. The first one to reach him must have brought him down, because he was on his hands and knees the last time I looked back. The three men were hitting him with their fists, kicking him with their feet and, as he screamed, I saw at least one of them on his knee with a raised knife over his head plunging it into him repeatedly. I faced away from them and kept walking. I heard their hurrying footsteps as they went in the opposite direction. By then I was accustomed to these things. I stepped back into the halfway house and sat down on the couch in front of the fan, which was our only refuge from the heat. A few minutes later another inmate came in. He casually remarked that there had been a killing on Fourth Street and that the ambulance was there.

The big meal at the Men's Shelter was served, I believe, between five and six in the evening every day. The doors were then opened for food and lodging and were locked again at seven o'clock. A good half of the city block, between Second and Third Avenues on First Street, was always filled at that time with a milling crowd of derelicts. The crowd usually stayed off the sidewalk in the immediate area of the entrance to the halfway house. They milled in the street. Sometimes there were three or four separate fights and assaults going on in the mob at the same time. A big strapping middle-aged City cop stood at the top of the stairs in his dark blue uniform with a large, heavy black billy-club strapped in his right fist. He tapped its end in the palm of his left hand and watched the crowd in front of him. It would not have been possible for him to enforce order. It was his job to guard the doors, which he did very well. It always happened that when someone was wounded he would make it to the vicinity where the cop stationed himself. We usually got a view from the front of the halfway house of someone staggering toward the cop, drenched in blood, everyday. Then the ambulance would come. Once I was standing on the sidewalk and talking with the cook at the halfway house when there was a shouting in the crowd. A man burst out of the crowd and ran past us, almost bowling us over. As he went by spurts of blood rained on us. His pursuer ran through the space we had given him. In his hand he clutched a French knife with a blade about ten inches long. We went back inside.

Occasionally I saw one of those vans from local television stations off to the side of the mob. I understand that during June and July of 1981 the situation around the Men's Shelter was aired regularly over New York television.

the rhythms

w i l l i e   c o l o n

My name is Willie Colon. I am. . . . Well, I really don't know what I am.
I do a lot of things. I have 11 gold LPs, two platinum. I act and have appeared
in movies and TV series. I've composed and recorded many songs, mostly in
Spanish, a few in English. I play trombone and sing. I've been nominated for
the Grammy five times.

In the last two years I have played most of the big cities of Western
Europe, the Amazon jungle, where the audience literally arrived in dugout
canoes, and, if this isn't contrast for you, I performed for President Reagan's
(barf) 50th Presidential Inaugural Ball in Washington, where the audience
was a lot rougher than the guys in the canoes. I also appeared at a few clubs
in Queens where you can rent a submachine gun in the bathroom . . . if you
forgot yours.

> willie colon has been a community activist for 15 years,
> and is currently running for office in the 17th Congressional
> District in the Bronx. As of date, he has released 36
> albums—15 gold records, five platinum, and ten Grammy
> nominations. His latest album is *Hecho en Puerto Rico.*

My maternal grandmother, Antonia Pintorette—who everyone calls Abuela (Grandma)—came from Puerto Rico in 1923 looking to start a new life here in the promised land. She was 21. She's now 85 and still refuses to answer in English unless it's absolutely necessary.

She met a boy, Felix Roman, from her hometown, Manati, and got married. She had three children: a boy, Gilberto, and two girls, Gertrudis and Aracelis.

Gilberto, who was taking saxophone lessons, died of meningitis at the age of 7; Trudy got married to Maximo Rodriguez, a Cuban, and left for Florida; Ara met Willie Colon, the son of a family from Abuela's hometown, and soon after, very soon after, I came into the picture. April 28, 1950.

139th Street in the South Bronx in the late 50s and early 60s was no longer a part of the United States, much to the chagrin of the Italian and Irish working-class population who would come down with serious cases of "White Flight" anytime more than six of us moved in.

We easily turned 139th Street into a tropical _barriada_. All the stores in the area had Spanish signs in front. In the mornings you could hear the radios blaring those Latin rhythms in an eerie but reassuring echoey unison—and the smell of hundreds of pots of Cafe Bustelo filling the air.

Abuela came to live with us when Felix died of undetermined causes. (Abuela said it had to be because of that damned motorcycle he had. He used to ride Abuela around town in a sidecar.)

She used to look at me with glazed eyes: you see, psychologically to her, I think, I was Gilberto, reborn. She would tell me that Gilberto was my guardian angel and was always with me. But I needed an instrument to play. Yeah, she pushed the rhythm on me.

But the rhythm was very important to all of us. On 139th Street it would be my lullaby. Conga drums and chants echoing through the streets and alleyways in the late afternoon. I would lie in bed with my bottle (baby bottle) and listen to the _coros_ as I watched the light from the headlights of the cars that would come down the hill track across the wall of my bedroom.

Occasionally, someone would start banging a bottle or tin can. He would usually stop soon afterwards either from fatigue or by popular demand if he fell out of time. "Don't come around messing up our jam, Bro'!"

The night had . . . rhythm.

So much so that when the music outside stopped, we'd say, "What the Hell was that!" There was something wrong. Like in those old Tarzan movies when he'd stop and notice that the drums stopped. That made a lot of sense to me.

Soon after, our rhythmic security force would start up again and we could all go back to sleep.

The rhythms protected us . . . .

In the 40s, the rhythm was the rage. The upper class congaed and sambaed and rhumbaed at every movie gangster's posh bougie supper club. Lucille Ball and Desi Arnez brought the rhythm into the American living room in the 50s.

Now we had our foot in the door; Pepino (Cucumber) from the real McCoys, and Ricky, Mr. Babaloo.

The rhythms gave us . . . faces.

The 60s was the Roots generation. We saw the emergence of Black Power, Weathermen, Radicals, Anti-War Activists, Flower Power, the Young Lords (with Felipe Luciano and Pablo Yoruba Guzman) and the Flower Children.

Meanwhile, back on 139th Street, I was starting my first band, the Dandees. My mom dyed some shirts pink for us and printed The Dandees on the back with a magic marker. It was a quartet: a conga, an accordion, a clarinet, and me on the trumpet that Abuela had bought from the pawn shop for $50. I was on my way!

The Beatles, The Animals and Paul Revere and the Raiders were burning up the charts. But I was playing _bombas_ and _plenas, son montunos_ and _merengues_. I recorded my first LP in 1967.

I was discovered at one of the dances that were the new thing. Most of the Hispanic and some black teens were learning how to "Latin."

Clubs like the Cheetah, Colgate Gardens, La Mancha, Casino 14, the Hotel St. George and Chez José were constantly filled to capacity. Thousands of teens getting into the rhythms 3 or 4 nights a week!

Our generation was mostly U.S. born, so when I started a song with a Puerto Rican *aguinalco* that went into a Cuban *son montuno* and then into a Dominican *merengue*, with occasional English or Spanglish choruses, nobody flinched... except for some of the old timers who nearly had apoplexy. It was blasphemous! It was incorrect! It was... *salsa*!

From the late 60s thru the 70s *salsa* was international: not only in New York where it started, but in Panama, Venezuela, Santo Domingo, Peru, Colombia, Mexico. Madison Square Garden, the Cow Palace, Yankee Stadium, Hiram Bithorn Stadium, the Hollywood Paladium. We travelled to Tokyo, Paris, Cannes, Zaire! Santana's Black Magic Woman and Oye Como Va were No. 1.

The rhythms brought us together. . . .

Today we hear Frank Sinatra, Miami Sound Machine, Paul Simon, Debarge, Shelia E., Madonna, Yes, Prince, Herb Albert and almost every pop and rock group has the rhythm on their record tracks and performances.

Listen to the commercial background music, some of it is even way up front like the Citrus Hill orange juice and the "Wouldn't you rather have a Buick" commercials.

The other day I was playing Television Roulette when I stopped on the Nashville Station, Channel 30. There was a Blue Grass group with long beards and all, and in the back was an 350-pound fella wearing coveralls and banging away on a pair of conga drums. I said to myself, "That's it . . . now I've seen everything!"

The rhythm has become part of the "Heartbeat of America. . . ."

better *looking through chemistry*
taxi with veronica vera

I am the original Taxi and I've been around the New York scene for seventeen years. I am thirty-two. I didn't come from a dirt-poor family. I came from a very nice family, but too demanding. I was just too New York. I wanted to be independent, so I came up here with a bunch of hard rocks who stole a car to come from Richmond. Then they left me. I was scared. I was alone. But I didn't want to go back.

The girls in Richmond, they were . . . they were country. They were loud. They were fags. They dressed in drag but everybody knew they were men. I was into Soul Train fashion: bare midriff and sandals and big hair and I looked real feminine. But when I came to New York, I was really shocked. I couldn't believe some of the people I met were queens. They looked so real. Wow. Now that I look back, some of them didn't look that real. I can say: "She was really a beast, she just had tits or hips. . . ." Some had those unnatural big cheek bones. But to me then, well, I was in a daze. There were probably some who looked so real I didn't pay them any mind.

taxi, who once headlined at the Gilded Grape, is still on the
scene. This text is from an interview by Veronica Vera.

I live full time as a female. I really don't know how to live as a male. I wouldn't know where to begin. I felt like a little girl even as an infant. I always played with dolls. It was no surprise to my family. I would walk down the street in high heels. One time my step-mother came home and caught me in the whole thing—the girdle, slip, bra, hair and make-up. I was ten or eleven years old and she thought she was going to pluck my nerve. She said: "Oh, you want to dress in my stuff. Well, you walk down the street and let everybody see you." She gagged 'cause I didn't come back for three hours. Not only did everybody in the neighborhood see me, everybody in town saw me. So I always knew what I was.

I was already dressed when I came on the scene in New York. I was very feminine, not like a lot of children who when they come out they look hideous. I looked like a little girl. I had no idea what hormones were when I arrived in NYC. I took hormones in order to look better 'cause I saw that they could make people look gorgeous. A lot of the girls used to tell me: "Girl, if you took hormones, you would be a threat to society." And they were right. I took hormones for a little while when I was sixteen, then stopped. I ran around for a while without them until I got a little older, and when things started changing on me, I had to hurry up and get those hormones.

At age seventeen, I started taking them again, from a doctor called Jimmy Treetops. He was a white man, real tall, tall, tall. Every kid in New York had his hormones. He didn't have an office. Well, he r-r-really didn't p-p-practice, you know what I mean. I was living in the Embassy Hotel on 72nd Street. I used to call it punk palace: it was home to just about every queen in New York, young and old. When Jimmy Treetops would show up, he made his rounds to each floor, like the Avon Lady. All the girls knew when he was coming and they had their money together.

When he first saw me, I was coming out of the shower. I was sixteen, young, innocent, soft and fresh. I had braids in my hair down to my shoulders. He saw me looking like this little, little girl and he fell in love. 'Cause you know, he was a pervert, he liked 'em young. He was old, trust me honey he was old. He was at least fifty. You know how when you're sixteen, everybody looks fifty. He had blond hair and a light beard. He said to me: "Miss Taxi"— he used to talk in a real nasal voice—"I want you to come over to my house." I'd come over to his house and get my hormone shot. He used to feed me, he used to give me money, pills, clothes. He told me: "You come back over here in four days," and I went over there every four days.

Jimmy Treetops's hormones were French. They were the best hormones and they made you look absolutely gorgeous. In the life of a transsexual, hormones are a top priority. I've heard girls say: "I don't want to take hormones, but I'm getting silicone." Silicone will not make you feminine. Silicone is like sticking a pillow under your stomach. Hormones will transform you.

Hormones work you in different ways. If you don't look like a girl in the beginning, they're not going to work any miracles. If you have a great big manly body, you're gonna have that same form on hormones. I mean, I've seen some girls take hormones and they don't look any different because they weren't meant to be women. Some just have to go get plastic surgery. Lucky for me, I didn't. When I first started taking hormones people did notice the change. Like: "Oooo, you're looking absolutely flawless these days." Your skin does get absolutely flawless, ultrasoft. Your features change and certain parts of your face fill out. I had never grown hair, so I've never had to worry about that.

The best thing to do regarding hormones is take 'em while you are young, because if you start taking them when you are thirty-one years old, do not expect you can walk down the street and someone is not gonna throw a brick at you. Hormones work better when you are younger. When you are very young, you grow on hormones, but it means you are growing as woman. I started Jimmy's hormones when I was seventeen and I stayed on them until I was twenty-one. I ate 'em like candy. I got his for free, sleeping with the enemy. He was like my sugar daddy—not only mine, a lot of others too, but I was his favorite at the time.

Jimmy was also known in the clubs. He was known for taking pictures, too. He had pictures of every queen in New York, dating back to Holly Woodlawn. He took pictures of me with Grace Jones. He used to go to all the functions, take pictures and then if you needed some hormones, he'd give you that, too. He gave me the shots every four days and then I also took pills. I took oravils and premarins. The injections I took were French. They come in French, German, etc. They were estrogen. The oravils were very strong. They made me sick. I'd get morning sickness. I'm talking: "Please don't come near me, I can't stand it. Please, I don't want to be bothered today." I would look at liquor and it would make me sick.

You must eat when you are taking hormones. You must eat and drink liquids because they will dry you out. You can't take too many because they are bad on the kidneys. Usually the best time to take hormones is at night before you go to sleep. It's good to go to bed so they can work on you while you are sleeping. They also knock you right on out.

In developing breasts, you get the sensation of the nipple first. The nipple gets sensitive. From the nipple, you'll feel a knot way in the back and then that knot will grow and grow. But if you are older, it may take much longer because you are not growing anymore.

You gotta wash all the time. There is an odor that will run you out of the house, especially on a hot summer day when you've been out all night. And being that queens tuck their dicks between their legs and have it all wrapped up in g-strings and things, it sweats. The testicles get smaller and smaller and they can almost disappear; the penis shrinks a little but it is not always unusable. I think it depends on the person you are with.

The smell of those hormones coming out is horrible, horrible, so you gotta always wash. And if you plan to sleep with someone, go to the bathroom first. You know what I mean: FDS, everything—if it smells like it could kill the odor, use it. Sometimes it's so bad, you can smell it through your clothes. So you gotta wash morning, noon and night, and sometimes in between. I would say it's best, especially when you are first starting, to keep a dress on to give it air.

It affects your mind, too. Hormones can make you moody—to some people it does, to others it doesn't. I get very sensitive to things. I want to fall in love. When I first started taking hormones, I was in love with a couple of people. When I like someone for real, I'm as innocent as little red riding hood, but if I lust for someone, I'm the tramp around the corner. I was on hormones one time and love was driving me crazy. I mean crying all the time, little things would bother me.

At times when I don't take hormones I'm kind of paranoid about a lot of things, but when I take them, I feel I could walk anywhere. I mean, I don't go to Harlem, but I could walk down 125th Street on hormones because you just feel like you are the world's only woman and you look it. It's basically all in the mind, but it helps to look good, too. Hormones make you look and feel womanly.

I get stared at all the time but it's not because people look at me as a man. I learned that lesson a long time ago when I thought that people stared at me because they were spooked. I was on the train in the late 70s—I was young and stupid—and so I asked this lady why she was staring at me, was it because she couldn't stand that I was a queen. She told me: "You know, you're stupid. I was admiring you because of how pretty you are. I never even knew." People look at me now and I know that I'm giving them a bump. "A hot chick, tall, she must be a model." I'm more confident.

In the late 70s, shots cost about $15 apiece (today, for a once-a-week shot, they cost about $40 in a drug store). Girls would get like $100 worth. Most of the girls in the scene were hookers. Some girls worked in bars. I did shows and worked out of the bars. When I first came to New York, I was introduced to the streets and I had nothing but problems. I mean, I was robbed. I'm from down south, so I thought everybody was sweet but I was taken advantage of. That lasted a couple of months until (thank God) I found the Gilded Grape—my Savior!

At the Gilded Grape bar I got into shows. On Monday, they had talent shows and I started winning. On Wednesdays, they had go-go boys and on

Sunday, there was a theme show every week, a movie, like "Guess Who's Coming to Dinner." Everyone who won the talent contests would be in the plays. We had to go early on Saturday or Sunday and rehearse. Timmy Scott was the director and he was a genius. People would come from miles around to see these plays and then at 11:00, they would have the finale. They served free food every night at 7:00 p.m., so you know I was down there early. They had hamburgers and french fries. It was like a family.

I started meeting men in the bars, and being I was really young they really liked me a lot. Because when you are young, trust me, especially young and stupid, men love you. Not stupid, I would say "naive." They like that because when you get older you seem to have a little too much knowledge for them, you're not having certain things. I had a lot of admirers running around.

These days the queens are not like what they were in the old days. In the old days, the queens were gorgeous and they were very real and they had a different kind of class to them. Today, there's TV—men in dresses who want to be women, or you get these husbands for twenty years who dress up in a dress and they want to start taking hormones and they think it's going to make them look like total women. I don't knock anybody for what they do, but don't believe they are not obvious.

After a while I stopped taking hormones from Jimmy. I got really sick of him. The hormones did that to me. I mean, I got the point where I just didn't want to be bothered anymore. I wanted to buy them and he didn't want me to buy them—he wanted me to sleep for them. So I went on to other people. I used to buy hormones from a girl named Crystal La Beija and she used to get them from Germany. I would take one of those and they were like time-released hormones. They would stop and then four months later, there they go again.

I haven't seen Jimmy Treetops around in a long time. I don't know what happened to him. He did have the best hormones. French gave you a certain glow; they made you just radiant. I could take them now and you would see a big, drastic change. The older you get, the stronger the hormones have to be—I can't take American hormones now because they are weak. I have to take something strong because of my age. I'm so full of hormones from taking them over the years, they still work for me, but it takes longer.

My doctor now is Dr. Schiffman. He is a regular M.D. He does women, men, everybody. He does noses. He sells hormones, liposuction. Does the best breasts. He's a very, very good doctor. I'm planning to start hormones again before the summer and I plan to get a little work done, too. Not a lot. Well, I did decide not to touch my nose. So what I had planned to do is a tiny, tiny pinch in my chin. So small you would not know it was there, you would just say: "Oh, she's been sleeping forever." Hormones will fill your face and hips out. I plan to get a little surgery down there, too. And a little roll in my cheeks, so when I smile there is a little roll, but just a little. I want to stay natural.

things he did

m a r c   e l o v i t z

Things he did that embarrassed me:

1. told the ER nurses that we were lovers
2. left green shit stains on the waiting room couches
3. talked about how big his dick was
4. sat in a hot tub in Key West where the water jet burst open the big lesion on his right foot.

The funeral is on December 31 and could cut into our New Year's plans. Kevin and I are on our way to it. He's still in his fear-of-driving stage so he goes faster to get it over with. We're speeding through the cemeteries that separate Brooklyn from Queens and I'm enjoying the Chinese tombstones flashing by and the heater blowing on my legs, thinking of my hands on Joe's chest, his arms and his back. Later Kevin will grimace through the service and I'll call Joe as soon as we get back to the City. I'll kiss him on the roof as Anne distracts Kevin and we all stumble in the dark, looking for fireworks at midnight.

marc elovitz is a writer and lawyer living in New York City.

Things he did that disgusted me:

1. stuck the thermometer under his sweaty unwashed arm and then put it back in his mouth
2. shit purple ooze in the bedpan
3. picked boogers out of his nose and stuck them to the wall by his bed, making a circle
4. threw up in a coffee can and let it sit by the side of the bed.

He was getting out of the shower and he looked in the mirror and he saw his bones and he thought he should eat more. He saw the lesions on his stomach and chest, and he paused and he stared and he walked away from the mirror. After that he never looked at his body. I had to endure stories of Oprah and applesauce and painkillers to get this gem from him.

Things he did that pissed me off:

1. wouldn't talk about dying
2. didn't thank my mother for visiting, just talked about her rings
3. walked away from the mirror
4. said, "you play, you pay."

The fish is heavily breaded and bland. I'm cutting it with the side of my fork as I stare at Nick's hands. The people at the next table brushed past us to leave and I start —"I had this cousin who I took care of"—and I'm feeling my fingers underneath Nick's sweatshirt—"I went to the hospital every day"—sliding up his smooth chunky sides—"his parents did nothing"—I've got to stop thinking of Nick's body now so I can answer his questions slowly—"six months"—softly—"just twenty-five"—with the right look in my eyes—"I don't know . . . don't think I ever knew him"—and then it's paydirt, his eyes red and wet as I look up at him, so much taller than me, so much bigger. Now I can think about his big legs and the way his hand can grab my entire shoulder. Now I can eat my fish because it will be another six weeks before he pins me on the bed and I lose him. Six weeks until I'm back out at sea.

Things he did that I can't do:
1. say no to the Key West hotel manager who tells me to cover my lesions when I lie by the pool
2. beg to go home for Thanksgiving and then silently shovel food into the thick white thrush of my mouth
3. meet my mother and sister in Grand Central wearing bedroom slippers
4. walk away from the mirror.

leonard freed

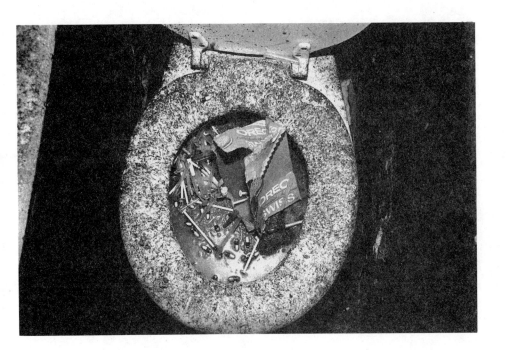

leonard freed was born in Brooklyn. He has several books
of photography, including *Black in White America, Made
in Germany, La Danse des Fideles,* and *Police Work*, from
which these photographs were taken. Photographs published here are courtesy of Magnum, NYC.

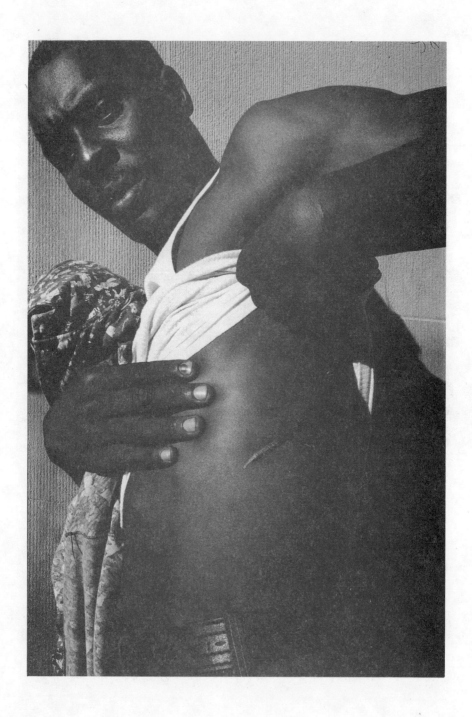

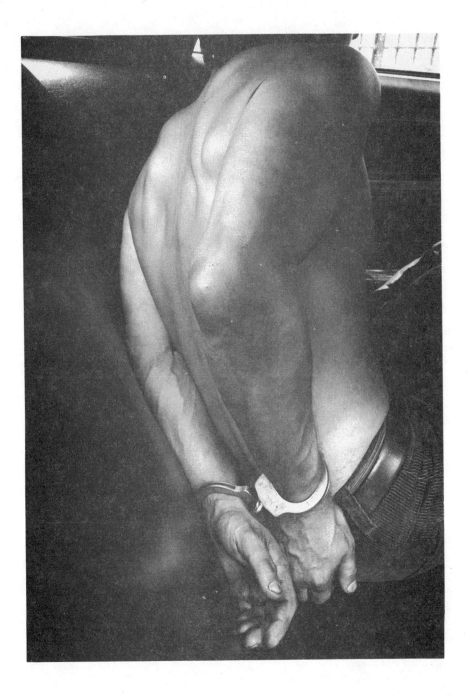

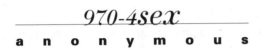

970-4sex

a n o n y m o u s

If you're under the age of 18, hang up now.

Oh, hi. I'm so glad you called 970-4SEX. I've been waiting for you. If you have a touch-tone phone, press ❶ now for hot women yearning for big dicks. For hot lesbian, two-girl action, press ❷. For kinky bondage or freaky sex, press ❸. Push ❹ for the hottest in sucking and fucking. If you don't have a touch-tone phone, I'll select for you. Make your selection now.

❶ Oh, excuse me. I'm sorry, it's just that it's so crowded in here. Oh no, I wasn't trying to steal your wallet. Oh, that's not your wallet? Oh goodness, I'm sorry. I just never would have believed that anyone could have a dick that big. Oh, let me feel it. Mmmm, what a nice bulge you've got there. You know, since it's so crowded in here and I can't help being pushed up against you, maybe I should fool around with your big tool for a while. No one will ever notice. Oh yes, I'll just lean my head against your shoulder, reach down

970-4SEX was a $3.00 toll call in New York City in 1991.

with my hand . . . oh there, doesn't that feel better with your pants unzipped and your enormous dick freed from the constraints of your pants. Now let me stroke it. Oh, it's getting harder. And bigger. It's got to be eight inches at least, and getting bigger still. Oh, do you like it when I stroke it with my nails. Oh, you seem to like it. It makes your already enormous cock grow. Oh, I'd like to give you a private handjob right here in public. Oh, that's it, rub that gorgeous piece of meat against my skirt. Doesn't that corduroy feel nice. I want you to come right in my hands, baby. I bet you have a lot of juice stored up in that enormous cock. Oh yes baby, oh come on. I'm stroking you harder and harder, harder, oh yes honey, shoot it in my hand, oh yes, faster, faster, oh yes, do it do it, fire it, oh, oh yes, yes, that's it, oh, ahhh, wow, what a big boy.

❷ Gina and Heidi's woman massage—welcome to your sex drive. We give the feminine touch and make you moan with pleasure. First we wrap your beautiful nude body in hot towels to ease tension. Heidi, start with her back. Feminine probing hands and an erotic tongue will make her cunt swell with ecstasy. Oh, thank you Gina. Touching another woman arouses feelings that only another woman can measure. It's natural. Oh, your pussy is wonderful. Oh, let my touching massage overcome you slowly. You have a wonderful figure. When I take off the towel, your magnificent ass and upper thighs make me want to play with your clit. I'll put my hand between your legs. Gina likes to watch as I fondle you, but don't watch her, let me describe what she's doing. Oh, she's rubbing her clit watching us. Now two fingers go in and out of her vagina, as I continue to massage your ass and pussy to loosen your back. Mmmm, mmm, it's so wonderful. I love your body, it's so smooth. Your tight rear end is so shapely. Now Gina will take over while I finger my pussy. I'm so wet. Lie on your back, love. Your breasts are two gorgeous melons that need to be kissed. Mmmm, mmm, your nipples. Oh, harder, oh, you're fingering her pussy, oh, they're both turned on so much, such wonderful erotic titties. I kiss your flat stomach and work my way to your mound of lush, full pubic hair. Oh yes, oh, I'm going to make you have such an orgasm. Oh, I'm going to eat you, oh yes, gggnnn, I'm coming, oh oh ah ahhh. . . .

❸ Did you bring the goodies that I ordered you to bring? You did? Let me see. I wanted a dildo, a riding crop and a black leather mask. Good, you got everything, you stupid asshole. Now, undress. You want me to undress you? Well, we'll see about that. You like my sharp, high heels, don't you? Huh? Answer me. I can't hear you. Talk louder when I'm talking to you. Look at your little cock, what a shame. You can never make a woman satisfied with that. Now, put the mask over your face as I take off my clothes. You'll never ever see my naked body—you don't deserve that privilege. God, you make me sick. I wish I had a real man here. I'm going to hit your cock, squeeze your balls. Don't cry out, I hate babies. Get on your knees and start crawling until I tell you to stop. That's right, pig, crawl on your knees. Uh huh. You wanted to be a baby, now you're a real baby. You see this dildo? I'm going to strap it on and shove it up your ass. You don't like that? Well, that's too fucking bad. I'm violating your asshole, you asshole. I don't give a fuck if you hate it. Take it. That's it, uh huh, uh huh. You'll never learn your lesson, will you? Now hold the dildo up your ass and keep on crawling until I tell you to stop, fucker. What a stupid cock—look how hard it is. I didn't tell you I wanted to see it hard. You better make it soft, and I mean now. I don't care, make it soft. If you come, you'll have to lick it up. That's right, I'm pulling and jerking on your cock, how do you like that? Pulling real hard on it, too. Now come on the floor, pig. That's right, shoot it all over the fucking floor. Now lick it off the floor, you slut. Uh huh, you like the taste of your own scum, don't you? Now call me back, you cum-sucking slut.

❹ Oh, baby, it's such a long drive and here we are stuck in all this hot traffic. Oh, oh, I can't wait until we get home. Maybe we don't have to wait. Why do you always make me wait until we get home. Oh, there goes your goddam car phone. I'm not your secretary here. Oooh, you just keep right on talking and I'll just let my fingers do the walking. Oh, your cock is so hard. Mmmm, mmm, mmm, oh baby, it's so hard. I love to squeeze it. Let me taste your cock. Mmmm, it tastes so good, yeah, yeah. The traffic's clearing up and we're almost home. Oooh, yeah, that's so great, in the car right on the street. Ooh, that's it, oooh baby, crawl right over the seat, ooh baby, mmm, ooh, yeah, put that nice big meat right into my cunt, oh, oooh, feel how tight it is. That's it, let me put my legs right on the dash, ooh yeah, ooh, deeper, harder, oooh, oooh, harder baby, harder, press them, press my titties, squeeze the nipples. It feels so good, oooh, I just love what you're doing to me, baby. Go faster, baby, faster. Oooh baby, ooh, you're coming, come deep inside of me. Oh baby, I'm coming, too, oh, oh yeah, that's it baby, take that cock out and come into my titties, mmm, ooh, that's it, shoot that gorgeous cum all over me, mmm, mmm, that's it, oh yeah, squirt it around, rub it into my chest, let me lick it off, oh, oh there, that tasted so good.

Call back now for new messages each time. For hot B&D action, call 970-BEAT. And for hot dating action, call 970-EASY. Bye.

junk
m i k e   m c g o n i g a l

Junk is no good baby. Brion Gysin

I cannot conceive of a life without junk food, without the rush of getting high, of getting off, of feeling light, of feeling lighter, of the chocolate melting in my mouth and not in my hands, of a weekend that doesn't end with a good nod, of a day where my blood sugar level does not soar through the roof. I do horrible things to my body under the pretense of pleasure. My teeth are plaque-damaged from years of sugar abuse, my stomach a massive monument to Milky Way bars. I'm trying to figure out a lot of shit, like: what is junk, and why do I like it so much?

The junk gets in you and it never leaves. Picturing the insides of my body, along with the usual red meat and gristle and nerve bundles, I imagine an invisible system: a capillary-like complex of plasticky tubing that pulses nonstop, sending a foamy, cream-colored insulation-like liquid to every cell. (Since I was a kid and saw biological textbooks with their cross-sections of human anatomy, this is how I've conceived of my "soul.") I've daydreamed that

mike mcgonigal is a writer living in Brooklyn. He is the
editor/publisher of *Chemical Imbalance*.

if I were to kill myself, I'd slice very deeply into my wrist, but no blood would come out. Instead, white foam would issue forth from the bursted soul tubing, very much like a can of Reddi-Whip being turned upside down and emptied. As I slip away into the warm bathtub water, I bend over and put my tongue to the creaminess. Its taste is the same as the center of a Twinkie.

I was birthed through the mouth of instant gratification. I grew up, sort of, with *Sesame Street* and Oscar M-a-y-e-r and Hamburger Helper and Goofy Grape, and if I need it I need it now and it better have lots of red dye number two. What is the taste of modernity? A glass of Tang, or a bottle of Coke? Does Coke really take the paint off a car hood? Did the astronauts really drink this gross fucking orange-flavored sugary shit up on the moon? Well, I didn't mean for this to be a pop-culture quiz. The point is that if desire is not brightly packaged I am not interested in it. I crave processed sugar molded into strange little shapes, covered in brightly-colored bite-sized artificial flavorings, wrapped up in plastic and aluminum foil. I have a great trust in prepackaged, individually wrapped junk food; I guess it was one of the first things that really made me feel good.

Sugar has flavor, but it has no taste. It has calories, but no vitamins or minerals.

When you overdose, your blood pulses so fast you seem to trigger a second heart. When the sugar heart is pumping inside you, the blood squirts underneath your skin miles per hour faster than ever, and you're rocking back and forth in your sneakers, looking up at the cumulus clouds. There's a smile on your lips, the double-scoop chocolate ice cream cone is slowly melting its way out of the base of the cone onto your arm. You try to enjoy it as slowly as possible without having it leak all over you, but even an expert can fail at that task. Your lips, chin, mouth, and hands are stained with a shit-brown color. You run to the street corner and you think that the world really does spin around.

Should the body be a reservoir for junk? You have to abhor the *idea* of the body to be a serious devotee of junk food. Though it is through this weird meat contraption that I find this quick solace, the heart-heavy pulses of relief and release, I am repulsed by the reality of flesh, of fat, of my ugliness. This conception of the body strikes me as very Catholic and regressive and in the end only good for medieval saints who can fly up to God after years of brutally pummeling themselves. But there's a little of the saint in every junkfoodie; we're all persecuted in this fatist society and we all secretly want to leave this body behind.

My mom threw me out 'til I get some pants that fit/
She just can't approve of my strange kinda width. Pere Ubu
At some point in the last few years, I stopped being chubby. I became fat. And I can't say it's like I didn't notice or something, 'cause I notice every new stretch mark, every extension of the little fat roll on the back of my neck. But I don't stop eating processed sugars. If I'm addicted to anything, it's instant gratification itself; hence, I never seem to, never want to put two and two together and make myself aware of what the results of my actions are. I just wanna get off now.

Sugar is culture. Sen. Jesse Helms
Civilizations that thrive on excess—like, say, ours—are inherently self-destructive. That sentence probably didn't blow your mind. But what differentiates the time we live in from any other is the type of awareness we have regarding our demise. True, there's been some fucker standing in the corner shouting, "The end is nigh!" since man learned the missionary position (see *Quest for Fire* if you don't know what I'm talking about) and thus became *sentient*. I'm not talking any biblical end-of-the-world shit, because that presupposes somebody or thing will do the offing for us. I'm talking about how it's the end of the world as we know it and I'm doing it and I feel fine. We all know the excitement of participating in the destruction of something infinitely huger than ourselves. We are David to our own Goliath. This is more than a projection of our own mortality on the rest of the world, it is a built-in desire that only the greatest men and women are able to sublimate: the desire to rip yourself apart and shred up everything that's around you.

The only way to self-destruct is slowly. The culturally acceptable pathways to self-immolation are always the slowest ones. The chemical things, legal and illegal, natural and unnatural, that get packaged up and sold to us as pleasure-inducing, these things are all poisons. It's not my intention to get moralistic about this because I have known the myriad pleasures of slow self-destruction all my life. It is a great part of the thrill of getting off on chemicals.

I think too much about offing myself. Almost every morning I lie in bed and imagine my body being annihilated all at once. I hear the skin rip, see the red blood and the white fat and the brown guts as I elaborately draw and quarter myself. But then I get up and take a long hot shower, and I'm OK again. Where does all this self-hatred come from? It's the flipside of total immersion in instant gratification. . . .

It's important to remember that junk food has nothing to do with food itself. It frequently bears no resemblance to the original, nourishing variety. You eat junk food to get off. Junk food is many kids' first dope experience, first religious experience, perhaps even first orgasmic experience.

> *Sugar, aw honey honey/ You are my candy girl,*
> *and you got me wantin' you.* The Archies

I suppose I should mention my great, uh, interest in porn from an early age. Porn is to sex what junk food is to food: a hyper-inflated, prepackaged simulation of the original. It gives it to ya ALL (the orgasm, the rush) AT ONCE. It often forgoes the nourishment, but again, that's much of its appeal. The crucial difference is that porn is infinitely less damaging to the body and soul than junk food. Porn and junk food can breed similar, voyeur-in-your-own-body feelings with regard to corporeal existence, however.

Where we can tie the junkfoodies together with the junkies is through their relationship to their bodies. There's a shared view that the body exists just to get you off right now, which is combined with the knowledge of the horrendous consequences of the action as well as the actual drug/sugar rush—and the eventual crash which often leads to the search for more.

I lived with this guy who was totally unhappy. He was in his mid-twenties and living off his parents and doing dope all the time, snorting it. I watched incredulously as he metamorphosed into this scary zombie creature from outer space. He never worked, the heroin made his balls itch all the time, and his junkie ghost girlfriend and he would just hurt each other, constantly. Break windows, sleep with each other's friends, quarrel over who hogged more of the bag. I stopped snorting heroin pretty much altogether while this guy lived with me, but after he moved out, I started doing it again. Duh. I don't need to drive around with the carcass of the victim of an auto accident in the passenger seat to stop myself from going too fast on a slick road, but I apparently did find it necessary to see the carcass of a living heroin victim to keep myself from heroin.

The junk gets inside you and it never leaves. A study written up in some Tuesday's *Science Times* found that "untreated" (no formaldehyde) corpses of Westerners decompose markedly more slowly than those from India, where Hostess products are less common, I think. When Americans kick, we're already pickled from all those preservatives we've consumed.

So how do you wash the junk out of your head? How do you cut it out without cutting out the desire part altogether? My head is this little green pond full of wriggling need-monsters. I want to fucking soar like Silver Surfer right over the orange buses and kids on their bikes on my way to school; I want to brutally murder everybody on the subway; I want some clothes that fit; I want to fuck that girl in the bodega down the street up her tight fifteen-year-old ass; I want my ninth grade Spanish teacher to seduce me that time she drove me home in her car; I want my dick to grow four more inches; I want everybody to like me; I want Winona Ryder to beg for it; I want a Guggenheim grant to fall out of the sky, hit me on the head, and make me dizzy.

Maybe I'll stop doing junk food this week. But these new Milky Way Darks have been really satisfying me lately and if I can just scrape together another four bucks I'll have enough cash for a wicked speedball, which will carry me blissfully till tomorrow.

on finding an old tarsadalmi szemle on st. marks place

george konrad

As I walk along Avenue A, relaxed young men, comfortably loitering, casually hiss between their teeth, "Smoke, smoke." They have fallen on bad days, the cops are after them, and the residents of 9th Street are in an uproar and want to chase the drug traffic out of the neighborhood. The dealers have already begun to move their headquarters to the shade of the trees of Union Square.

I stroll along, a young man sidles up to me and hisses. I ask how much? Thirty. Too much, I'd pay twenty. He doesn't have enough change, he wants the twenty up front. I'm an idiot, I give it to him, he gives me his ID's for security, one of them has his picture on it. He's back, he puts something in a small torn plastic bag, not enough, it seems to me. Exotic, he says, and runs away. Next time I'll call the Chelsea Hotel for a certain woman who's got sensemilla and is reputed to be a witch.

george konrad was born in Hungary in 1933. He has worked as a social worker, sociologist, editor and professor. His novels include *The Case Worker*, *The City Builder*, *The Loser*, and *A Feast in the Garden*. He was recently the president of PEN International Center.

We intellectuals are also reputed to be witches, we also get the respect due to witches. But we cannot aspire to be tribal chieftains, that's reserved for the venerable imbeciles. The wizard must conjure up his own dignity. We see into the future and the past. We are the healers of the spirit and the body. Literature is psychoanalysis in reverse. It is the master that lies on the couch. He talks nonsense, but he talks sense.

The Auden memorial was held in the auditorium of the Guggenheim Museum. Poets recited the poems they had written for him and dedicated to him. Brodsky chanted his poem in English, singing words like state and dictatorship in episcopal and rabbinical tones. Ashbery, slender, with his fine-boned, squarish head, reminiscent of Eliot's, and wearing a well-cut grey suit, read his cool, elliptical, self-ironic poems with his cool, elliptical, elegantly self-ironic voice. The eastern and western poets sat side by side, apparently in mutual respect.

Auden lived here on St. Mark's Place, in number 77. This was the place he chose for himself. He became an American citizen. He came here during the war. He was chancellor of the Academy of Poets. He loved this Ukrainian-Jewish quarter, which perhaps even then was one of the nests of bohemia.

The East Village, as opposed to the West Village, is now, along with Soho and Downtown, the avant-garde of the avant-garde. The wedge moves through the city, followed by the bourgeoisie and established art, and the academic world. The artists go in first, they occupy the industrial sections, the poor sections, the ruined buildings, the lofts, little restaurants begin to open, and the street grows more colorful. Then they are evicted, and the galleries take their place. Capital supports, capital squeezes out. Capital loves bohemia. Nowadays everyone loves W. H. Auden.

Our apartment is on 4th Street, between First Avenue and Avenue A, four blocks from St. Mark's Place, where I first turned up with J. one morning during a street festival. Bands played, a woman was jumping around on stilts, coaxing the children to dance.

We bought a table lamp for two dollars: the vendor wanted to show us that it worked. We went into a police station in search of a socket. His honor was at stake, he told the policemen. They smiled, and pointed out the socket: the lamp did not burn. The policemen, white and black, men and women, burst out laughing; then they took pity on the vendor, now sweaty and pale, his virtue crumbling. They pointed to the good socket and lo! the lamp lit up.

The vendor was grateful, his sense of dignity was revived: he said his mother was Hungarian, too, and he was glad we moved into this part of the city, which some people accurately call the East Village, and others, inaccurately, the Lower East Side. Why are you glad, I asked him. Because you look like such nice people.

We were happy; due to my sister's wizardry we had found a terrific, spacious, old-fashioned apartment in the neighborhood, just where I have always wanted to be. We furnished it with comfortable, functional, enormous steel writing desks. Mine is black; it has deep, rolling drawers, and a gray linoleum top. J.'s is yellow, with the same drawers, but she covered the top of hers with a lightgreen blanket. On her window, which has the fire escape on the outside and safety bars on the inside, she has hung some sort of bamboo curtain. Our bed is in her room, constructed of piled-up mattresses covered with a big yellow spread which we got from Yvette (who got it from Patricia).

The goods, lamps, teacups, migrate. Richard Sennett gave us the sofa. We walk along the street with eyes open, looking down at the sidewalk, hoping to find a good tea kettle or pot for a buck or two at one of the vendors.

My grant lasts until the end of April; we'll stay in New York until then, in this apartment, which was certainly not easy to procure, as people responded to the ads by the hundreds, and the rents are rising abominably. When my sister found this apartment for us, through an old Lithuanian-Jewish agent, and the old man said, We Hungarians should stick together, I felt as if providence had taken us under her wings, and in this neighborhood, in this apartment, we were blessed.

I am standing among steel pipes, plate-metal sheets, and wrought-iron gates, in front of a Tarot reader; his shop is also marked with a drawing of a huge palm. The destiny-reading, moustached old gentleman habitually snoozes in a rickety old armchair in the display window. Close by are two bookstores, both of them carry *A Cinkos* (The Loser), which could only be published underground in Hungary. It was here in New York that I saw the new samizdat edition from home. I'm happy to see it; it is densely typed and hard to read.

Ivan and I wrote our book on intellectuals like that, too, single-spaced. We typed like madmen, just to get it going, just to get one copy to a safe place outside the country, because inside there are no safe places.

Oh, my Lord, how bored I was with writing the words "rational redistribution" hundreds of times. I decided then that I would no longer write ostensibly scholarly works, because they require linguistic monstrosities. The weight started to lift from my chest; I can write novels again, I thought, as I walked enthralled down the little streets of Budafok, the autumn leaves falling, past the vintners' houses and wine cellars.

Suddenly Biki came to say there had been a raid at Tamas's house. They were looking for pornography, but it was our manuscript they swooped down on, and as soon as they had it they weren't interested in porn any more.

The Intellectuals' Road to Class Power is a one-hundred and thirty-two page typed text which contains anti-State agitation. I am particularly fond of that phrase in German: *Staatsfeindliche Hetze*. This is your genre, said the pleasant, fat lieutenant colonel. I really should heckle something else, this state is so little, why should I provoke it—the bloc-system is a much bigger morsel, after all.

I am standing with J. in St. Mark's Place, absentmindedly browsing through the things on the sidewalk. The excitement of nine years ago has shrunk into a humorous anecdote. It is the custom here to put coats, shoes, books, anything, out on the sidewalk, in the hope that someone will buy it, that perhaps by the grace of the god of the market it will find its owner. This is what's happening now. On the sidewalk, there among English language pulp novels and one or two good books, are two yellow and red journals, with a familiar Hungarian title: _Tarsadalmi Szemle_ (Sociological Review), the theoretical journal of the Hungarian Communist Party. Two volumes. One is November-December 1949, the other May 1955. It is at times like these the heart must pound.

Stalin on the cover. What a birthday celebration we had for him! Everyone sent him gifts, the grateful Hungarian people sent a trainload full, too. They even organized an exhibit of the more imaginative presents. Scores of miniature locomotives, machinery, children's drawings. The shop windows were filled with statues of him. At the butcher shops, the _Generalissimo_ was sculpted in frozen pork grease. I know a sculptor who struck it rich then, since he got as much lard in payment for his lard-busts as the weight of his work. He was concerned that his big Stalins should have dignity and weight.

I pick up the yellowed pamphlet/journal. This convinces the vendor, a young black man, that the most unlikely stuff has a chance of finding an owner. Here, now, I am not afraid of the _Tarsadalmi Szemle_. Lying there on the ground, it isn't very threatening. It does not quite succeed in impressing upon me what I must avoid if I know what's good for me.

translated from the Hungarian by
Istvan Csicsery-Ronay, Jr. and Etelka Laczay-Szabo

darrel ellis

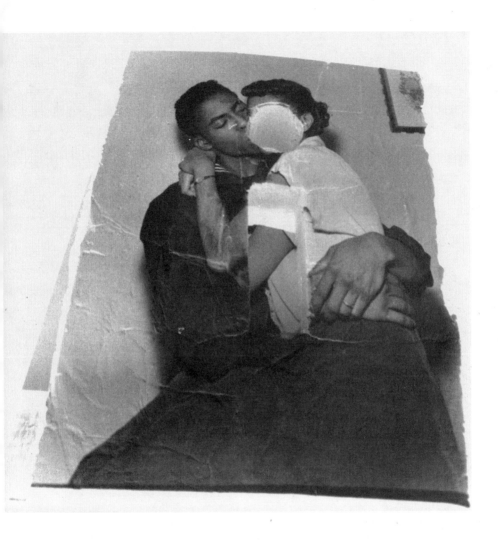

<u>darrel ellis</u> was born in the Bronx in 1958 and died of AIDS
in 1992. He was a painter and photographer. Darrel used
old photographs taken by his father and manipulated
them by projecting them onto plaster forms and rephoto-
graphing them. These photographs are courtesy of the
estate of Darrel Ellis.

diary of a nicotine queen
linda yablonsky

My tongue, my tongue! What is happening to my tongue? I feel like I have tongue cancer. It's all fuzzy and swollen, like it's growing a fungus. It's the color of coffee. It feels too large for my mouth-size to contain it, and looks so ragged and cut up, like a sun-dried riverbed, the way the desert looks from the air, brown and burnt to hell.

I don't think I ever gave a great deal of thought to my tongue before. It's got to be the most overlooked, undercared-for organ in my body. I read somewhere recently how the tongue is the site of thousands upon thousands of tastebuds, more than was ever known before or believed possible to exist. Thousands of taste buds. Small wonder I get such a kick from the lighting of a cigarette: it's like getting shot in the head with a scatter gun, like spraying my tongue with a thousand points of taste. My tongue is no longer my tongue but a vehicle of taste.

linda yablonsky is a writer living in New York. She has just completed a book of essays, *Nicotine Queen: A Quit Journal*, and is the curator of the "NightLight" reading series at Pat Hearn Gallery.

No one eats tongue anymore. You hardly see it in the delis. I like tongue in my ear, human tongue. I like the sound of it, I like the feel of it, I like the way it centers my attention while another special someone's legs, arms, hands, feet and eyes explore the rest of my busy body. I could go for a plate of sex right now, and a post-connubial smoke. Smoking and sex were meant for each other. They both speak a common language.

Who doesn't like a cigarette after sex. My friend Ira, who is still a smoker, says one of the things he likes most about having sex with another smoker is the "ritual cigarette" he has while mingling abed. "Think of it as punctuation," he explains, appealing to the literary turn of my mind. "If sex is a paragraph in the narrative of an evening, then cigarettes are like the periods at the end of a sentence." Ira says ritual cigarettes prolong arousal, and as obstacles to desire I understand it, but I'm not sure I'd want the same for me. I think stopping what I'm doing for a cigarette might only make me irritable, but then some people think it's fun to torture their sex partners— in an effort to intensify passion, as they say. I concede a place for sadism in every bedroom, but still I think deferring climax may have more to do with childhood fears of abandonment than the pleasures of smoking in bed.

Until one quits smoking, one cannot know the sheer joy of the pure narrative flow, the excitement that precedes the introduction of the endless, the torture of the antipleasure at its best.

My friend Angel Stern, the buxom blonde dominatrix, has a client whose love for degradation has become manifest in an ashtray. It seems he's made himself a great silver one, and fitted it with a mouthpiece. During his favorite sex ritual, he gets on his knees while she ties him up, and slips the ashtray into his mouth. Then, after lighting a cigarette and parading around the dungeon in her eight-inch spiked heels, she flicks her ashes in his waiting receptacle.

I think she enjoys this sort of role reversal a lot, but she says the best part comes when the ashtray is full. At that time, still bound, the man eats her ashes, and they do it again. That's his whole kick, eating ashes from his own personal tray. Kind of makes you wonder about his family, briefly. Madam Stern, who may have seen it all, doesn't think this too peculiar, but then she doesn't really smoke. I guess she doesn't have to.

Franco, my kind Italian upstairs neighbor, just came by and knocked on the door. Some of my mail had been delivered to his box by mistake. I asked him if he thought smoking with sex was different for men than for woman. He said no, but he doesn't speak perfect English. Then he confessed how much he hates smoking and wishes he could stop, like me. I smiled. But that's easy, I told him. You can stop right here, right now. Just give me all the cigarettes you have left, and then you can forget about it. For some reason lost in translation, he thought I was joking and left me standing in the doorway, empty-handed.

I came back inside and called my friend Mr. Leonard, who's always good in a crisis. I called Leonard because I know he doesn't smoke, but then it turned out he does—one, or maybe two, a day. That's all he needs, he told me. I wanted to slam down the phone. I can't stand it when people I like have this much control over things that are bigger than we are; it makes me think they're lying.

But Leonard never lies. Leonard is one of the most honest people I know. How, I asked, could he keep himself to just one or two cigarettes a day?

Oh, it's not every day, he told me, which of course made it that much worse. He only smokes when he can stand naked in a mirror, and watch. "Half the pleasure of smoking," he says, "is watching yourself. The rest is like putting a fish hook in your lungs." This is his way of describing the tobacco kick—as good a description of antipleasure as I've ever heard.

Also, Leonard says, he won't smoke unless he has a Camel Light or a Marlboro—"no cigarettes with white filters." I laughed at this, because I knew what he meant. I hate all cigarettes with filters, especially those that are white. "If they have white filters, I don't want to look," he told me.

I hate them because they smell. They smell worse then anything in creation. I don't know what manufacturers put in those things, but to my mind it's ten times worse than anything in tobacco. They're putrid.

"Are they?" Leonard asked. He never noticed. Make a comparison test, I said, if you dare. You'll see what I mean, right away. I know people think smoking white-filtered cigarettes is supposed to be easier on the lungs, but I think this is just a move by the tobacco industry to get people smoking more. They have to smoke more, to get any taste, any kick, any pleasure. Leonard didn't disagree, but for him "there's just something not right about them, visually."

As I put down the phone I heard Franco moving around upstairs and only pride kept me from crawling up to bum a smoke from him. As Leonard says, if you bum cigarettes you can pretend you're not a smoker, but if you buy them, well, then you are. Franco smokes Marlboros, which have brown filters, so maybe it'll be all right.

I have another friend named Sarah, who doesn't wait 'til after sex to smoke. She recently confided that when she was a youth and just starting out in the world, she only enjoyed sex *while* she was smoking. She puffed away while someone else sucked on her. It sounded right to me. But Sarah says she put an end to this practice after her first lover, who didn't understand Sarah's brand of eroticism, accused her of affecting boredom. I know other people who would find this situation seductive, but evidently Sarah hasn't met them. Now, she says, she keeps it closer to home: she masturbates when she smokes.

I asked her if she could apply herself without a cigarette, and she said maybe, but she never did. The bigger her smoking habit becomes, the more often she pulls her own chain. They're inextricably connected.

People like their leisure cigarettes, as I call them. They're not the same as ritual cigarettes, or any other kind. A leisure cigarette is not a cocktail cigarette nor a pre-bed cigarette nor a beach cigarette nor even like the very special alleyway, after-gym-class cigarette. It isn't a cigarette to keep an edge on: it's the one that takes it off—the after-burner cigarette. Nicotine is a lucky drug; nicotine can do it all.

But what if you can't do with nicotine anymore? Is sex really different without it? I'd have to say yes. Not smoking affects the way you choose partners. Instead of smoking after sex, you have to talk—unless, of course, you can pay them to leave.

My mother was very clever dealing with this issue in her life after cigarettes. If she couldn't smoke in bed, she wouldn't go to bed. I don't mean she didn't sleep. Every night, when the day's demands were met, she'd sit in a big old armchair in front of the TV, her legs propped on an ottoman, a newspaper or book in her lap, and slowly peel a couple of oranges. This done, she'd just as slowly eat them. Then she'd read awhile and watch TV, and eventually doze off. When the station she was watching went off the air, she'd wake up and go to bed, exhausted.

I have to say this made me feel kind of bad. I didn't know what it was about and I thought she seemed unhappy. I don't know what this did to my parents' sex life, since my father retired early, but they stayed together thirty years, so there didn't seem to be anything wrong. My mother just didn't know how not to smoke in bed, and my father still smoked a pipe. Maybe that was what kept her up so late, but I really can't be sure. Someday I'll ask him, if I'm still feeling curious.

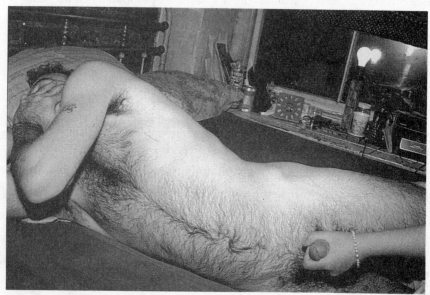

my hand on brian's dick, 1983

nan goldin

brian after coming, 1983

nan goldin is a New York City photographer, teacher, writer and curator. Her books of photography include *The Ballad of Sexual Dependency* (which is also a multi-media slide show), *The Other Side: 1972-1992,* and *A Double Life,* a collaboration with David Armstrong.

chemical holiday
alfredo villanueva

Soon after we had met, he told me he dealt with substances, which did not surprise me since he was a biochemist whose specialty was botany. He had worked all his life investigating the properties of plant-based chemicals and their effects on the human brain. Mine was experiencing chemicals of quite a different type, probably a mad rush of whatever it is that incites instant lust. But it would be unfair to attribute my escapade to Paris to mere gonad action. I was curious about his work, and there was the small but essential matter of having fallen head over heels in love with an older-scientist type, and broken every mold I had ever snuggled into in an effort, not to bed him, which was quite easy given his erotic free-for-all attitude, but to make him love me. And believe me, I wasn't his type.

No sir, I wasn't his type. About twenty years too old, I'd say. Chunky, short, compact, hairy, balding, cowardly, (un)happily married to a sexual

alfredo villanueva was born in San Juan, Puerto Rico. He is the director of the English Department at Hostos Community College. He has published poetry and essays on Latin American literature.

athlete for whom I played the applauding public at every virtuoso performance. A teacher, for heaven's sake, dragging himself every day of his life to a high school masquerading as a college. Feeling sad for himself and crying his eyes out early in the morning to the strains of the final aria from "Salome," yearning for something that a popular songstress had labeled "*amor total*," total love, begging for one great wuthering heights sturm und drang emma bovary whitman and dickinson type of romance.

A poet.

I knew I had to get under his (fore)skin—bagging this ancient love monster was not going to be easy. I baited my hook with poems related to alchemy. He baited his hook with the promise of chemicals; I would have tried anything he'd given me, but there was more; I wanted to do things I had not done, I wanted to learn things I had not learned, things that the other, my permanent Mate, had tried and/or done but would not let me do. He was afraid for my mental sanity. He had also been a reluctant witness to my previous experiences. None. Or to be exact, one. Another guy, his friend and my "impossible" flame, had slipped me a "mickey mouse" and left me alone to imagine I was drowning in my own body fluids. It was quite a trip. Mate had warned me about such things. He was quite pissed off when he got home and found me on the floor, with a death gargle in my throat, muttering that my lungs were full of water, that I could follow the pumping rush of blood in every last vein, artery and capillary, that my bladder felt as a bag bursting with acid wine, that I was afraid I would never stop urinating if I started, would become the source of a gigantic river of waste and ultimately dissolve, much like a certain evil witch.

Stick to grass, Mate commanded. And so I did, wine and grass, and tears and poems, and joyless, guilty, anonymous sex with amputees, hunchbacks and blind men. Or so they seemed to me, whenever I found the courage to look up. The beautiful ones were not for me but for my erstwhile Mate. Mate was beautiful, you see, as they were; a body like vanilla ice cream, baby blue eyes, golden hair, equipment that had figured prominently (no face, please) in the front pages of Honcho. I was just one of the seven dwarfs, or a gnome, working night shifts (actually, early mornings) on the dark galleries of his poetry. At times, though, I could be a teddy bear, or, when I was feeling exceptionally sure of myself, which wasn't often allowed, a small hairy faun. Emphasis on small. Emphasis on hairy.

Well, Mr. Scientist, though more of a chickenhawk than a chicken, belonged to the first category. If things had gone their usual way, Mate would have gotten to him first, I would have gotten seconds. But they didn't. It must have been that first night. One hell of an enchanted evening. He had this total look about him. A mature man, a handsome, not a pretty man, a man who placed you at the edge of a precipice and dared you to jump, find out whether you could fly or just fall, a man who said: "You are not a poet, no one reads what you write." And: "Why don't you come to Paris this summer? You can try some of the stuff; no need to worry, I will make it myself, totally pure, for you."

And so, three months, seven passionate/playful letters and a manuscript of alchemical poetry later, I found myself on the plane, feeling totally afraid because of what I had done (leaving home and Mate) and because of what was expected from me (sex, drugs, rock and, *ay papi, uy papi*, roll).

Mr. Scientist had a surprise for me; we were leaving on the evening of my arrival to Paris for Bonn, where one of his former disciples, a woman, worked at the university on plant research and chemicals. As soon as we had settled down I was taken to a lab where a clear, slightly bitter liquid awaited me in a test tube. I was to drink it and walk back to the apartment with him, there to await the effects of the *pharmakos*. I was lucky: it was a sunny, warm, early afternoon as we were crossing a mall and I felt my feet leave the ground. I notified my companion: *ça marche*; barely twenty five minutes had passed, not the expected hour. My accelerated metabolism had played a trick on us. I was up and away.

The first sensations: light-headedness, clearness of vision, the sun soaking my entrails through the skin. And at my side, a man who had turned into something else: a guardian for the road, an angel. (And why not? He looked like a cross between Terence Stamp—remember *Teorema?*—and Jean Marais—remember *The Beauty and the Beast?*) He asked what I wanted to do. I answered I wanted to walk through a park. He told me not to be afraid, he would take me to the botanical garden which was part of the university grounds. He made me place my hand on his shoulder, and we started walking. I am sure now that he knew that my altered consciousness was being bonded to him as a guide and master through the images flashing before my eyes. I played among the plants. I kissed trees. I stuck my head in fishponds all the better to see the fish. I was becoming each thing I touched. How brilliantly illuminated the world was! He watched but did not interrupt my delighted explorations. After a while, he suggested we go home.

Once in the apartment, he made me strip in front of a mirror. He sat on the opposite side of the room, holding a small pad where he scribbled notes. He told me to identify the reflection. I couldn't—I did not know who he was. At some point he came over and made love to me, but I can't recall his having his clothing off. He held me. And then I noticed this really interesting-looking male staring back at me from the mirror. I went to him, full of erotic curiosity. He showed an identical emotion. I asked who he was, I was told to remember his identity. I could not stop from staring—and then I realized it was me. It was myself as the faun! It was my animal self, my playful self, my earth-creature self. I also recall talking about Mate's pickups, whom he would sometimes share with me. Mr. Scientist asked: What will happen when Alfredo brings the (sexual) bacon home? I said I did not know. Then he asked me to lie down, try to sleep, try to remember my dreams. As it happened, I didn't have any. But I woke up ravenously hungry.

And that was my experience with the drug commonly called Ecstasy.

Emboldened, I did not wait for Mr. Scientist to get home and supervise the proceedings a second time. Levomed, the more hallucinogenic isomer of MDA—the love drug of the 60s (I found this out years later, like barely yesterday). Recommended dose, 125 milligrams. To start, erotic stirrings, including a very intense burning, painful sensation in the groin, which I associated with my mother's cancer (as if it were housed in my body) and my own embarrassing inability to enjoy surrendering to another male. Then, hallucinations. The phone rang. I panicked. I knew I had violated house rules and, in my state, my linguistic promiscuity had turned on its (high) heels and left me. A male voice, in French, of course, asking whether Angel was at home. No angels here, I said (or think I said). This is the home of a respectable scientist, I said. Click. Ring. Again, the voice. I have no time for joking (pleasantries), the voice said. Is Angel at home? No, I said. Tell him I am to be found at la rue d'Arènne (rue d'Arènne? There is no such word in French but in Spanish, sand, *arena*). Click. No angels, no angels, only a very scared would-be faun waiting for a scolding.

Boy, and did I get it. He would not deal with me but went to bed directly, leaving me to my own (hallucinatory) devices. Thermal hurricanes, freezing and boiling alternatively; a dark tunnel, a road of sand, a sand tunnel, a time tunnel. Cold sweats. I am talking to myself all the while but I cannot hear what I say. Meanwhile, I am crossing an old Latin American colonial house, down an open corridor flanked by banana trees, yucca plants, fat geraniums on the walls, women coming out of rooms chattering among themselves. They all know me. I am in a place I have been before, I walk youthfully naked toward a well under an enormous tree at the end of the pathway. I throw myself backwards into the well. I descend fearlessly, weightlessly, through an orange-colored space, hit the bed, bounce, I'm back.

Daybreak. Mr. Scientist checks on the prodigal faun. You are still under the influence, he says; twelve hours have elapsed since I took the fatal pill. I am at the still point, suspended in the amniotic fluid of total indifference. My groin is on fire; I don't care. I make an effort to shower. The pain is so intense I can't feel anything else. This has not been a shared experience. Extreme individuation, a passive acceptance of emptiness at the center of Being. I jerk off. No fluid comes out, but a gummy white matter. Curdled male milk. I ask for explanations. The cold and the heat are all in your head, he says. You are what you feel. It is good that you allowed yourself to fall backwards, he says. You are strong. No angel in the house, an angel in the house, think twice. That voice was not asking for me.

Montpellier, La Bastille Day. A brief digression on Pastis: Anise-based, sugar, 45% alcohol, colorants and plant substances.

Everybody drinks it from early on in the morning.

Everybody wears disconnected, silly smiles.

Everybody looks *real happy*.

A glorious sunset, a balcony, thousands of swallows, two would-be lovers, sharing the sky and the milk of the gods (as is proper, mixed with water).

Which is full of iridescent flakes.

There is sudden shift of intensities. The noise from the birds increases; the pinks and blues and golds of the horizon deepen; what the breeze is doing to my skin would not go well with the National Endowment for the Arts ruling on "socially useless material."

I tell Mr. Scientist.

Yes, he says, this is related to absinthe. I'll have it analyzed.

And so he does, by a friend in California. The mica flecks are in reality particles of anethole, which may be metabolized into the hallucinogenic PMA.

And perfectly legal.

Then, the third drug. DOB. Orgies in the Bois de Boulogne! Mad groupings under the *ponts de Paris!* Mr. Scientist keeps them on hand only for close friends and fellow satyrs. I am nervous. I have a slight stomach ache. Mr. Scientist asks ceremoniously: What do you want out of this experience? I sense a change of mood in him. I answer: To envision the structures through which my thoughts move. And: To meet all the beings I am. I lie down while he sits at his desk. I stare at him.

He lies dead on a battlefield, covered by ice. I crawl among the dead, his flag bearer, searching for him. Eighteen days I survive the hunger and the cold. Finally, I die myself next to his frozen body.

A gang rape. I am about four years old. Probably, this is the beginning of my sexual handicaps. Hallucination? Reality? This life, or another? I don't want to dwell on this, I don't want to remember.

Inside the trappist monk, whose face reminds me of mine and whose text on how angels replicate I have laboriously copied in my journal. His thoughts are made of stained blue glass. He fights Eros with mysticism. Does not know they are one and the same thing.

I climb onto a chair as Mr. Scientist snaps pictures for the record. Happily naked I rock violently until I roll on the floor, the chair having fallen backwards. I cut my arm on the shards of the glass of the Pastis I have been holding. Blood flows, Mr. Scientist worries, takes me to the sink, bathes the wound. The blood stops flowing suddenly. How strange, Mr. Scientist comments, I had never seen that reaction before.

We make love several times. I pour myself into the body next to me, I am flowing freely into an ocean of peacock blue, salmon pink, sunset orange, bands of iridescent gray and green. It is already dark. He wants me to listen to something while we lie together, arms around each other, on the floor.

Wagner.

The Norns.

I barely see his face; his eyes glow, a phosphorescent blue spreading over his naked body. I know what he wants. He wants me to tell him what I see. We take each other's places, I say. I have no shame either of the soul or of the body. I have never felt so entirely another's. There is a word on my lips but I dare not call it out; the name of the dark mistress who comes into the room in the music and lies with us, covering us with her mantle. His eyes turn into unearthly sapphires. He holds me, and we both know who is there with us. No mystery to it. We have consented to sharing her between us, will show each other the way, but there is no bypassing the grief we feel, and the acceptance of that grief.

So, a drug others use for sexual play has made me get in touch with mortality, my own, his own; I have acquired one more skill. (*Amor y muerte*,

how did I know then I would live my own version of Wagner's *Liebestod?*)
One last drug to be done, taken the day before I am due for departure. Mr.
Scientist does not work on Saturdays. DON (a nitro analog of DOB, practically
invented by Mr. Scientist). I am to take it on an empty stomach, early in the
morning, before he wakes up. I ask about possible reactions; he smiles and
refuses to explain. I wake up early, do as told, sit at his desk to write and wait,
perfectly at peace. There is a slight breeze; a bird trills a simple melody. And
then. From the very site of my burning pain, pleasure emerges, moves in
ripples through my organs, reaches all the forbidden places, softens them,
makes them receptive. I know I am on the threshold of another world, I am
being possessed by Eros. He beckons and I move in waves, this time it will
be different, I do not fight it, he tears into me and images of erotic Japanese
prints flash through my head. I find myself insatiably biting the edge of a
pillow. No more just a faun, but also a geisha; I have not ceased to be the one
while becoming the other.

I want to fuck the world.

Or rather. . . .

We shower and dress in a hurry; it is barely nine o'clock in the morning.
No underwear for Mr. Miniature Macho Man today; Mr. Scientist smiles;
DON frees the mind and the. . . . No need to comment, I carry the sensation
with me, I run through the streets of Paris, my eyes ablaze, recognizing
buildings I have not seen for a hundred years, asking for those which have
been torn down, naming stores, parks, intersections. Mr. Scientist is careful;
he knows there is no way for me to know these things except one. You must
have lived here, he ventures; but he doesn't believe his own words. We get
to a park which I do not want to cross. I turn to him accusingly: You brought
me here to have sex with young proletarian males when I was twelve and you
were twenty, I say. When? he asks. At the turn of the century, of course, I
answer, so sure of what I am saying that his eyebrows go up.

Another park. He asks me to undress, covers me with leaves, takes a
picture, leaves me. It is high noon and the sun bounces off my skin, I feel no

heat, but a glowing warmth makes me drowsy, men periodically approach and play with me, I let them. Covered in radiance, I turn my head and there he is, a few feet away, watching. I want out, I tell him, this is a hell we have made for ourselves. I want the green on the other side of the fence, where families sit and have lunch under the trees. He smiles, and says it is about time. We come to an enchanted grove; I have never seen such colors, shimmering green encased in shimmering orange. You are inside the stones you wear, he says. I want a picture. He warns it will never capture what I am experiencing.

The African Quarter. We are looking for kaftans for him, for me, for Mate. I have not come down yet, and it is late afternoon. Periodically I experience a violent shudder in the groin, my pants get wet, *coño*, orgasmic pulses rake me while walking down a street, *carajo*, while sitting at a cafe having a glass of Pastis, *puñeta*. Mr. Scientist is very amused, says my pipes must have been quite clogged, he must take care of that.

Back to the apartment. I simply can't get enough, but other needs beckon. I am starving. Good, he says, we will go to a Latin restaurant. I wear red pants, a white shirt and a big red, bohemianly floppy silk bow tie. One last picture records the transformation. The place is not quite Latin American but more Caribbean, Martinican, to be exact. We sit under Jean Marais's picture; looking at it and looking at Mr. Scientist makes me feel doubly lucky. We have codfish and banana fritters, some spicy stew, but for dessert I want a further and more exotic delicacy, a mango, freshly chilled. It is brought together with a fork and knife. I peel it with my teeth, the way we do it back home, bite the flesh, suck the seed, lick the juice. A smiling black woman comes out of the kitchen, talks to Mr. Scientist. It seems she has recognized my mango-eating style. Aha, she says (by this time I understand her), a fellow islander!

The next day, already at the airport, I ask whether it is necessary for me to do more of these wonderful chemicals. He says it will not be necessary; in fact, for the rest of my life I will probably "fall into" hallucinogenic states quite on my own. No monsters inside, only a need to be filled or fulfilled which now I will know how to manage. He defines loving: living apart from each other, always being present in the other. He says I am a rare plant, he has seen to it that I will survive, and bloom.

I still talk to Mr. Scientist, once in a long while. He lives far, far away with a young male dumb broad. My own Mate is gone as well, far more tragically and permanently. Having remained in love with both, I await my own fate à la Piaf, no regrets. And Mr. Scientist was right, you know. Just let me tell you what happens when I dream!

williamsburg seizure sites
christopher o'connell

There are no footprints in the city, no paths to be worn. The impression we leave is obliterated the moment our foot rises from the concrete. We walk the same blocks, pass the same buildings, but there's no rapport to be built up, no intimacy to achieve. We could leave at any time and another would immediately take our place. Come springtime I'm always walking. Anywhere. I'll pick up a bottle of beer and wander aimlessly for hours. I've lived in my neighborhood long enough to have a store of memories for specific locales— houses I used to visit where I had a friend or lover, corners where I used to cop and the brand names peddled at each location—"No Way Out," "D.O.A.," "On De Down Low," "Deuces Wild," "Crazy 8;" the Hasidic bakery, now a Chinese joint, where I would stop in every morning for a pastry before walking to work; buildings I watched burn, now rehabilitated and bustling with people moving in. A street can lead me back over my past, then jolt me back to the present so it seems I can round a corner and as I step off the curb seven years of living have passed before me.

christopher o'connell was born in England, has lived in the
U.S. since he was fourteen, and currently lives in Brooklyn.

Springtime brings something else—for some reason, perhaps a spring fever change in hormones, it's the time of year when, if I have one, I'll have an epileptic seizure. A seizure breaks up the hard logic of the urban landscape. Sites where I've had a seizure exist outside the rest of my experience; they're imbued with an almost sacred significance. At them, the linearity of my consciousness has come to an abrupt and violent halt, they're the spatial coordinates of the little black holes I've fallen into.

Like small batteries, neurons contain a voltage charge across their cell membrane, at rest approximately -55mv. A sodium-potassium pump is the most common way this charge is maintained, with the sodium channel inside the membrane, the potassium outside. Neurons are digital in their M.O., switching either "on" or "off" and communicating with adjoining neurons via a transmitter, often acetylcholine, which diffuses across the narrow space between the terminal of one neuron and the dendrite of the other. There's a constant level of electrical activity in the brain, higher or lower, depending on whether the brain is at work or resting. The hallmark of a seizure is an abnormally excitatory electrical discharge within a cluster of neurons, which spreads over the brain as the inappropriate firing of one cell kindles the firing of cells it communicates with. If the snowball effect goes unchecked, you have a full, grand mal seizure; if it's stopped, you experience a partial seizure, perhaps a sudden jerking of a limb, a momentary blackout, or an inexplicable sensation of smell, depending on the location of seizure in the brain. The notion that epileptics experience an aura of *déjà vu* prior to blacking out is the case when the seizure begins in the temporal lobe, where memory is located. My seizures always begin in the occipital lobe, where visual phenomena are controlled. Photosensitive is the term. An EEG revealed a marked susceptibility to colors in the red/orange end of the spectrum, and at frequencies between ten and thirteen pulses per second, the alpha frequencies. I know a seizure is impending when my vision becomes a wild array of violently shifting images, liquid patterns, and exploding lights, and I feel a giddiness down to the pit of my stomach.

• • •

Broadway under the El. In the perpetual half light it's always the grey New York of 30s, 40s and 50s newsreels and *noir* films I see. Collars upturned and faces downcast against the gloom as a paperboy hawks the *Evening News*. Today's inhabitants and places—men playing dominoes on upturned boxes, families in their Sunday best attending storefront churches, cuchifritos joints, anonymous doorways and holes-in-the-wall where a ten dollar bill exchanges for a glycerine envelope are like ghosts haunting a forgotten landscape.

A spring afternoon several years ago. Sunlight plays down through the sleeper of subway tracks above, my steady pace imparts to the light a rhythmic flickering. At Broadway and Flushing, I can feel an attack approaching. The screeches of subway cars overhead are the sounds of neurons firing too fast, the brilliant sheen of a metallic hotdog cart flashes explosions of light in the back of my head. I see the street scene in fits and starts, as one moment people, cars, corners are in the distance, the next, they're upon me. I should shade my eyes, sit down and try to calm the electric storm in my brain, but my bowels feel like they're fit to burst. I bought a Cuban sandwich by Havemeyer Street and ate it as I walked along Broadway. Later I realize my previous seizure came after eating a ham sandwich, and I formulate a theory that pork, being a particularly rich food, requires more blood for digestion. More blood in the stomach means less in the brain, something that would help trigger an attack. Walking, too, directs more blood to the lungs and muscles—simply being upright can drain blood from the brain. Just past the corner of Flushing, outside the Burger King and across the street from Woodhull hospital, I fall to the sidewalk. My loss of consciousness is precipitated by a paroxysmal discharge of neurons from a focus in the cortex of my occipital lobe. Linked to the spinal cord, this misfiring of neurons fires other neurons throughout my brain. Axons in my spinal cord controlling muscle activity fire abnormally causing disordered contractions of muscles, especially those in the face, hands, and feet. The first phase of the seizure is the contraction phase—my body becomes rigid, respiratory and jaw muscles contract, and oxygen supply in the blood is rapidly depleted so my skin turns a dusky blue color. Normal movements of swallowing are lost, perhaps there's some saliva dribbling from between my tightly clenched teeth. Disordered contraction of bladder muscles could cause incontinence. After one or two minutes, the seizure passes into its convulsive phase, with rhythmic movement of limbs and trunk muscles. These cease after a few minutes, color returns, breathing regulates, consciousness returns gradually.

I come to in an ambulance that's taking me to the hospital across the street. There's a crowd of people, a couple policemen and the emergency workers. For the first moments I have no idea where I am or how I got there. They ask me questions, what's my name, what day is it, how old am I, where I live, and I struggle to answer. Later my friend tells me I was recognized by some of the secretaries from the Home Care service that shares the building with the program I taught for. They thought I was having a heart attack and unbuttoned my shirt to massage my chest.

I'm wheeled into the hospital on a stretcher. I don't know what day it is, or why I'm here, but I know enough to know I don't want to be here. My memory's stuck at some arbitrary point a couple weeks back. Everything in my short-term bank gone, piecing together the events that led me into the emergency ward is a matter of finding new paths through the neurons to the spot where each memory is stored. Flanking me, a curtain to separate us, is a man who's just been wheeled in with stab wounds, his screams piercing and angry, but alive; and an old man who keeps repeating he wishes he were dead, his weak groans hollow with resignation. I'd like to be away from this atmosphere but I'm getting the full treatment, fussed over by the nurses and doctor, pulse, blood pressure, blood test, the i.v.—the horrible needle burrows into my vein—taped to my arm. I can feel it, an unwelcome violation, touching the inside of my vein.

The saline solution is hooked up. The doctor's administering liquid Dilantin, something new for me. She says I need a certain level in my blood stream quickly, so I don't have a repeat seizure. After a previous seizure I was given Dilantin (phenytoin sodium) in capsules. I was to take five or six a day, but I soon gave up because I felt miserable. A dullness engulfed me, I was lethargic and slow-witted, then zits began to sprout freely, and, to top it off, two or three beers and I was completely debilitated. Also, if I became acclimated to the drug, the possible long-term effects would be a coarsening of the facial skin, a darkening and increase in facial and body hair, as well as gingival hyperplasia (a severe overgrowth of the gums). I kept the pills around until I decided no way I was going to palm them off on anyone for non-prescriptive use. Here in the hospital, I'm hooked up and no arguing about it. A syringe is inserted in the tubing that runs from the saline bag to the needle in my arm. The doctor squeezes off doses at regular intervals. It sears like acid travelling through my vein, my forearm's burning from the inside out. I grimace and jerk uncomfortably. "Stop that! This doesn't hurt so much," the doctor says, her strong German accent sounding particularly admonishing. She's wearing heels that look less than practical, the sharp retort of their clip-clop advancing down the hall transmits a Pavlovian alert. Each time she pumps more Dilantin into me, the piston moves in excruciatingly small increments down the tube of the syringe.

• • •

Northside Williamsburg, the location I choose for my next seizure, is a completely different world from East Williamsburg of Flushing and Broadway. Polish and a few Russian immigrants predominate. If you were to walk from one neighborhood to the other, you could take Graham Avenue, aka the Avenue of Puerto Rico, north from Broadway, a bustling shopping street festooned with the colorful merchandise of clothing, discount, and variety stores, piled onto the crowded sidewalk. In summer the street has a carnival atmosphere. Storefront hawkers armed with microphones, ice-cream trucks spinning out tinny jingles and the ever-present salsa music—escaping from apartment windows, blaring from radios placed on the sidewalk, and booming from the extra bass of passing car stereos—combine in a mad din. Once across Grand Street you enter the quieter and older Italian neighborhood. Ave of Puerto Rico yields to Via Vespucci and groups of people dragging young ones in tow, pushing strollers and shopping carts in front, and clutching parcels and bags to their bodies, become old men enjoying the pleasures of a stoop and a cheap cigar. A feature of the neighborhood that makes every walk worthwhile are the explanatory signs hung out in front of the business establishments—a coffee cup at the coffee shop, a hammer outside the hardware store, a bull's head at the butcher's—it makes me think of a medieval guild town. Between Grand and Metropolitan you pass a bar, complete with a massive frosty stein above the door, where I like to stop in for a drink. At the time of my first seizure, when I was teaching, my friend José and I would go by after putting recruitment posters up in the Greenpoint projects, before hitting the low-rises further down Graham Avenue at Ten Eyck Street. A few years passed before I went back. When I did, I was curious about Al Capone, who I had learned lived in Williamsburg. "Sure," one of the old-timers said. "He lived on Park Avenue, over by the Navy Yard. Used to be in gangs around here 'til he got run outta town."

Continuing north, McCarren Park sits directly across from the dilapidated W.P.A. swimming pool. Sunlight glints off the steel of the newly erected razor-wire. I note it with disappointment because I used to clamber over the fence and wander about the colossal structure, going into the eerie blue belly of the drained pool, once jammed with thousands of young Brooklynites, now a receptacle for graffiti and, amazingly, stolen or abandoned cars. Hungover and tired, I'm kicking a soccer ball around with my Brazilian friend. Sylvia is sitting under a tree, reading. We've just started together and the nervous energy of not knowing one another is what kept us up all night drinking, before going to bed. Ten minutes of kicking and I'm getting hot, not just hot and sweaty, but hot in my head. The ball comes at me in jagged lurches. There are moments when it doesn't move, when everything's frozen, then suddenly it's upon me and my muscles have to jerk into action. I recognize the symptoms and sit down under the tree, out of the sun. "I'm feeling dizzy," I say.

When I come to I don't know where I am. There's the leaves of the tree overhead and the clear summer sky, but I feel like I've been away for a long time. I'm looking straight up and gathered around are Sylvia, my Brazilian friend, and a man I don't recognize. "You alright?" someone asks. "I don't know," I say. "What happened?"

"You had a seizure," the man says. He's shaggy-haired, scruffy, and smells of alcohol. "You want some water?" I sit up to sip it, but I'm shaky and it dribbles down my shirt. "I passed out? Did you call an ambulance?" They didn't and I'm relieved.

It seems the shaggy-haired gent had taken charge. He sent Sylvia off to buy some water and a banana, which he hands to me, explaining the benefits of potassium. I ask what day it is, what I'd been doing, what had happened, then let them talk. I'd been under for around ten minutes and my brain is slow and sludgy, emptied out. I have difficulty formulating sentences, my syntax garbled like verbal dyslexia. The boozy guy is real friendly. He'd been drinking with his buddies at a nearby bench (he gestured, they were still there) and had seem me go into convulsions. He knew something about seizures, though I didn't gather where his expertise came from, maybe the drinking life. Alcohol, as a depressant, acts as an anticonvulsant. Seizures aren't as likely to occur when you're drunk, but far more likely to during the hangover. I'd earned mine. Added to that, a lack of sleep will lower the seizure threshold, too. Hippocrates believed seizures were caused by an imbalance of the blood, phlegm, yellow bile and black bile—the four humors—and that they originated in the brain. He was closer to the truth than later men of learning, physicians and priests, who viewed epilepsy a sure sign of demonic possession. But most epilepsy is idiopathic, though tumors or head injuries can be a direct cause.

The man attending me is from Greenpoint, a Pole, and his dad owns a business in the area. He lives in Far Rockaway, in a house his old man has there. As far as I could tell, drinking seems to be his full-time occupation. Anytime we want to come out to the Rockaways, we're welcome. "Party the whole weekend," he says. When I'm strong enough to get up and leave, I thank him for his help. For the rest of the day I try to refill my memory. "We went to the Sunlite for breakfast, then sat down by the river," Sylvia prompts, but much as I try, nothing's there. Remembering what happened before a seizure is like remembering the events in a dream—for a long time I'll be stuck, then an association will prompt a sudden flood of memory. It can be days until I'm able to fully reconstruct the events that led to my seizure.

• • •

When I pass by spots where I've had a seizure, I often pause to stare, as if there might be some clue in looking, or I'll remember, or be able to imagine, what happened in the time I was blacked out. Sometimes I think I'd like to try to capture the event with some sort of marker, like the memorials painted for young kids by their friends after a killing. Often these are on a nearby wall, but I like it best when they're painted on the sidewalk, marking the exact location of death like a chalk outline, the paint where the blood has just been washed away. Some memorials are in the shape of a tombstone. There's one for "Raul 7/23/91," a crack dealer shot in the head last summer. Others are done graffiti-style. One of my favorites is "In Memory of Robert," a site lovingly kept up with fresh flowers and a lighted candle for many months. I take care never to step on them.

learning how to grow old
g r a c e   p a l e y

My father was teaching me how to grow old. My daughter didn't like this. If I knew how, she thought, I would do so too easily. No, I said. This is for later . . . years from now. It's in case he's not around then, he wants to make sure I know how to. Like I've told you things about growing up—you know. (In fact I hadn't ever told her anything useful. I knew I'd better begin pretty soon so that I could peacefully grow older without her interrupting questions.)

But listen to me, my father said, you're so distractible. Send the kid out to play. I want to tell you. Now, first there are little things—putting cream in the corners of your mouth or on the heels of your feet. But here is the main thing—oh I wish your mother was alive.

This remark surprised me because she never knew anything about cream. She was famous for not taking care, though she was a fine woman, extremely neat and clean with excellent posture. Well she died too soon and full of secrets.

grace paley is the author of several books of short stories, most recently *The Collected Stories*.

Forget it, my father said sadly. I must mention squinting, he continued. Don't squint! Wear your glasses for godsakes. Look at your Aunt Sonia—so beautiful once. I know someone said Men don't make passes at girls that wear glasses, but that's an idea for a foolish class of person.

Now I said sit down didn't I? The main thing is this: When you get up in the morning you must take your heart in your two hands. You must do this every morning.

That's a metaphor, right?

Metaphor? No, no, you can do it. In the morning, do a few little exercises for the joints, not too much, then put your hands like a cup over and under the heart. Under your breast. He said tactfully, It's probably easier for a man. Then talk softly, don't yell. Under your ribs, push a little. When you wake up you must do this. Massage—I mean really pat, stroke a little, don't be ashamed. Very likely no one will be watching. Then you must talk, to your heart.

Well what do you say? I asked feeling timid—embarrassed.

Say anything, say—maybe say—Heart, little heart beat softly but never forget your job, the blood. You can whisper also remember, remember. For instance, an example: I said to it yesterday, Heart, heart do you remember my brother, how he made work for you that day when he came to the store and he said, Your boss's money Yasha and right now! How he put a gun in my face and I said Rubin are you crazy why don't you ask me at home? And he said Who needs your worker's money. For the movement, he said, only from your boss. Oh little heart you worked like a bastard, like a dog, like a crazy slave banga bang bang that day, remember? That's what I told my heart yesterday, my father said, and what a racket it made to answer me I remember I remember I remember till I was dizzy from the thumping.

Why'd you do that Pa? I don't get it.

Don't you see, this is good for the old heart—to remember—just as good as for the old person. Some people go running till late in life—for the muscles they say, but the heart knows the real purpose. The purpose is the expansion of the arteries, a river of blood, it cleans off the banks, carries the junk out of the system. I myself would rather remind the heart how frightened we were than go running in a strange neighborhood miles and miles, with the city being so dangerous these days.

I said Oh, but I said then, well thanks. I understood this was only the first lesson in how to grow old.

I don't think you listened, he said, as usual probably worried about the kids. Another lesson tomorrow.

tracy mostovoy

<u>tracy mostovoy</u> is an artist and photographer. These
photographs are from a series entitled *Naked Women in
Public Places*.

the coat

h u b e r t　　s e l b y

Harry loved his coat. He had gotten it toward the end of winter and it saved his life. The winters on the Bowery were tough under any conditions, but without a coat the winters were deadly, bodies picked up each morning, some frozen to the ground and having to be chipped loose. But Harrys coat became more than comfort, more than protection against the cold, even more than a life saver . . . it was his friend, his buddy . . . his only companion. He dearly loved his coat.

It was long, reaching almost to his ankles, and heavy, and he could wrap it around himself almost twice and when he raised the collar he felt completely protected from the world. It was an Army surplus coat that he had gotten from the Salvation Army, one of the last ones they had. He loved it right away. But keeping a coat on skid row during the winter was not easy.

hubert selby is the author of several novels, including *Last Exit to Brooklyn, The Room, The Demon,* and a collection of short stories entitled *The Song of the Silent Snow,* in which this story appears.

He had to be alert. There was always some person, or group, ready to take it from you and they were willing to kill you for it.

But now the weather was getting warmer and he could relax a little. He didnt get careless, but it would be progressively easier to protect his coat. He had seen men sell their coats when the weather warmed, for enough for a bottle of wine, but he would never be that foolish. Winter always returned. He had spent part of one winter with newspapers wrapped around his body trying desperately to keep out the cold, each day an eternity, but that was only a memory he kept alive during the heat of summer when keeping the coat seemed such a burden. Winter always returned.

During the cold weather he often worked as a dishwasher at night. When he first got to the row a couple of old-timers tried to show him how to panhandle, how to size up a mark and know whether to lookim in the eye and tellim you need a drink, or try the painful look and old vet approach, and all the variations. And they warned him that the most important thing was to know who not to hit. They have a look in their eye and theyre liable to killya. You gotta stay clear of em. . . . And Harry would watch them panhandle, always staying south of Houston Street—the cops dont botherya down here, but north of Houstons bad news—but Harry just could not go up to a stranger and ask him for money. He even had a difficult time, finding it almost impossible, to ask for his money after a nights work. He had been that way all his life and had given up trying to change.

He liked to work at night because it not only gave him a job, but a place to stay warm during the long, cold nights. It was easier to find a place that was safe during the day to drink his wine and sleep. When he worked he always hung his coat next to the sink and watched it the whole evening. No one was supposed to be back there, except him, but that was no guarantee that someone wouldnt suddenly rush in and try to grab his coat.

Being alone was another reason he liked washing dishes. It was just him and the dishes, and his coat. Harry always had a difficult time being with people, having left school early because of the daily terror of being with so many people in one room and having to stand and talk when called on. He just spent more time by himself and less in school and eventually they left him alone and he drifted away, spending as much time as possible alone, longing always for companionship, never able to talk about his fear, no one, including Harry, understanding why he did what he did.

The nights washing dishes went easy enough. He had his warmth, some food, his solitude, and he would take a drink from time to time, being sure no one saw him take the bottle from his pocket. Survival depended upon keeping certain things secret. And dishwashing jobs were always available. Its not the kind of job guys keep. Some place always needed a dishwasher.

When he finished work he would get breakfast and his money, then buy a bottle of muscatel and find an abandoned building somewhere safe. The rest of the row was waking up and starting their day and he could nestle somewhere and not worry about people stumbling on him. He always went as far back in the deserted buildings as possible. There were gangs that roamed the Bowery who were worse than crazed dogs and you had to be careful you didnt let anyone think you had something they might want. He always put his bottle in the huge pocket of his coat and walked as aimlessly as possible. He didnt know how many men he had seen beaten, and killed, for a coat or a bottle of wine.

You had to be careful on skid row. You had to be your own counsel . . . your own friend.

He climbed over the rubble and garbage in an empty lot to an abandoned building and worked his way around battered walls and fallen beams to a distant corner in the shadows and sat, wrapped his coat around him, and opened his bottle. He took a long drink, almost half the bottle, then gulped air for a moment, then let out a long sigh. . . . He looked at the bottle admiringly . . . affectionately, as he felt the wine warming his gut and flowing through his system . . . then took another quick drink . . . then another . . . then licked his lips as he put the top on the bottle and placed it carefully beside him. He took out his money and rolled it up, except for a dollar, and shoved it through a small hole in a pocket into the lining where it could not be found, then leaned back against the wall, wrapped his coat around him, cradled the bottle on his lap, holding it tightly, closed his eyes and smiled and wiggled as he felt the wine going through his body, feeling nice and warm and sending a glow through him right down to the tips of his toes.

Fantasies used to come with the wine, but somewhere, sometime, they stopped, or maybe they just drifted away. There just did not seem to be any energy available to bring them back and no material for new ones. All hopes, fantasies, dreams, now centered on this one moment of Harry and his bottle nestling safely and warmly in the corner of an abandoned building. . . .

But there were memories that sometimes haunted him . . . or others that eased their way across his minds eye with gentle waves of pleasure. . . .

He was driving through the Appalachians once when he pulled off the road to watch a sunset. He watched the sun go out of sight, then the changing layers of colors turned from pink to red, from blue to purple . . . sitting alone, tears rolling from his eyes and down his cheeks as he was overwhelmed by the beauty of the incredible spectacle . . . sitting there still when there was only a faint hint of blue/gray in the distance as it got darker, and when the moons brightness started to bring light to the valley below and the sky softened into a thick dark velvet, twinkling stars slowly emerged and dotted the darkened sky, he was still there immersed and transfixed by the wonder of it, experiencing its beauty and miracle in some secret place deep within him. . . .

But much time had passed since he was last visited by that memory.

He took another drink, recapped the bottle and looked around. . . . He had everything he needed right now. A bottle . . . a place to park himself for a while . . . and his coat . . . his wonderful, beautiful coat. He kissed the collar, I love you coat, and chuckled. He took another drink and closed his eyes and felt the warmth, then looked at his coat. I can always depend on you. Youre my friend. My really true friend. My buddy. You/ll never let me down, right? And I/ll never let you down. I swear to you—raising his right hand in a solemn oath—I/ll never let you down. Unto the death I/ll never let you down. He lowered his hand and took another drink, then looked at something shining in the darkness. He stared hard, frowning, until he finally made out the form of a huge rat staring at him. A shock of disgust and fear sickened him and he closed his eyes and huddled deeper into his coat, then opened his eyes, but the rat was still there, his eyes looking like two beacons in the dark. He stared at the eyes, swallowing a mounting nausea, then forced himself to pick up a piece of debris and throw it at the rat, the rat quickly disappearing in the dark. He took another drink and relaxed. At least it was real. If it wasnt he couldnt have gotten rid of it so easily. He had had d.t./s, but he never saw anything like rats. He knew some guys did and he didnt know how they survived imagining that rats were crawling all over them . . . he shook his head, Arghhh. He opened his bottle and threw the top away, took a long drink, then pulled his coat even tighter around him. He cant bother us, can he? He/d never be able to get me. My buddy would keep him away, wouldntya? Nothin, no one . . . no one, nothin. Right? Cant bother us. He snuggled deeper into the corner and his coat. He closed his eyes momentarily and listened to the wine singing through his body and smiled, then started singing, Nights are long since—he started giggling and nodding his head— I dream about you all thru—he started laughing—hehehehehehe—thru hehehehehe—ishh . . . ishh . . . my Buddy . . . my Buddy—he started waving his hand in a small arc conducting himself—Watch the bounding ball—all through the—hehehehehehe . . . ishh. . . . Nobody—hahaha—Nobod— ishhh—Bod—hahaha . . . he gulped and swallowed hard and shook his head—Nobody hehe—ishh . . . he took another drink, his off-key singing continuing in his head, a few mumbling words coming from his mouth, nobody but a buddy, hehehehe . . . continuing to stammer and giggle and nod his head, then emptied the bottle and tossed it as far away as possible, deep into the shadows of the rubble and listened to the tinkle of broken glass reverberate through his snug nest like the tinkling of sleigh bells as his head slowly lowered, his chin eventually resting on the lapel of his great coat, and drifting into sleep.

He moved, jerked spastically and mumbled as he was slowly dragged back to consciousness. It was much darker in the building but he was long accustomed to waking up about this same time so he knew it must be late afternoon. He got to his feet and brushed off his coat, then slowly, and carefully, made his way past and through the shattered walls out of the building.

The shadows were long as he picked his way through the rubble of the lot, slipping and stumbling, rats squealing and skittering off as he staggered and inched his way to the street.

The traffic was heavy this time of the evening and Harry huddled in his coat as he walked along the street, the people fulfilling his need for human companionship without being a threat. He had spent many, many years alone, and lonely, but they had not eliminated his need, and occasional desire, to be with people. As long as he was free to just be there on the street without having to be a part of them, he was alright.

Soon he became aware of the need for a drink and he bought a bottle of muscatel, putting the bottle in his pocket before leaving the store. He rushed from the vicinity of the store and went to a deserted, safe area to take a drink. He rejoined the activity of the street, huddled deep in his coat against the cold, a feeling of triumph and love flowing through his body as he turned his back to the cold wind, aware of his bodys warmth.

He decided he would work again tonight so he made the rounds of the joints and soon was standing in front of a couple of sinks. He took his coat off and hung it right by the sink where he could keep an eye on it.

● ● ●

Spring passed easily enough. During the day if it got too hot in the sun he would go to the shady side of the street and though it was warm he was still able to wear his coat. A few times he was tempted to take off his coat and carry it, but he knew better. That was inviting trouble. It would be too easy for some guy to knock into him while his partner yanked the coat away from him and ran down the street. No, he could not afford to take chances. No matter how hot it got, his coat was always valuable to winos. It could always be hocked for at least a jug.

And anyway, there was always the relief of the evening, his coat being perfect for the springtime coolness. Then, as the spring rains passed, everything seemed to be a little easier. For a month or so he had a great apartment. He had found a huge packing crate and spent hours dragging and pushing it to the remains of an old building. It took a tremendous amount of will to not just leave it in the first room of the building but to push and tug it around corners and back into the recesses of the building where it would not so easily be stumbled upon. He set it up in a corner and cleared some of the debris away from it, not too large an area, he did not want it obvious that someone was living there, he did not want to leave a trail, just enough so he could roll in and out of bed without stumbling over something. And he found an old calendar, maybe five or six years old, and hung it on a wall of the crate. He collected a few rags and the remains of a cushion and made himself the semblance of a chair.

He spent as much time as possible in his apartment, loving the feeling of security and the smell of the wood, and if it was exceptionally warm, as it usually was in the summer, even at night, he would take off his coat and wrap it carefully in some old plastic sheets he had found and bury it under the rubble where it could not be seen, secure in the knowledge that no matter what happened his coat would be safe. Then he would lean back in his chair and drink and sing or talk softly to himself, or sometimes be silent and watch the various creatures that shared the abandoned buildings and lots with him, coming from deep under the buildings, from caverns of deserted cellars or basements, or perhaps deeper, from some unknown area beyond that created by man and his buildings, where darkness and moisture fostered and nurtured its strange inhabitants. He watched with fear and disgust trying, from time to time, to close his eyes and thus eliminate them from his world, but he was more afraid of not knowing where they were, so he was forced, beyond will and desire, to watch them when they suddenly appeared, scuttled about, then froze still and looked, eyes reflecting light, eyes that seemed to get brighter and larger the longer he stared, so large and bright they appeared to leave the creatures head and float toward him . . . his body tense, becoming stiff, a panic and nausea knotting and constricting his gut and throat . . .

until the creatures suddenly ran, jumped, or just disappeared into the unknown and fearsome world they had come from.

Sometimes he watched, fascinated, as they would slink through the shadows and rubble, unaware of his presence, intent upon not being seen by their prey or predators. One day, while there was still faint light finding its way into the inner recesses, he watched a huge tomcat slowly, stealthily, stealing up on something. He was battered, with a piece missing from an ear and large clots of fur torn from his body. He was obviously a fighter and survivor . . . no, more than that, he was a prevailer and Harry developed an instant affection for the cat. He watched him, not knowing what it was the cat saw, but it was obviously tracking something as he crawled along the ground, his belly rubbing the stones and rubble, moving a few feet . . . stopping . . . staring . . . nose twitching, tail beating. Harry followed the direction the cat seemed to be looking, fascinated and curious, and thought he saw some sort of movement . . . then was certain there was something back in the shadows. The cat continued crawling . . . then stopped, its tail beating rapidly, his entire rear portion wiggling . . . then he leaped and Harry saw the prey as it squealed and tried to escape. It was a huge rat and it continued to squeal as the cat hit it in mid air. The rat rolled over and got to its feet quickly and found itself cornered against an old sink. The cat slowly . . . cunningly . . . forced the rat back into the corner until it could no longer move and when it leaped the cat leaped too and grabbed it with his large paws and they both landed, hard, on a piece of steel, the rat squealing so loud it almost hurt Harrys ears. The rat managed to get out of the grasp of the cat but had nowhere to go and the cat continued inching closer and closer to the now bleeding rat. Harry continued to remain immobile and stare, barely breathing, trying to shut out the sight of the blood, yet glad the rat was bleeding and had to fight himself not to shout encouragement to the cat. The rat leaped again, and the cat caught it, and this time as they landed the cat sunk his teeth into the back of the neck of the rat and shook it violently, the squealing of the rat piercing the stillness, and shook the rat until there was a loud snap and the rat was instantly silent as it hung from the jaws of the cat. He shook it a few more times, then dropped it and looked at it for a moment . . . then pushed it with a paw . . . looked for another second or two . . . pushed it around for a few minutes as if it were a ball of yarn . . . Harry becoming very uncomfortable . . . then picked it up and carried it into the shadows, out of sight, but not out of hearing, the silence broken, from time to time, with the crunching of bones. Harry clamped his hands over his ears and pinched his eyes shut. . . .

Eventually he allowed his face to relax and his eyes to slowly open . . . everything looked as before. Then he removed his hands from his ears . . . and sighed with relief at the silence. He took a long, long drink and sighed again and soon realized that his mind was back into an old habit of wondering about the violence of nature but pushed it from his mind with another long drink.

● ● ●

The coat was hot in the summer, even in the shade, if you could find any, but he did not mind. He knew that another winter would be here before you knew it and he was going to survive that winter. His coat would guarantee that.

He gave up his dishwashing in the summer and did a lot of junking. He got a pushcart as early in the morning as possible and stayed away from the row and the gangs who might rip him off when he collected a load of paper, or after he got his money. And, when he was safely distant, he took off his coat and put it in the cart and covered it with paper.

He concentrated on paper and cardboard. He had seen some other junkmen bring in sinks and pieces of furniture and haggle with the guy and eventually get a few dollars, but when he tried it the guy told him what he had wasnt worth anything and he just nodded and went out again for a load of paper. He knew the guy was going to keep it and sell it, but he just didnt know how to bargain with him the way the other guys did. So he stayed with cardboard and paper.

He took it nice and easy, knowing he would get enough for what he needed. He always had a bottle of muscatel with him and would take a drink from time to time and go leisurely about his work. Usually he would stop in some greasy spoon and fill himself with beans and bread before going back to his apartment with a bottle of muscatel.

Eventually he had to give up his apartment. One night he came back with a bottle and before he turned the last corner he could hear voices. He stopped. Listened. . . . Sounded like a couple of guys, maybe more . . . could be three . . . but who knows? Their voices were muffled and indistinct and he could just barely make out what was happening. They were fighting over who was to get the next drink, or who got more than the other. He listened . . . not moving . . . the voices got louder and angrier and suddenly there was a thud and a gurgling scream, then another thud . . . and another . . . and he recognized the sound as someone being hit on the head with a rock or a pipe, or something similar. Then the thudding stopped and there was the sound of a falling body, and then silence . . . then the sound of someone drinking. . . . Fear and disgust almost panicked him, but he forced himself to quietly leave. He stood in the evening air for a few moments, swallowing his nausea, wanting to get away from there as rapidly as possible, but feeling weak and sick. He took many deep breaths and closed his eyes from time to time, trying to push away the sound and the image. Soon he was able to take a drink, then work his way through the rubble to another building and find a corner to nest in and dissolve the incident in wine.

Even with the heat summer was easy time. He slowly pushed his junk cart through the streets looking around, taking an occasional drink, watching kids run and play a thousand and one games, looking at the trees, bushes, shrubs, and flowers, feeling free and unencumbered with the sun and air on his face. In the evening he would go to whatever abandoned building he was using, and drink, sing and talk softly to himself until he lost consciousness.

Then autumn turned the leaves and the breeze and he would pick up an occasional red leaf streaked with yellow. Now, with the cooler evenings his coat was always around him, keeping out the chill and keeping in the warmth, the tip of his nose cold, making him more aware of the friendliness and comfort of his companion . . . his soft singing and talking not so much to himself, but more to his buddy . . . his great coat.

Then the leaves stopped turning colors and fell, the trees becoming bare and naked and exposed. He sought out the sunny side of the street, constantly awake to the chill in the air that meant another winter would soon be blowing its way through the Bowery. It brought him even closer to his coat, knowing that it would protect him from that wind and the cold that would soon make the entire row shiver and nightly leave in its wake the bodies of winos who had passed out in doorways and abandoned buildings, their bodies blue and rigid.

But winter was yet to come and Harry picked his way through the rubble of a lot, happily aware of the sudden change in temperature as he walked from a sunny spot into a long shadow and then once more into the late sun. He heard voices and laughter and looked at a couple of older kids dancing around a wino staggering through the lot a short distance ahead of Harry. He saw one of the kids pouring something on the wino. Harry assumed it was water and shivered momentarily as he realized what it must feel like to the guy who was wet, but then one of the kids lit a match and tossed it at the bum and he suddenly exploded and was engulfed in flames and the kids ran away, laughing, as the wino screamed and tried to run but kept falling down. Harry reacted instantly and ran toward the bum, slipped out of his coat, quickly knocked the wino to the ground and wrapped the coat around him smothering the flames, the wino screaming in agony, Harry having to fight to keep his coat wrapped around him, but mercifully the guy soon passed out and Harry was able to suffocate the flames. He kept his coat wrapped around him to be certain the flames stayed out and to cushion his body against the sharp edges of the rubble.

Others had seen what happened and soon the police and an ambulance were there. The attendants carefully rolled the wino out of Harrys coat. He was charred, but alive. They placed him in the ambulance and then asked Harry if he was alright. Any burns? Harry shook his head. Why dont you take a ride with us and we/ll check you out at the hospital. Harry shook his head, holding his coat close to him and staring at the ambulance. The attendant shrugged, You saved his life . . . for now anyway. Dont know if it/ll do much good though.

The ambulance left and the police questioned Harry briefly. Harry clutched his coat to him, still in a state of shock. A couple of people told the police that they could describe the kids who did it, probably the same kids whove been doin it to all the others.

Yeah, they think its some kind of game.

They call it burn a bum.

Harry managed to work himself into the coat and stumble away from the small knot of people to the liquor store. It was when he shoved the bottle in his pocket that he noticed how much his hands had been burned. The sudden pain snapped him out of his shock and he became more alert as he went to his corner nest in the abandoned building. He looked at his coat and though it had a few black spots there was no real damage done. He hugged it to his breast as his body unfolded in the corner and almost cried with relief as he leaned against the wall. He continued to hug and kiss the coat, overwhelmed by the fact that it was alright, realizing that the flames could have destroyed his coat when he wrapped it around the wino. His relief was so great that he spent many, many minutes hugging and kissing his coat, telling it he was sorry if it got hurt but he had to do it, he couldnt just let the guy burn, and his coat reassured him that it was alright, it understood and agreed that Harry had done the right thing. . . .

Eventually the shock was completely drained from him and Harry put his coat on and wrapped it snuggly around him, but even the fact that his coat was safe could not stop the feeling of sadness that flowed through him. Harry took a drink and once more looked at his burned hands. They werent too bad. A little red with a couple of blisters. They were starting to hurt now. He took another long drink. Soon the wine would take away the pain. In the meantime he would hold a few cold stones in his hands to keep them cool . . .

but the cold stones, and even the wine, couldnt seem to stop that terrible sadness that was taking control of his body and mind. He took another long drink trying to drown out the screams of the winos agony, but when they finally faded he could still hear the peoples voices, its some kinda game . . . its some kinda game, its some kinda game. . . .

He suddenly groaned and tears burst forth from his eyes and he folded his arms around his head as he sobbed from the depth of his being, O God . . . O God . . . he squeezed his arms tighter around his head hoping the pressure might in some miraculous way ease the sickness flowing through his body and the pain of his mind and soul . . . O God . . . why is life so fragile???? Why???? Why????

There was still a faint glow in the sky as he walked along the street, his hands deep in his pockets, talking softly to his coat, telling it how much he loved it and appreciated how warm it was keeping him and how he never had to be afraid of the winters because of it; and sometimes he would whistle for a few minutes, or even hum, and then continue talking to his coat and tell it how theyd get a bottle of muscatel and go back to that nice warm place they had fixed up last night and just drink and sleep, no worries no cares, ju—A couple of bums suddenly shoved him in a doorway and he knew they were after his coat. He swung out and screamed HELP!!!! HELP!!!! AAAAAAAAAAAAHHHHHHHHHHHHHHHH!!!!—Shut up ya son of a bitch—Harry

continued flailing his arms, screaming, AAAAAAAAAAAHHHHHHHHHHHHHH!!!!—
Fa krists sake grabim—What the fuck ya think Im tryin to do—Hitim fa
krists sake—and Harry continued to swing his arms and fight to get out the
door, still screaming, hoping someone would come to help him,
AAAAAAAAAAAAHHHHHHHHHHHHHH!!!!—and the three of them continued to
fall over each other and bounce off the walls in the cramped hallway, Harry
flailing and screaming as he lunged for the door, the bums trying to grab him
and hit him with a piece of pipe one of them was holding, and Harry finally
crashed through the thin door—AAAAAAAAAAAAHHHHHHHHHHHH—just as
the guy hit him on the head with the pipe and Harry staggered forward onto
the street and the guy hit him again and Harry fell to his knees, his arms
wrapped around himself so they couldnt get the coat off, and he was hit again
and knocked flat on his face and was kicked, but still he kept his arms
wrapped around himself in his semi-conscious state, muttering, no, no, no,
as they tried to yank the coat off, and people passing by glanced at first and
then looked and soon a few asked what the hell was going on and the guys
looked around at the people, still tugging on the coat, and then a prowl car
turned the corner and they let go of the coat and ran. . . .

The cops got out of the car and walked over to where Harry was lying on
the sidewalk, blood seeping from his head, his arms wrapped around his
body protecting his coat in a death grip. The cops looked down at him for a
moment. . . . Seems to be alive.

Yeah. . . . Guess we/d better put in a call.

The other cop nodded and strolled back to the car and called an
ambulance.

A dozen or so people milled around Harry, asking what had happened,
shaking their heads or relating what they had seen or surmised; some
passersby stopped to join them or to look for a moment then move on, others
slowing slightly and seeing it was just a bum hurried on their way.

The doctors did what they could for him but Harry was not expected to live
through the night, and at 4/00 a.m. his heart actually stopped beating, but an

alert nurse pounded on his chest, his heart responding with a feeble but constant beat. Every function of his body was monitored and checked with amazement, there being no known medical explanation for his still being alive.

The fourth day they started having hope that he would live. Not because there had been any improvement in his condition, everything was still the same, but simply because it somehow seemed inevitable. Then, about 4/30 a.m., his body started to convulse from alcoholic withdrawal. His condition got worse and worse rapidly, yet still he lived, something inside him refusing to give up.

Treating the convulsions was in itself a simple matter but the treatment tended to aggravate his other condition, and so the hospital personnel had to maintain a delicate balance so they would not bring about his death from one condition while treating the other.

Miraculously he survived the convulsions and the treatment, and after being in a coma for a week he regained consciousness for a brief period, his eyes barely focusing, but able to nod his head when asked if he could hear, then mumbled something about his coat before drifting once again into unconsciousness. From that moment on his recovery was slow, sometimes barely discernible, but steady.

A week later he was able to talk and was visited by a clerk from the records office. She smiled and sat down next to the bed and explained that as he was unconscious, and had no identification when he was brought in, she had to ask him a few questions. Alright? Do you feel up to it?

He nodded. They didnt get my coat, did they?

What? What coat?

The one I was wearing. They tried to get my coat.

Oh . . . Im sure its down in the clothing room just like all the others.

The information seemed to take a while to register, but eventually it did and he sighed inwardly . . . then nodded his head.

Now then, I need a little information. It wont take long. Name?

Harry. Harry Wright.

Address?

Harry spoke softly and slowly with obvious effort.

The Bowery.

The Bowery? Dont you have a permanent mailing address?

He moved his hand in a negative motion. The Bowerys permanent. It aint movin.

Nothing more specific?

He moved his hand slightly.

She smiled and shrugged. Age?

Forty.

In case of emergency who do you want notified?

I dont really care. . . . He smiled slightly, Gallo Brothers.

Gallo Brothers?

He smiled a little broader, Ernest and Julio.

Oh???? Then she understood and smiled. The winemakers.

Harry blinked his eyes.

She was still smiling, Well, I guess we had better leave that blank. Occupation?

He moved his jaw in a shrugging gesture. . . . Dishwasher.

Have you ever been a patient here before?

I dont know.

Dont know?

He shook his head slightly. . . . I dont know where I am.

Oh. . . . Bellevue.

Nope. He winced as a pain pierced his head, then exhaled sharply, exhausted and tired.

The clerk looked at her form, then at him, I think thats enough for now. You get some rest. She got up to leave.

Do me a favor? See if my coats alright?

She started to say something, then just smiled and nodded. Sure.

Thanks. Harry closed his eyes and slept.

When he awoke he asked the nurse if the clerk had called about his coat.

Coat?

She was going to check to see if its alright.

She probably hasnt had time to yet. Im sure she/ll take care of it.

Harry nodded within himself, unable to really think about it, not sure when he saw the clerk . . . not sure about anything actually. Every now and then there would be a slight glimmer of light, but it would be quickly absorbed by mist and he could not find the energy to really grasp a thought for any length of time and would just drift off into sleep.

Through the following days whenever he was conscious Harry would wonder about his coat and if it was alright, if he was still wearing it when he got here and, if he was, what had happened to it after he got here. Everytime someone came near him he wanted to ask them about his coat, but couldnt seem to summon up the energy. Eventually he felt a couple of days must have passed since he spoke with the clerk, not absolutely certain because he spent so much time sleeping and was still confused about time, but whether it was or not the pressure was building to the point where he had no choice but to ask the nurse again if the clerk had called about his coat.

She frowned agitatedly, What coat?

My coat—Harry could feel himself starting to tremble—remember I asked. Oh that. No. Nobody has called about anything.

But she said . . . can you call her?

I dont have time to make calls about coats. I have all I can do right now.

But I have to know. I dont know if—he started to get up, but a sudden pain took his breath away and he fell back on the bed.

Pain in your heart?

He could hardly mutter.

The nurse rushed from the room and quickly returned with a hypo and soon the pain subsided and Harry once more drifted off to sleep.

Harry continued to ask about his coat, never being certain if he was asking many times in one day or once in many days, but when the pressure built to the point where he no longer had a choice, he asked, and when he was given an evasive answer he got so upset he usually had to be sedated and another note was made on his chart. Eventually the doctor asked about the notes on his chart and the nurses told him about Harrys preoccupation with his coat and the doctor wrote a request that Harry be interviewed by a psychiatrist. And for krists sake, in the meantime tell him his coats alright.

When a nurse told Harry that his coat was alright he seemed to change instantly, tension draining from his body almost visibly, a hint of color returning to his cheeks. He could feel an endless sigh flow through his body as he drifted back to sleep.

Harry was relaxed, but still a little groggy, when a young psychiatrist visited him one morning. Harry had not been shaved for three or four days, his head was swathed in bandages that were stained with blood and antiseptics, and he was still wired so his bodily functions could be monitored. The psychiatrist looked at him for a moment. You look depressed.

Harry just blinked.

How do you feel?

Harry shrugged slightly. Okay.

The psychiatrist made a few notes. You seem to be concerned about your clothing.

My coat. I wanted to be sure it was alright.

Were you wearing it when you were admitted?

Harry looked at him for a moment. I dont know.

The psychiatrist made more notes, then looked at Harry. I see. Do you often have lapses of memory?

Harry looked at him, blinking, feeling more and more intimidated. He started sweating. I was unconscious.

The psychiatrist peered at him for a moment, then made another note. Are you often so obsessive about your possessions?

Harry stared, his head shaking slightly, trying earnestly to understand what it was the doctor wanted. He listened hard, and heard the words but he just could not seem to make any sense out of them. They did not seem to have anything to do with him . . . or anything he could think of. Harry did not know what he had done wrong. All Harry could do was look and twist his face into a frown. . . .

The psychiatrist stared at Harry then made more notes. Are you always so insecure about your clothing?

Harry could feel himself wilting as the psychiatrist stared at him. . . . Eventually he shook his head.

Harrys sweating and trembling increased and he was no longer capable of even trying to understand what the psychiatrist was saying or what it was he wanted. He just stared, on the verge of tears, and shook his head.

The psychiatrist made a final note about the patients hostile and uncooperative behavior and infantile regression, then snapped the metal binder on the chart shut. That will be all. He left.

Harry was still trembling an hour later when a nurse came into the room.

Are you alright?

Harry shook his head slightly.

Youre so pale and sweaty—she touched his forehead—and clammy. Do you have any pain?

He nodded.

Harry continued to tremble many minutes after having been given a hypo, feeling cold and lost, wanting so much to run and hide and just cry . . . cry. . . . He looked at the wires going from the various parts of his body to the machinery around the bed knowing that he could disconnect himself easy enough, but he would still be unable to move. He was trapped. He knew his legs would not support him if he tried to stand. And even if he could, he could never find his way to his coat and he could not go anywhere without his coat . . . not now . . . it would be suicide . . . and he did not want to die. Not that way. Not anyway, but especially not that way . . . just a hunk of frozen flesh. . . .

He shut his eyes and squeezed them together as hard as possible to shut out the image, then suddenly opened them so his senses could be enveloped by his surroundings and blot out the cold and the stares of the psychiatrist. . . . He tried to change his position on the bed, but didnt have much freedom of movement. His eyes got heavy . . . sleepy . . . his body started to feel light . . . the tension slowly started dissolving as the opiate flowed through his body . . . he knew that soon he would fall asleep . . . his body got lighter and lighter . . .

his eyes heavier and heavier . . .

he

could no longer think . . . was only vaguely aware of his body . . . still he felt like he was drowning in tears. . . .

• • •

Harry Wrights condition continued to improve and soon he was able to walk to the bathroom, at first with assistance, then alone. Another month and he was able to walk around whenever he wanted and spent some time in the tv room, when it wasnt too crowded, staying in the back of the room, but spending most of his time playing solitaire or looking at magazines. He was still too weak to do much of anything else and was content to rest and eat, feeling relaxed and secure now that he knew his coat was alright.

He was unable to eat the Thanksgiving dinner, but he did participate energetically in the Christmas festivities, enjoying the food and the entertainments that various organizations presented and the little packages of candy they passed out. He also laughed at their jokes and smiled in recognition of their greetings and MEEEEEEEERY CHRISTMAS.

Now that he was well enough to move around without any ill effects, the first thing he did in the morning was to look out the window and check the weather. The area around the hospital always had a gray, cold look, but he watched the people walking, knowing by the way they moved just how cold it was. He also checked the morning shift and listened to them. Everybody talked about the weather and on the really cold days they were still rubbing their hands together when they got to the ward and hunched their shoulders when they talked about the wind and snow. He watched and listened to the radiators letting out their hiss and smiled. . . . Even when he got out he/d be warm. He had his coat. He had nothing to worry about, and he would wrap his bathrobe around him and pretend it was his coat and stand by the window and put his nose against the cold glass and feel the heat coming from the radiator. . . .

And, from time to time, he would sit, his hands in his bathrobe pockets, thinking about his buddy . . . and how it felt and looked . . . closing his eyes and seeing every inch of his coat, even the black spots from the fire, feeling its weight on his shoulders and the texture of the material against his cheeks and the almost bottomless pockets . . . and he experienced another warmth, the warmth of friendship . . . the warmth of affection.

One morning he was looking at the paper when he recognized the area in a photo, an empty lot on the Bowery. There was a bulldozer in the lot and in front of it were four or five bodies, " . . .inhabitants of the Bowery who had frozen to death sometime in the past month and were just discovered. They had to be broken loose from the ground with a bulldozer." Harry felt a wave of sickness and panic twist his insides, but then he slowly relaxed as he wrapped his bathrobe around him once again, closed his eyes and affectionately talked with his friend. His friend loved him and would never let that happen to him. He didnt have to worry about that.

• • •

Harry had been in the hospital three months and with the return of health and strength came an increased feeling of nervousness. There was a vague tension within him, a gnawing anxiety that grew with each day. He gradually retreated further and further within himself, becoming less communicative and spending more time just sitting with his robe wrapped around him, occasionally going over to the window and staring out at the grayness. It had always been like this, ever since he could remember. The only thing that changed it was drinking. When he had enough to drink things around him seemed to change . . . they became friendlier, more comfortable and pleasant and he didnt feel threatened or sickened by what he saw. But the longer he went without drinking the darker things became, the more painful life became . . . everything around him became unbearable. It seemed like there was nothing but killing and hurt . . . always hurt . . . the kind of hurt that stays inside and just keeps growing and gnawing until it takes over everything in you . . . always hurt. . . .

That was why the Bowery was so ideal. In other places when everything got gray and ugly there was always a small part of him that would remember and remind him that it wasnt always like that, that he had actually looked around and liked what he saw . . . at times loved it . . . loved it with a depth of feeling and involvement, and all he could do was drink to try and re-kindle that feeling of love . . . of beauty . . . the conflict consuming him.

But the more he drank the more impossible it became to stay, so he had to move on, always feeling the pain of a crying child or a straggly cat, occasionally being brought to tears by the beauty of a flower or a budding tree.

But on the Bowery when he felt that all the beauty had been squeezed from the world and there was nothing but grayness and hurt, he could look around and know he was right because the world he saw was precisely that, and so there was no conflict. The ugliness was real and the wine painted over that and he could go his way, alone, washing dishes, junking, finding some place to nest alone and talk and sing softly to himself and his coat, and drink himself into a state of unconsciousness.

Harrys feeling of anxiety and grief increased with the passing of each day, and so, though it was snowing and cold when they told him all his test results were fine and he would be discharged soon, he was relieved.

Before he was discharged he was visited by the psychiatrist again. He asked Harry what he was going to do when released. More alert than before, he was still confused by the psychiatrist. It seemed that he just could not mean what he said and Harry was trying to understand what it was the psychiatrist wanted. Go home.

The psychiatrist looked at the chart, Wheres that? They dont seem to have it on here.

Harry frowned. The Bowery.

The Bowery? Why would you go there?

I live there.

The psychiatrist made a note. But wouldnt you like to do something better with your life? Like get a good job and be a productive member of society?

Harry shook his head. I work.

The psychiatrist made another note. Washing dishes isnt much of a job.

Harry just looked, trembling slightly inside.

Now that you are free from alcohol you should be able to find a place to live with nicer surroundings.

Harry shook his head, his confusion showing in his expression.

The psychiatrist made a note. Would you like to go some place to rest and get some help in evaluating your—Harry was shaking his head—life and not go back to that old environment?

Harry was still shaking his head, No . . . no, no nut house.

Well now, thats not really—Harry continued shaking his head—the proper way to . . . the psychiatrist looked at Harry intently, disbelief in his expression and voice. Dont you want to better yourself?

Harry stopped shaking his head and stared at the psychiatrist, almost wanting to explain to him that he had found the most comfortable life he had ever had and was going to stay there, but could summon up neither the necessary energy nor the desire. Now at least the psychiatrist was no longer a problem to Harry, the enigma was solved: he was just another dogooder trying to get involved in someone elses life. Harry stopped frowning and even started to relax slightly. . . . Im fine.

The psychiatrist looked at Harry, exasperated, then slammed the metal binder on the record shut and left.

On the day of his discharge a ward attendant was sent to get Harrys
clothing, and Harry started to pace. The tension in his body became more
and more acute as he looked at the drab ugliness around him, then out the
window at the snow and the trees bending in the wind. He felt the heat from
the radiator, then touched his nose to the cold window. . . .

then

turned and started pacing again.

After half an hour he went to the nurses station and asked where his
clothes were. He was told to relax, that the attendant would be back shortly.
He started pacing again, his anxiety and tension becoming so intense he felt
brittle, walking from one end of the floor to the other, from time to time
looking out the window.

Eventually the charge nurse decided to call and see where the attendant
was, assuming he was goldbricking. When she spoke to the clerk in the clothing
room she was told that the attendant was still there, that Mr. Wrights clothing
could not be found but they were still looking. Well, you tell Walter to come
back to the ward and when you find his clothing give us a call. Ward B3W.

Harry caught bits of the tail end of the conversation, Whats that? Cant
they find my coat?

They seem to be having some difficulty Mr. Wright, but—

The color instantly drained from Harrys face and his legs weakened, Ive
got to have my coat. He leaned against the counter in the nurses station. I got
to have my coat!

Just relax Mr. Wright. Dont upset yourself.

Harry was trembling and staring at them, Wheres the clothing room? I/ll
find it. Where do they keep the—

Mr. Wright—spoken authoritatively—you must relax or youll have a
relapse and—

Just tell me where the room is. I/ll find my coat. I/ll find it . . . Harry was
clinging desperately to the counter, feeling weaker by the second, the room
starting to spin, his vision blurring . . . he could no longer feel his feet or legs.

He started to sag, semiconscious and sobbing almost incoherently as he relived his long fight to save his coat, feeling the death-like emptiness of separation from the most valuable thing in his life, a friend that was at least as valuable as his life itself. . . .

He pulled himself to his feet and pleaded with them to tell him where the clothes room was, I can find my coat . . . I know I can . . . I can find it anywhere . . . I—

Mr. Wright please, you must con—

Walter returned from the clothes room, dropping the clothes receipt on the counter, They cant find his clothes anywhere, Miss Wilson.

Let me look, I can find it . . . and Harry continued to plead and tremble and cling desperately to the counter as a nurse tried to quiet him.

Miss Wilson glanced at the papers quickly then asked Walter what name the clerk had looked under?

Whatever names on there I guess.

She showed him the admission sheet, He was a John Doe when he was admitted. See, theres also an I.D. number. Mr. Wright, what sort of clothing did you have?

A big army coat. I can find it in a minute. . . .

Miss Wilson called the clothing room and told them what to look for, and what name and number.

It seemed like forever to Harry as he remained suspended between life and death, the only thing proving to him that he was alive was the curious pain twisting and clawing within him, but in just a few minutes Walter was back with Harrys clothes. They had been sterilized, but they still looked and smelled funky and Walter carried them at arms length from him and wrinkled his nose. Harry grabbed his clothes and hugged them to him, almost crying, and rushed to the mens room to get dressed. He sat on a commode half laughing, half crying, hugging and cradling his coat, telling it how much he loved it and had been waiting for it and he would not have let them keep him away that he didnt have to worry that no matter what happened he would have found him . . . rocking back and forth, tears rolling down his cheeks, sobbing and laughing with relief. . . .

Harry started down the hospital steps when a gust of wind blew snow in his face and momentarily blinded him. He grabbed the hand rail, feeling the cold metal on his hand and the wind biting his face. He pulled his watch cap down around his ears and yanked the large collar of his great coat up around his head and nestled deep into his coat like a butterfly in a cocoon and smiled from deep inside himself. He could feel the cold on his nose and the warmth of his body. His coat was even warmer than he remembered. His lovely and wonderful coat.

The wind stopped and he went down the stairs, holding the railing, the ground slippery and treacherous. When he reached the bottom he shoved his cold hands in his pockets and looked around. There were large snow banks on the sides of the street, its gray filth showing through the whiteness of the newly fallen snow. He started walking cautiously, over the patches of ice everywhere, feeling his body moving inside his coat, hearing the wind and feeling the snow and laughing at them.

He walked carefully down the street to the first liquor store and bought a pint of muscatel. As soon as he got outside he took a drink, standing still long enough to experience it going down and through his body, knowing soon the drabness and ugliness would be tolerable. He put the bottle in his pocket and started walking toward the bus stop. Soon he would be back on the Bowery and he would find a nice deserted building to nest in and leisurely drink his wine, then softly talk and sing to himself and his coat.

He stood with the wind at his back, cuddled in the warmth of his coat, his entire being happy and glowing. He rubbed his cheek against the collar, its roughness reassuring him. They were together. They could take anything together . . . do anything together . . . survive anything together. . . . He loved his coat . . . and his coat loved him . . . and they were together. That was the important thing. No one . . . nothing could separate them. And as long as they were together theyd make it. Yeah . . . theyd make it. . . .

The bus came and he hopped aboard and Harry Wright headed home. He was warm. . . . He was safe. . . .

go-go
d i v i a n a   i n g r a v a l l o

Nick hired me for my leather G-string, garter and corset. After my audition all he said was: "You like leather, huh? We should talk. You can start work tomorrow."

That's how I ended up working in what was known as the best go-go bar in New York City, which meant that the prerequisites to work there were blonde hair and big silicone breasts. The sight of my leather accoutrements blinded Nick, so that he ignored my small tits, black hair and olive complexion.

Nick was Italian. From Brooklyn. His big belly, the gold crucifix emerging out of his hairy chest and the pony tail combed out of an almost bald head, made me deny the fact that I was an Italian from Italy, and so I said, "I'm from Brazil."

Nick was the persistent type. He wouldn't lay off the subject of leather and screwing and kept on inviting me to play in his office. What Nick didn't know was he was dealing with a dyke from no other place but hell who

diviana ingravallo is a writer, actress and performance artist, author of the theatrical piece "Thru Our Blood."

despised him. This dyke knew that all Nick really needed was to be fucked in the ass with a 12" dildo, and how boring, this dyke thought, if I have to be the one to show him that.

Besides Nick's strong cologne, crucifix and sliminess, I hated working there because I was the only dyke. I know I was. Let's face it, it takes a dyke to spot another one, even if she's in disguise in a stripper or nun's uniform.

That's why I was so relieved when Kamala auditioned. Blonde hair, so fake it shined from a distance. Full, real breasts, pierced at both nipples, a gold chain connecting them, smooth curvy hips, muscular legs, thigh-high red boots. And a big personality. Nick hired her on the spot.

Kamala, whose real name was Kim, would ride her Harley to work, looking like an urban cowboy on an untamed horse. Her black riding boots made a statement at each step. Come to think of it, she was a walking statement. Leather jacket with dangling chains, spiked hair, a myriad of buttons with mottos like "Shit Happens" or "Butch Girls Rule." But the Kamala coming out of the dressing room was something completely different. A true femme fatale out of the cheesiest porn magazine. I loved that transformation so much that I wanted to mold it with my own hands. I wanted to fuck Kamala out of Kim. Sucking the femme out of a butch girl is my favorite game.

The weeks that followed were torturous, but at least work was finally spicy. I'd always be creeping glances at Kamala's cleavage, spying on the moves of her hips, sneaking peeks of that special place between her legs, where her G-string was just a bit too tight. I became the drooling stripper.

That's why I jumped on her Harley when she finally offered me a ride after work. I squeezed my legs around her hips and placed my hands on her inner thighs. I said: "Drive to the darkest alley you know. My cunt hurts. The vibrations of your bike are not gonna do it for me, baby," and I sunk my teeth in her neck to embellish my frank approach. A tremor ran through her body down to her cunt, which I cupped, firmly, with my hand. Kim followed my orders.

She stopped. And it was so dark, so hot, so sultry, so New York. I pulled her leather off and, before she knew it, I had her wrists tied behind her back.

"You bitch . . ." slid out the corner of her lips. I jumped off the bike to finish off my bondage job. Kim knew not to resist. Her Harley's balance was at stake.

Her nipples were instantly hard in my mouth. I pulled her tit ring with my tongue, twisting it a little, sucking on it, tugging the chain with my teeth. I felt like Audrey, the undulating teenager in Twin Peaks.

I pulled her G-string up, it actually slid up from her wetness, and pushed it against her clit. "Fuck me," she whispered. "So soon?" I replied, pulling her G-string higher up, bringing my knee between her legs. "Now, honey, where's the butch girl gone? In my lesbian manual femmes get off first." I started masturbating in front of her, rubbing my clit with one hand, fucking myself with the other. I felt Kim's desire transform into pain. Sweet revenge.

I came and started licking her all over, pulling off what was left of her clothes. She got so excited that a long, warm stream came out of her pussy. I put my hands and face under it, nourishing a thirst I didn't know I had. I felt like a kid trying to drink for the first time at an Italian fountain.

"So," she hissed, "are you going to fuck me now?" I said: "No, I'm just gonna lick you." I moved the soaking wet G-string to one side. I pulled the hood of her cunt by a ring that had mysteriously popped out and started sucking her, spreading her cheeks open. My tongue became an animal with a mind of its own.

"Fuck me, fuck me now!" she yelled.

"You butch girls are all alike," I whispered, and fucked her with as many fingers as her cunt could take, slowly and then fast and slow again, pulling on her tit chain with my mouth. I would have fucked her with my whole fist but did not have the right ingredients.

Kim's toughness was now melting on the bike seat which smelled of leather, cunt juice, motor oil and piss. The residue was all over my sticky fingers.

I untied her as if undoing the ribbon of a present. I told her to drive back to work. She did. Nick was closing up the place. I ran up to his face and said: "Hi Nick, let's go to your office, Kamala and I want to show you some kinky lesbian sex." He believed me because my words smelled of Kim's cunt.

Nick followed my orders. As I suspected, he was a fine slave, a trained slave, in fact. It was easy to have him undressed and on his knees. I started whipping him.

"You're a bad, dirty boy."

"Oh yes, mistress, I am a dirty bastard." I ordered Kim to blindfold him. The marks of the whip on his ass were the sign of the victory I had been longing for. I shoved a dildo without lube and without finesse up his butthole and kicked it with my pointy shoe and an exquisite sense of cruelty.

Then we took all the money the club had made that day, which was sitting in the jerk's pants pocket, and left him there. I thought, Goddammit, I'm giving up my favorite dildo. But it looked so good up his butt that it was a small sacrifice. Kim/Kamala and I parked her Harley in her garage and took the first plane to Rio de Janeiro.

guilty of everything
h e r b e r t   h u n c k e

When I got to New York in 1939, the first place I hit was 8th Avenue, between 46th and 47th. Cold turkey. I didn't know anything except that this was near 42nd Street. I began hanging around Bickford's, Chase's and several other spots. Now around the area at that time were a few rooming houses on West 43rd Street. There was even a place just off 7th Avenue right across from the old Paramount Theater. The Paramount's gone now, but there used to be a building there where you could rent studio rooms. They were cheap enough and you could live halfway comfortably, so after the first couple of scores I made, I got myself a place to stay. I soon discovered that my clothes just didn't go with the New York scene at all. I had to get a couple of pairs of slacks that at least fit properly, and one or two little items that bespoke New York and not a hick from the hinterlands.

herbert huncke was born in Massachusetts in 1915, and grew up in Chicago. He hit the road for the first time when he was twelve years old and has since lived all over America, New York City being his home base. This excerpt is from the autobiography of the same name, published by Paragon House in 1990.

I was quick to catch on. I was always quick in picking up on the scenes. I took to 42nd Street—I was a natural for it. It was exciting. I didn't see all the tinsel and tawdriness about it. It took me quite a while to finally detect the horror of the whole surroundings, but the Pokerino with its neon flashing, and the little passageways from one street to another and little things that were off the record, like the guys sitting around talking about the clip they'd made—all of this was completely new to me. I had led a sort of open life in Chicago, but still it was comparatively protected. I had never really been out where I had to scuffle on my own. No matter how bad things were in Chicago, if I couldn't get it from my father, I could bum it from my mother. There was always some member or friend of the family that I could put a sob story on. But in New York I didn't know anybody—I was strictly on my own.

The one thing that I didn't want to become was an open faggot. I drew the line at that. I didn't mind being known as a 42nd Street hustler, but I sure didn't want to be known as a faggot. Faggots have a hard way to go. They're everybody's property. They have that defense mechanism of theirs—that screaming at people and so on is mostly a defense mechanism. That may be partly why they're so bitchy and why they pick that particular aspect of the female as a defense to keep people away. For example, if you go to jail and the word goes out that you're a broad, it's a foregone conclusion that anybody in the joint can fuck you. That's all there is to it. They either fuck you or sodomize you or they get a blow job or one thing or another. I've always had a horror of getting involved in that sort of thing. Why, I don't know, because I have had sex with men and I have been both passive and aggressive, but they were people that I chose, people that I was attracted to. They certainly weren't some big galoot that I would be terrified of that was going to browbeat me into a situation. I learned all this the first time I was sent to Riker's.

One night I was stoned out of my mind on goofballs. It was about three o'clock in the morning. This guy that I'd seen around the neighborhood had been pointed out to me as being a pretty tough customer. He came on over, sat down and said, "Hey, I've seen you around. My name is Roy. I'd like to know you." I said, "Well, my name's Herb, Herb Huncke. Most people call me Huncke. Hi. Give me a little skin." We went through that bit. He said, "Listen, I'm going out and I'm going to make a little money. Would you like to come along?" I said, "Sure, I'm almost tapioca. That's great. Let's go."

So the two of us staggered out onto 42nd Street and over toward the East Side. We passed a car that was packed with luggage. There was a portable radio and I don't know what all. We fucked around with the vents trying to get into it. Neither one of us had a tool. Later, I learned to crack a vent without any trouble at all, but this was a new thing to me then. What he did was run up into Bryant Park, where they had these signs—"Stay off the grass." He pulled one out of the ground, came back and, man, he walloped one of those windows. Glass in every direction. "All right," he said. "Let's go. C'mon, let's get all of it we can."

There we are, we got the portable radio, and he's still going through this stuff not worth bothering with. Meanwhile, I'm doing everything but having a heart attack. I'm really so out of it that I'm not sure exactly what is happening, but I know this isn't right. Anyhow, we settled for a portable radio and some socks. We're shoving socks in our pockets, and he found a watch in one of the suitcases and a ring of some kind. I guess that was about it, and we just dumped everything else, left it there in the car with a broken window.

Nobody had paid the slightest bit of attention to us. If they had, they'd gone right on about their business. So there we are, arm in arm, staggering down across 5th Avenue. You know when you leave 34th on Lexington, how it sort of goes up a little hill? Well, we got over there somehow. Right in front of a building with a doorman, Roy spots a car. Now both of us had to be just crazy. Neither one of us knew what he was doing. He'd been carting his goddam two-by-four piece, having knocked the "Stay off the grass" part off of it. We walked up and again he let loose, whammo, and the car busted open. He said, "You go in this time."

I'm climbing in the car and I'm throwing things out to him when all of a sudden somebody grabbed my shoulders. I'm dragged out of the car and thrown down on the sidewalk. I look up and there's a cop. "You rotten little bastard, what do you think you're doing?' Meanwhile Roy is putting up some kind of fight. He's swinging at the cops and the cops are swinging at him and, man, they've finally got him—almost broke his arm trying to get him in line so he'd quiet down. He's calling them everything he can lay his tongue to. Of course, I thought that the least I should do was say, "Why don't you guys leave us alone. You're nothing but cops anyway." Whammo! "Officer to you," one of them said. So, officer it was.

I look up and everyone and his brother are hanging out the window, and the doorman is strutting around like King Tut. He had put in the report and had kept an eye on us to make sure that we didn't get away. He didn't have to worry because I was right smack in the car. Until then everything had gone so smoothly that it was almost like we had a license. Well, the next thing you know we're over in the precinct and I'm being slapped around. I wasn't beaten, but I was pretty mouthy and they knocked that mouthy shit right out of me.

Now I'm beginning to sober up and things are beginning to change a little bit. I think, "Jesus, I'm in jail. Now what do they do? God, we've destroyed two cars. We've stolen this merchandise. Nothing shorter than five years, surely." It never occurred to me that there were such things as misdemeanors and felonies. I didn't know any of that yet.

Well, the next thing you know we're downtown in the old Tombs. I wish you could have seen it. It looked like an old fortress with towers at each corner. They had used that awful red stone brick. It really was a fortress. They had two buildings, one was the annex for the drug addicts, and, of course, they just took it for granted that we were drug addicts, because we were falling all over ourselves. Roy turned out to be an ex-junkie, and I still had a few needle marks on my arms.

Well, to make a long story short, after going back and forth to court and talking to legal aid, they finally got me down to a six month bit for accessory. Roy got a year, and we were separated.

In those days, Hart's Island was being used as a prison for city cases. Riker's Island had just been finished. It had been the old garbage dump, and on top of the old dump they built Riker's Island. When they first moved in Riker's Island, there were rats big as your arm running around, and the guys were scared to go out into the yard. It was really funny when you look back on it. They'd just gotten over this big scandal on Welfare Island. They weren't going to have a second Welfare Island, so this was going to be run as it should be run. Everybody was going to toe the mark—the prisoners, the guards, the principal keeper, the warden, the whole thing.

Hart's Island, of course, is Potter's Field. Out at the very end of the island they have a section where they bury the dead. All the so-called drug addicts in those days were sent up there, because they had some theory about the fresh air. Also, they needed people to bury the dead. If you were lucky, you were a dormitory clerk. They used to have a little tailor's shop, so you worked in the tailor's shop or you got on the paint gang. But, if you were a fuck-up, you made the cemetery gang. You were known as a "ghoul," and those guys were tough customers. They used to come back with rings off the fingers. The blood would still be dripping out of the boxes.

You went to Riker's Island first, the reception prison. Then, twice a week they sent the stiffs up the river on a boat to Hart's Island, and along with the stiffs they sent a load of prisoners.

I thought I had really reached the end of the line. I couldn't begin to understand half of what was happening to me. The first shot out of the barrel I was locked in a dormitory, fifty-two on one side and fifty-two on the other. One guard for one-hundred and four men. There were four dormitories, one on top of the other, with a cement yard in between. The mess hall was a short distance away, and in the winter they used to tie a rope that you could hold onto to get to the mess hall. It was pretty rough.

They gave me a bed in the dormitory. I was a pretty cute kid, and when I came down the aisle, people were looking. I could feel what was going on, and I was really kind of scared. I didn't know what I was going to do. I had already learned of one case, a guy named Joe, a musician's musician. No man could play a piano like Joe. He had soul, he really had soul, and he was a beautiful guy, not only inside but outside. All that inner beauty emanated from him. He had gold curls and innocent blue eyes, soft skin, and he was thin. He didn't know anything except music. That had been his life, that's what he loved. One day he had been given what was known as a "blanket job." Seven big black guys got him down at the end of the dormitory, threw a blanket over his head, and each one took a crack at him. The experience was so awful for him that he went completely off his rocker. He was never the same.

Well, I'd heard about this. Now I'm in the dormitory. The beds were not far apart, with a little locker there for me, and the next guy had his locker on the other side. For about three days nobody bothered me. I made a few friends. I can play cards pretty good, so one night one of the guys said, "You play cards?" "Yeah." He said, "You play bridge?" I said, "Yeah." He said, "We need a fourth for bridge. Come on over." So that was the first crowd I got into. No hanky-panky. It was straight, guys that just wanted to be friendly. But the guy that slept next to me. . . . I have always had a theory that people who constantly see homosexuality in other people invariably are afraid of it in themselves. Nobody ever walked into that dormitory that whole time I was there that this guy didn't say "broad," unless it was some old man or something. Well, he had me pegged for a broad.

One morning, about three o'clock, I'm sound asleep and somebody reaches over. I wake up, and there's this, "Sss. Hey, hey." He lifts his blanket up and he's lying there with a hard. He says, "C'mon, give me a blow job." I said, "Man, are you crazy? You've got the wrong guy." Jesus, what am I going to do? They used to give us heavy shoes with thick soles, and the only thing I can think of was the fucking shoes. I couldn't hit him with my fist, and I'm not supposed to holler "guard" because that makes me a rat, so I said, "Hey, man, just leave me alone." I reached down and I said, "If you don't leave me alone I don't know what I'll do, but I'll do something." He said,

"You can't do a fucking thing. All right, if you won't blow me, give me a hand job." I said, "I'm not going to give you fuck-all."

I picked up my shoe and I clobbered him across the top of the head. I cut the whole side of his head. He started to bleed. He said, "You motherfucker, I'll get you for this." I put the shoe back down. I didn't give a fuck what happened. If there was going to be any ratting it was up to him. What he told the guard, I don't know, but the guard let him go. I hadn't cut him that bad, but I had really clobbered him. He never bothered me again, except verbally. Every time he'd see me he said, "You're gonna get it before you leave the fucking island, I'm telling you."

the boy who cried wolf
n i c k   z e d d

I'd like to say a few words on behalf of the late G.G. Allin, an individual I once knew but never took very seriously. For those too square to know, G.G. was a singer in a series of punk bands that never made it big but he was on the verge of becoming famous before he died of an overdose. I don't think his life particularly deserves a eulogy and if he were here he'd probably tell us all to fuck off. Not that that matters. Having witnessed more than a few of his celebrated performance pieces and successfully eluded the flying turds of this warrior poet, I can now pass judgement on his barbaric antics. Perhaps those of you less familiar with Mr. Allin's oeuvre are looking to me for an opinion upon which to base a consensus. Think for yourselves, assholes.

Far be it for me to speak unkindly of the dead, but as far as I'm concerned, G.G. was a fool. Since he's not here to defend himself, I don't feel too good

nick zedd is a super-8 filmmaker (*They Eat Scum*, etc.) and is known as the founder of the Cinema of Transgression. He is working on a novel entitled *Bleed* (from which this piece is excerpted), chronicling his experiences with whores, junkies, drag queens, bikers and art fags.

about having to say bad things about him, but the same thing will probably happen to me once I'm gone and in a way, G.G.'s death serves as a challenge to all of us to face the truth, which I've always tried to do anyway.

G.G. went out of his way to be hated. He spread hatred and stupidity everywhere he could. One theory advanced for his psychopathology was a childhood of sexual abuse. Who knows? Furthermore, who cares? I consider it a joke that I'm even writing about him. His minimal talents were focused on a crude form of infantile self-promotion manifested in public filthiness.

Allin was an overgrown kid who believed passionately in some kind of twisted rock 'n' roll myth wherein he could run roughshod over everyone else's feelings and rights in order to exalt his status as a shit-covered asshole at "war" with the underground. His understanding of the politics of confrontation and the aesthetics of late twentieth-century dadaism was limited and anti-intellectual and ultimately boring. I was too bored with him to bother attending any of his last few gigs. I am not a masochist. I never would enjoy being picked out of a crowd and assaulted by a fat nude punk rocker covered in his own shit. Some people maybe do. Some of you might deserve to be assaulted for being jaded, cynical voyeurs looking for a spectacle to turn your noses up at. In every crowd there's someone who deserves every drop of saliva and excrement that can be thrown on him. I myself, when I did go, would place myself directly behind the recording equipment and technicians taping the proceedings, hoping that Allin would avoid injuring anything near it since he considered the preservation of his sound and image so important to posterity.

I was never afraid of G.G. It was myself I questioned when in his presence. He had a way of testing your limits by being willing to go to whatever extreme there was to prove his manhood, his fearlessness and his willingness to do that which would be considered "outrageous" or "shocking" to his parents. He once proposed that I shoot a film of him killing someone. We were to rent a hotel room and go out looking for a suitable victim. He would then kill the person while I filmed. I was initially interested but the chance never presented itself when he failed to turn up at the hotel I was living in. I was relieved. I didn't really want to be an accessory to murder. Like his pledge to commit suicide onstage, unrealized due to a convenient arrest and prison sentence for assault lasting two years, many of G.G.'s more outlandish claims were nothing more than flatulence.

One Sunday afternoon I followed him with a video camera around Boston hoping he'd do something interesting. After kicking in a car window and blowing up a TV, G.G. inhaled a paper bag full of White Out. I was let down— nobody died. Later, G.G. half-heartedly attempted to undress and rape a girl who mistakenly walked into a room full of punk rockers and lowlifes like myself. I was the one person in a room full of seven who pulled G.G.'s arm off the girl and told him to let her go, which he did with no resistance. I don't think G.G. really wanted to rape the girl. What he wanted was to test us—to see how far we would let him go before stopping him. In this way he forced me to look at myself and recognize the limits I'd place on my own freedom. I could have joined in a gang bang like any other Cro-Magnon, but my own self-respect wouldn't let me. Or the pleading look in the girl's eyes.

Naturally, the media belatedly zeroed in on the latent entertainment value of this overgrown baby who would publicly shit on himself and his audience. The media loves to spotlight people like Al Sharpton, Oliver North and David Berkowitz for the same reason—they all have so little credibility. But then so does the President, Jerry Rivers (a.k.a. "Geraldo"), the F.B.I., Congress, Dan Rather, or most of the hundreds of venal celebrities we encounter over the airwaves. Michael Jackson probably ruined more young boys' lives than G.G. ever could. G.G.'s spectacle was real. Michael Jackson's and Madonna's are fake. Even though he cried wolf and never got around to shooting himself in public, as a performer G.G. had more integrity on a barbarian level than any of the posing frauds on MTV. Not that it merits praise. The world is too full of idiot hate and mindless brutality as it is. What we have always needed is more love, more compassion and more friendship (not to mention cash), all values G.G. opposed, just as Bill Clinton and Janet

Reno did when they immolated eighty-six Christians in Waco, Texas. Clinton is a baby burner. G.G.'s atrocities pale in comparison.

The number of civilians murdered by U.S. troops in Somalia, blasting lead into crowds of innocent people, was a direct result of decisions made by individuals in the highest levels of our government—people who are daily held up for admiration by a media that thrives on hypocrisy and lies.

To demonize clowns like G.G. Allin serves the interests of the ruling class which sets the media agenda, always looking for a distraction from any useful organizational opposition to its pervasive control. A genuine, though misguided rebel like G.G., as motivated by sheer self-promotion as he was, in some way exposed us to the essentially empty nature of what the media thought was important.

One night, a week before he died, G.G. threw a beer mug across a bar and hit a dancing yuppie in the face, drawing blood and opening flesh. It was an idiot act that served no purpose and had no point. G.G.'s final retribution came from his own hands, by accident, of a heroin overdose, a cowardly death, typical, predictable and disappointing to anyone dumb enough to have believed in him. (One of his bands was called The Disappointments.) Earlier that day in his last performance, G.G. punched out a heckler, took a shit and smeared it all over his nude body, then chased his audience out of the converted gas station on Avenue B, as the plug got pulled on his band. He then ran into the street nude and blocked a bus full of people before stumbling away and hanging onto a lamp post. He vanished as several cop cars arrived, blocking traffic and causing a chaos far worse than his brief performance. The spectacle of a squad of cop cars blocking four lanes of traffic in response to a club manager's complaint over his act, like the one I witnessed a year before on Third Avenue, was G.G.'s greatest achievement. He altered daily life. It was a revolutionary achievement, though a stupid one. By throwing shit on a fleeing audience, and with the help of New York's Finest who failed to catch him, G.G. managed to cause a tie-up that inconvenienced hundreds of strangers who didn't even pay to see him, spreading a little more hate and confusion in a world that would never appreciate it.

I once asked G.G. why he dedicated his life to such a selfless mission, injuring and poisoning himself to the point of hospitalization to simply entertain a few hundred strangers. He couldn't say. He was an imbecile. He insisted he hated everyone and didn't care about his audiences but in reality he cared deeply, far more deeply than they deserved. He really thought his audiences merited his hate—a hatred so misdirected it always ended up hurting himself more than it did the spectators looking for a cheap thrill. He reminded me of a would-be Hitler, a fucked-up little misanthrope who'd destroy the world if he ever got any power for no reason except his own inferiority complex which needed compensation through mindless acts of violence.

G.G. was a danger to himself and others and ultimately a failure on any artistic level. But as Robert Williams has said, "If it commands attention, it's culture. If it matches the couch, it's art." As a counter-cultural icon of mindless barbarism he stands alone. Few sociopaths have gravitated to musical entertainment as a realm for self-expression, that is, until recently. With the popularity of rappers like Tupac Shakur who makes videos extolling respect for women and then gang rapes one in his hotel room (innocent until proven guilty) one starts to miss the Mongoloid charm of G.G. who once recorded a tune called "Expose Yourself to Kids." Michael Jackson would tearfully lie about his acts to the world in much the same way his parents did, the Age of Denial being in full effect.

G.G. always was what he claimed to be—an animal, a sick, worthless piece of shit, Jesus Christ and Satan. His biggest flaw was his inability to see anything better in anyone else, to recognize something unique and beautiful in others, in short to transcend himself, the ultimate act of transgression by which one stops being a victim or victimizer. To love is the most revolutionary act, for it brings us outside of ourselves. To turn yourself inside out is the hardest thing to do in a world of corruption and pain, betrayal and lies. It involves an act of faith in yourself that few of us get a chance to do nowadays. Maybe G.G. experienced this, but his whole life was dedicated to making us think he didn't.

the only living boy in new york

a m e e n a   m e e r

Adam is in an Indian restaurant in Queens, little red plastic tables with yellow turmeric stains on them, styrofoam bowls of dal and chicken curry, slippery with orange oil.

Adam's fingers tear a chapati and dip it into the dal. He gulps it down, the smoothness of the dal mixing with the wheaty taste of the chapati. He eats some chicken, carefully licking all the masala from his fingers, almost tasting each spice alone, the sweet cinnamon and cardamom, the bitter cumin and coriander, the sting of the chilies. The smell makes him so homesick his eyes start watering. He thinks of his grandmother's chicken curry.

"Food all right, sir? Not too spicy?"

Adam swallows. The chicken is so sweet. He looks up at the waiter. "It's perfect," he says.

ameena meer was the managing editor of *Bomb* magazine for several years. Her work has appeared in *Actuel, Details, The East Village Eye, Interview, Paper, South* and *The Times of India.* This piece is an excerpt from her upcoming novel, *Bombay Talkie,* to be published by High Risk/Serpent's Tail.

The waiter looks worried. "You want some yogurt, sir? To make it less spicy. Some raita. That is yogurt with cucumber in it. You know, cucumber."

"No, thank you," says Adam, smiling. "I know what raita is."

"Oh yes, a lot of Europeans eat Indian food now. It's very popular in England as well. Yes, I can see you know how to eat like an Indian," leaning on the table now, he hangs the wet cloth over the back of the chair. "Me, I like American food. I never eat here. I eat at McDonalds or Kentucky Chicken. It's so funny, isn't it? Indians like American food and Americans like Indian food."

Adam laughs, "What's even funnier is that I'm Indian."

The waiter's face is incredulous. "You're Indian? How can it be? You look English." He scratches the baby hairs sprouting on his chin. "You are from where in India?"

"From Bombay."

"Oh, Bombay. Even I have my uncle who is living in Bombay. Bombay is a very exciting place. Like New York. Me, I come from Julunder. Do you know where that is? It's Punjab."

"No," says Adam, taking a bite. "No," he says through the dal, "I've never been there." He swallows and stuffs more chicken into his mouth. "Actually, I've been away from India for some time," he wipes the grease from his lips and gulps his Coke.

The waiter sits down in the chair. "Good food," he nods approvingly. "I also like chicken. What is your name please?"

"Adam." He doesn't want to look up again from his food. The waiter smells of old sweat. His face is brown and spotted with red pimples. He pushes his stained sleeves up to his elbows and taps his dirty fingernails on the laminate.

"I am Talvinder—but everyone calls me Tom. You can call me Tom. It's easier to say for Americans." He holds out his hand for Adam to shake.

"Mm," protests Adam, trying to keep as much of the food in his mouth as he can. "My hands are dirty. I don't want to get chicken curry all over you. But it's nice to meet you. As soon as I finish I'll wash my hands."

"No, no problem," laughs Talvinder. "You are eating. Eat. You want some tea also?"

"Yes, thanks, I'd love some. It's the perfect way to end this. The food, I mean."

"Yes, first you finish your food," Talvinder nods. "Where do you stay in New York? You have some relatives here?"

"No, I'm staying with a friend in the East Village. I have an uncle in America and his daughter, my cousin, her name is Sabah, comes to New York quite often, but I don't know where she is."

"Is she Indian? Then she must come to Jackson Heights. But why are you staying in Greenwich Village? It's very dangerous. There are all the strange people walking around there and taking drugs and all that." Talvinder looks concerned, then his face widens in a grin. "But you're there for the girls, aren't you? That's a good place for girls. They're all over there, the fast ones, wearing short frocks and all."

"It's actually the other side of Greenwich Village. There are all these Indian restaurants near there. On East Sixth Street."

"What? Those? Those restaurants are all owned by Bengalis. That food is terrible. Horrible. They should stay at home and eat the fish heads their wives make for them. You should only eat here in Jackson Heights. Only here. You just bring those girls with you. That's the way to catch them. This is the best Indian restaurant in New York. Really. Just read that newspaper there, the _New York Times_, that is an article all about this restaurant, just written last year."

"I promise I'll read it before I go," says Adam, taking the last bites of his food. "Could I have some tea?"

"Tea? Of course." Talvinder looks around the restaurant to make sure no one is in earshot. He leans forward. "Listen," he whispers, "you know a lot of American girls? I know some here, in Queens. They're not like our girls, yaar. They completely crazy–_puglee_–you know. You come out with me and you'll meet some wild girls. Really wild. And they'll love you. I promise you. _Masala chai._" He gives Adam a quick pat on the shoulder and gets up to bring the tea.

Adam sighs and piles all the little styrofoam cups into a little tower. He swings and slaps it with his hand. It topples down, orange oil splattering all over the tray, globs of yellow dal flying out, dripping down the sides of the cups and soaking into the paper napkins.

Talvinder plops a cup of thick milky tea on the tray.

"Thank you." Adam lifts the cup slowly to his mouth, inhaling the smell of cardamom. "Ow!" He jerks the cup back, splashing tea on his shirt and jeans, and squirming in his chair as the boiling liquid burns his skin. The tear is searing. His tongue is numb.

"Too hot, yaar," laughs Talvinder. "Hot, hot tea. Don't worry, I'll give you a shirt to wear tonight. I'm finished with work at seven o'clock. Then you come by my house. It's just here. Okay? No problem." He winks at Adam and picks up the tray. Adam watches Talvinder walk away, his eyes watering and his tongue still smarting. He touches his tongue with his fingers. It feels like it's covered with little stinging sores. He sticks his tongue out farther, like an eel curling out of his mouth. He thinks about his tongue tracing the ridges of Marc's ears or moving around the corners of Marc's pink lips like a paintbrush on a piece of porcelain. His tongue burns.

• • •

"New York is great, really great," laughs Talvinder. "Here I am working in restaurant and I meet the son of a movie star! It's great. You like this music? The best radio station in New York–hey, hold on–red light!" The car screeches to a stop, Adam flies forward, the seat belt slapping his chest, and then falls back, hard, into the seat, the springs creaking and poking into his legs. "Sorry, Adam, sorry. There's too many policemen in New York, you know?" Talvinder rolls down his window and turns up the radio. He puts his arm out the window and thumps the side of the car in time to the music. "My house is just here. Everyone will love to meet you." He pulls into the driveway of a split-level brick house. "Come on!" He jumps out of the car and runs up the cement steps three at a time.

A young girl opens the front door. She looks hopefully at them. "Hi Talvinder *bhai*, will you take me to a movie tonight?" She's wearing a pair of skintight stretch jeans and a tee-shirt, a long black braid hanging down her thin back. Adam compares her pointy face to Alia's soft one.

"Sorry, Chotu, I have my friend Adam here. Adam, this is Chotu, my niece. She's a real American, aren't you, Chotu? Chotu, who is Jimmy Al Hussain?"

"I don't care," snaps the girl, crossing her scrawny brown arms over her chest. "Some Indian nobody." She flounces up the stairs.

"Hey," Talvinder shouts after her. "Get me something to drink."

Adam follows Talvinder down the green carpeted stairs. He can hear the sound of a Hindi filmtrack, a dance number. A girl is giggling and a man is singing *Que Sera, Sera* in Hindi. Suddenly, Adam hears a whole chorus of off-key voices. "*Jubh meh choti larkhi thee* . . . when I was just a little girl. . . ." Talvinder walks into the darkness.

The television flashes colored lights around the room. Adam can make out people sitting on sofas along both walls, their faces alternately red, green and orange. "Sit, sit," says Talvinder, handing Adam the glass of brown liquid his niece brought and pointing at a crowded sofa. Adam takes a step into the room, tripping over something and half falling onto a body on the floor. "Watch out! Behave yourself," says Talvinder as the small body lunges for Adam's leg, teeth flashing. Talvinder gives the head a cuff, sending the child rolling into the others who begin shouting, "Stop it! Leave me!" Adam realizes that there are three or four children on the floor.

"*Chup*! Quiet!" warns a woman from one of the sofas. Adam leans against the door frame. "*Vilayet-ke-bacche*!" she growls. "Go and do your homework!" The children are instantly silent.

"I'll be right back," reassures Talvinder. "This is my family."

"Oh," says Adam, "they're very nice." He holds the glass in his hand, trying to guess what it is. He thinks it's Coke. The whole room smells of cold rice and dal and cumin and harsh drugstore perfume. With the curtains drawn and the door shut, the battling scents make Adam's eyes water. He leans against the doorframe, trying to get fresh air from the hallway. He thinks of Marc's parents and their clean, drafty house in Paris.

"Talvinder!" shouts the woman as Talvinder leaves. "Oh Talvinder! You don't even see your mother anymore? Come here! Where are you going?" She sighs and the person beside her pats her on the back. "What a son I have." She notices Adam in the doorway. "Come here, *behta*. You are Talvinder's friend? Come, come," she gestures for Adam to approach. "What a nice boy," she reaches out and grabs Adam's face as he steps over a child, squeezing his cheeks as he loses his balance. "Good boy. You are American?"

"No," mumbles Adam through his mangled mouth. "Fren... Indian."

"Indian?" She is incredulous.

"Indian?" say the woman sitting next to her. "No, never."

"What is your good name?" asks Talvinder's mother. "Where are your parents?"

"He looks *ex-dum* foreign," says a man on the sofa, putting his running shoes up on the table and crossing his legs. "Are you Kashmiri?"

"Adam," says Adam. "I just met Talvinder tonight, at the restaurant. I'm from Bombay, but I live in Paris. I haven't...."

"Oh-ho," laughs the man, "*Bumbai-wallah*! Are you a film star?"

"He's so white, he must be an actor," says another voice. Adam can make out three Indian men in salwar kameezes and sweatshirts lolling on one of the sofas. "Hey, Sandy!" one laughs.

"I haven't been in Bombay in a long time."

"Oh, you live in New York?"

"What is your family name?"

"Al-Hussain. No, I live in France."

"You are a Muslim?"

"Yes."

"We also have some Muslim friends," says Talvinder's mother. "They live just here," she waves her hand off into the darkness. "They're from Up, their name is Bothelwallah. Do you know them?"

"No, sorry. But I haven't been here very long."

"Muslims make the best halwah," she says. "Do you like halwah?"

"Yes, yes," adds the other woman, "remember they sent some halwah last month? It was so lovely. They're very nice. It must have been Eid. Was it Eid?"

"Muslim? Muslim?" says a quivering voice. Adam makes out a withered old woman on the edge of the sofa. As the idea sinks in, she starts coughing violently, her tiny body shaking beneath the swaths of white cloth. "Do you know what the Muslims did to us during partition?" she shrieks. "Get out! Get out!"

"Shh, shh, *Bari-ma*," soothes Talvinder's mother. "That was not all Muslims. . . . This is Talvinder's friend. He's very nice."

"You know, not all Muslims are dirty, like in India," reassures one of the men. "In America, they are very good. Just like us. At Quaker Oats, at the factory, I work with a lot of Muslims. I am forklift operator."

"They burned down our house in Lahore! Burned it down, everything was burned! I had nothing when I got on the train. Nothing! Get out!"

"But in Punjab, the Muslims are so bad," explains another man, shaking his head. "So dirty and they are stealing and doing all bad things, not like in America. In America, Sikh, Hindu, Muslim, we're all the same. My job also, I make pizza, and we are all *bhai-bhai*." He leans over and slaps Adam's arm.

"You stole everything! Everything my mother gave me! Get out!" shrieks the old woman. "Go!"

Talvinder walks back in and grabs Adam's arm. He starts shouting in Punjabi. "You don't have any *izzat*? This is my friend! His father is Jimmy! And look how you treat him! Come on, Adam," he says, in English. He takes the glass of Coke and puts it in the young girl's hand. "Let's go."

"Jimmy? The film star?"

"Get out!"

Adam hears the glass smash as he walks up the stairs.

courtesy: National Gallery, Washington, DC

robert frank

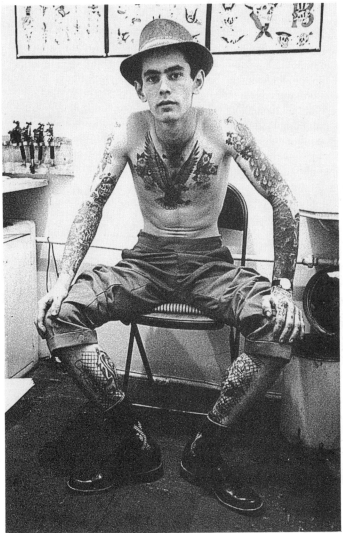

courtesy: Museum of Fine Arts, Houston, TX

<u>robert frank</u> was born in Zurich, Switzerland. His books of photography include *The Americans* and *Lines of My Hand*. He has also made several films, including *Pull My Daisy, Cocksucker Blues,* and *Candy Mountain*. There will be a major retrospective of his work at the National Gallery in Washington, DC this year.

this man and me

g u y - m a r k   f o s t e r

> *Some day I shall rise and leave my friends*
> *And seek you again through the world's far ends,*
> *You whom I found so fair*
> *(touch of your hands and smell of your hair!),*
> *My only god in the days that were.*
> Rupert Brooke (1887-1915)

I have been in love only once. I was twenty-one years old and lived in the city I think of sometimes as my pretend birthplace, though I was not born there. That city was small and clean and architecturally pleasing to the eye. I can close my lids and picture the slender cherry blossom trees, tall and pink-colored, lining the wide avenues; the Tidal Basin, and the two great rivers calmly opposite one another—the Potomac and the Anacostia—where my father sometimes went to fish. There was, I recall, an abundance of sunny days, people smiling, and the nostalgia of quickly-changing seasons. I remember nothing but happiness in that city; though to be sure there were sad times, too. But these I can't recall as clearly.

In that city, because neither this man nor myself had money, we often took long, rambling walks. Our shoulders now and again bumped one another, and the hair on my bare arms stood up and tingled. Some days we would stop at a sidewalk cafe and ask for a table in the uninhabited rear, near

guy-mark foster has published poetry and prose in the literary anthologies *Shadows of Love, Brother to Brother: New Writings by Black Gay Men,* and *The Road Before Us.*

the toilets, and split the cost of a large, wet fruit salad. He fed me from his fork and I was promptly awed by his attentiveness and, too, by the strange, new flutterings taking place in my body.

When he and I were together there was, when I walked, always a hardly perceptible, springy layer of cloud between the soles of my shoes and the hard, weather-beaten pavement. At night he would lay me on his single mattress and hover in the air above me. Often I would forget to breathe. I would leave my body and from a distance watch him trace the outline of my face with the sweaty tips of his fingers. He shoved a digit up inside a still nostril and withdrew an index hung with mucilage. He bit into my flesh until my body would jerk.

Downstairs, hardly out of earshot, his aged mother sat drinking can after can of Piels beer. She wore what appeared to be the same hairnet over her greying head every time I saw her. And her toothless jaw caved in under the despairing burden of what horrified me to imagine could be a person's memories. His weight lay pressed upon me, and I thought, as in Whitman: *This is not only one man!* His tongue lathered my lashes so that I could not see but with my body; it was as if I was surrounded. I could hear the television in the background: "Rowan and Martin's Laugh-In," or "Maude." It was this soundtrack of canned, vertiginous hilarity that punctuated my moans of pleasure, of gratitude, and simple lust. The fitted sheet on his bed was like his mother's hairnet, always the same one whenever I visited: a shade of dullest white with thick swirls of brown waves in the pattern. Smeared upon this threadbare fabric was the proof of our bond: there, mixed in with the undulations and food stains was his gummy semen mingled with my own, and the dark, oily excrement or fart fucked out to exhaustion from both our saliva-slickened bodies.

In the middle of the night he would awake to find me gazing at his uncircumsized penis, amazed at the now calm sheathe of flesh which had been, only hours before, violently chafing against the inflamed walls of my rectum. Sometimes, when he had to urinate, I asked if I could hold this warrior for him, pull back the shield of foreskin and guide the stream into the bowl. For some reason he always declined, amusement in his brown eyes. I thought, self-praisingly: *My love is so large and uncontainable that it will, sometimes, simply burst out with the most aboriginal of requests.*

Months later, because of the nature of his work, he told me of his plans to relocate to this other city. I did not know yet what kind of a city it was, of its reputation as a murderer and a cheat, as an unconscionable liar. And so I asked him to take me away with him—away from the cherry blossom trees and the wide, forking rivers; and because I was young and persuasive enough in my argument and I humored him, and because he loved me, too, I think, he did this.

The apartment we moved to was directly opposite a small park. But the trees had not grown of their own accord—I could tell this; but rather they were planted with questionable intentions by what seemed to me a vain and desperate city. I could never look at those trees without feeling a slight discomfort in my chest. At the beginning these trees were pruned regularly by a man in a dull-green, belted jumper. Under the pretense of an esthetically perfected landscape, bandages were wrapped around certain limbs to direct the growth of the branches. I thought, indignantly: *This would never have happened to the venerable cherry blossoms in my city.* In every way these trees were being prevented from flowering into the full extensions of their true selves. This horrified me, and yet I averted my eyes and behaved as if such oppression could not concern me.

It was at this point that I began to hold my love more and more loosely in my grip. Other men caught my attention. I would stare after them, smile, and once caught I would snatch my eyes away in embarrassment. I did not understand this behavior and when I was alone with the man I lived with I would lavish more and more attention upon him, to make up for having strayed earlier with my mind. But whichever direction I faced there stood before me always this implacable guilt. I turned and I turned and I turned my head until a kind of terror shook me.

"I'm lost," I thought.

Avoiding those trees, I began to leave the apartment when he was away and I would walk along dark streets looking strange men in the eye. If ever anyone displayed the slightest curiosity I would panic and accelerate to a brisk pace. I only wanted these men, for an instant, to witness my impossible interest in them. I played my eyes over their bodies until I sensed their arousal, and then, like a shot, I would bolt. I never wanted them to respond: for then I would be committed to them instead of to the man I had come to this city devoted to, and I could not risk such a betrayal.

During those days we seldom had friends over. But when they came this man I lived with would become suddenly more vivacious and brighter than he was when with me alone. I did not take offense at this. I enjoyed the many variant angles to his persona. With him I was always surprised and always, simultaneously, on the surest footing. In honor of the arrival of these people in our apartment he would drape colorful African cloth over his chest and sit cross-legged on our murex purple carpet and tell funny stories, gesticulating with his blunt, flat-tipped, expressive hands. White candles in tall cylindrical jars would be lit throughout the room and soft music would play on the turntable: Peabo Bryson or Brenda Russell, singers he liked. He was in the theater and so were many of these friends. I was outside all that. I had been inside but, in the end, he and these people I thought were more committed, not to mention adept, at this type of work than I ever hoped to be; and, anyhow, I felt the need to uncrowd them all by stepping down and out of, what seemed to me, their already too immense and overpopulated circle.

After a while I began to unbuckle my trousers on some of those walks I made at night and stroke my penis to erection. Sometimes, if it was cool, I carried a jacket to drape over me in case of an unsympathetic passerby, or a woman. I lived in an exalted fear of being seen by one of our many friends, and of them reporting back to my lover my nocturnal habits. In my worst hours I craved for this. In time I grew very brave, and often some man would stop to chat with me. He and I would stare at one another, each waiting for the other to grab him where he was most elongated; and both of us, too, incorrigibly lusty, full of a secret, exhilarating, nasty, dual fright.

The city was at its ugliest then; it was even common to see grown men taking a piss in full view out on the sidewalk. Besides, the buildings were all covered with soot and in various states of disrepair. Access to the sky was severely restricted by the ludicrous height of these block-shaped edifices. Each morning a new rash of killings covered the headlines. When I returned to our apartment, if he had come in I would tell the truth: that I had been out taking a walk. Or else, shamelessly, I would lie. During the night I somehow would lose sight of these wanderings and by the morning the memory was all but obliterated. At rest all those hours, next to his dark, regenerative body, somehow this absolved my soul: for he never judged me, or otherwise gave indication that I was not to be trusted. I felt it was therefore incumbent on me not to disappoint him. As in the beginning, by sunrise it was as if I had died and been reborn all in the long, purifying interval of night giving way to the diurnal. I became my old innocent, sweet-natured self: a bit irascible but harmless. I rolled over to him and we made love, or we simply kissed one another upon our fat, ancestral lips, and the trial began all over.

One evening I met a friend of his, a certain actor from the south who was not very attractive. He was tall and absurd with his body—the perfect hick. He spoke with the customary twang in his voice, and always leaned forward to clutch a person on the shoulder when talking. I remembered he had one of those highfalutin society names, as from a Henry James novel: Charles or Frederick.

It began simply enough. I loathed him. He had no sense of moderation and saturated himself in musk-scented oils. He reeked of it. Instead of making him more desirable, this repelled me. And it did. But then I felt bad for him. He so wanted to be a part of the "in" crowd, stylish and in the "know," like the man I lived with, and all the others in his profession—those who paraded themselves in bright plumage and behaved as if a camera were recording their every gesture. He reminded me of myself: the outsider who longs desperately to be inside but who simply does not fit; who isn't popular or even talented, or especially well-liked, but who is merely tolerated as the embarrassing love-object of one in their ranks; who has simply lucked in on a certain crowd, as I assumed I had with this man and his friends. But after a while I could not stay away from him, nor he me. We phoned each other and confessed in quick, movie-script voices:

"Don't you want me?"

"He'll find out."

"But you want me, right?"

"No."

"*Liar.*"

At his apartment we circled each other. He had already bathed himself in his favorite scent and it was all I could do to keep from retching. To my horror, he wore a short-sleeved, plaid shirt a size too small, and loose-fitting generic bluejeans with loopy stitching on the back pockets.

"No," I thought, when he held me. He did not remind me of myself, but rather of boys I had gone to school with, boys I had admired yet had not been friendly with since they had claimed a much stronger kinship with girls; or, as he told me, in his case, with large-hipped women. Nevertheless, that first time he exuded caution for only an instant. Soon he had bruised my neck with his uneven teeth and I had torn a button off his shirt. In no time both our jeans lay undone at our ankles and we ground or bodies together, liberally, as if to reach the core of something we both believed lay concealed in the deepest recess of the other. He did not have as finely muscled a body as the man I lived with. His was of a larger mass, but it was soft and there was a surprising opacity to his copper complexion; it did not give, but took. In our lovemaking there was no confidence: it was all crying out and mad panic, as though we were sure the world would end because of our illicit groping. And yet I knew it was too late to turn back.

Some nights I lay next to the man I lived with and did not know him. I was twenty-three or twenty-four years old and had grown very skittish. I began to hide my various new faces from everyone who entered our lives. When friends visited I discouraged them from staying long by storming out of the room, or by showing them the door when I decided enough time had lapsed. Leaving, they merely smiled at one another or said, "Oh, Mark's just being Mark. Isn't he cute?" I had lost my identity and I resented these people for telling me who I was, and when they'd gone I would become an emotional gymnast before that man; it was as though I'd gone mad. He was calm and loving, and sometimes he would say my name aloud to cool me off, or sit astride my body and ride my erect penis to exhaustion; other times he would take up his sketch pad and draw mythical figures of tall dark men with scales along their backs and a bit of schizophrenia in the eyes.

We never returned to that other city, the one we had left. He often went alone to visit his aged, alcoholic mother and I would wait for him after my nights of walking the streets. I had adapted too well to this new city. I misplaced all memory of the parades my mother had taken my brothers and me to see every year along Constitution Avenue, for the cherry blossoms. I forgot the picnics on the grounds of the Smithsonian. When I was with some other man, and not the one I lived with, I would be caught off-guard sometimes by a recollection. A vivid sadness would wash over me and I would drift back in time to when he and I would ride the Metro from the housing project where he lived with his mother into the center of that historic city. He would sit next to me and just as the doors closed he would shut his eyes. I sat in silence beside him, awed by his trick of blotting out the world through meditation, as I had been awed once by his fork between my lips. This mastery of myself was what I wanted, but I could not be confident that I would come back from such depths; therefore, I leaned upon the proven solidness of his frame for support and guidance instead of searching for it from within. I thought: *I dare not risk such a journey for fear of losing myself inside my vast, chaotic self.*

When I was twenty-five or twenty-six he came home from being weeks away and confessed his love for some other man over me. This was in the summer, and while he had been away I had undergone yet another rebirth and was more determined than ever to hold my love more firmly in my grasp. I had not seen that musk oil-wearing actor for some while, nor any other man. I had been cleansed this time not by his presence but by his very absence. It left a hole in me the size of that city which had initially nurtured our love, and I had stared bravely into it while he was gone. The depth of it stunned me; I did not want to ever be without him. I could not, I thought, survive it.

We tried to wait it out. When he left in the evenings to rendezvous with this other man I would fire up sticks of incense to burn the stench of jealousy away. I played his favorite records over and over like a mantra, especially "If Only for One Night"—a song he had serenaded me with in our courtship. I would extinguish all the lamps and, with a single white candle, sit in that heavy darkness and try to glean from Brenda Russell's mellifluous voice and, too, from the guilt I felt, what could be salvaged from my shattered world.

Eventually, it was no good. One night this occurred to me and I lay up in our loft bed, sobbing. The windows were opened and all our neighbors could hear the despair flying out of my body like birds being freed from an aviary. We had often lain there ourselves listening to the desperate fucking, and the curses in English, but in Spanish too, which was the language of that part of the city. For seven hours the deluge was unceasing. The man I loved lay listening in the next room. I did not know to what extent he was aware of my infidelities, but I was sure that this was the very reason that had pushed him, finally, to form this sudden alliance. The planet had abruptly come spinning off its axis and was now shockingly out of control: I had not truly imagined that this could happen, no matter how often or rarely I strayed. If anyone, I thought, reminded me of those adolescent boys from my youth—in whose arms I imagined lay my eventual salvation—it had been him all along; and yet for years I had felt that I was suffocating with him, and that simultaneously I was living the greatest pleasure a man could fabricate out of the stuff of his dreams.

Later that summer I moved out of the second floor walk-up he and I had shared in that city, into a one-bedroom affair across the bridge. I did this decisively, and yet in spite of my packed boxes I could not quite believe in my actions, or in the actions of those friends who assisted me with my belongings. It was not my body, I told myself, that this was happening to, but some other poor man's worn-out, adulterous body. I was very much like those trees across from our building, I thought, who had suffered, in years past, a similar asphyxiation of spirit. Like them, I felt paralyzed at having my expansive potential for love smothered so early in life, without having a say in the matter. I shut my eyes to what seemed a ruling beyond my self-government and, instead, I fashioned an alternate reality to compete with the obviously untenable one that faced me. For months afterwards, and then for years, I convinced myself that as far as those trees were concerned, the filthy pieces of sackcloth would eventually rot and drop from around their bark-covered bodies, and with a vengeance an unprecedented blooming would occur. In my patience I willed for a similar reconstitution of justice to happen for this man and me. I clung with fingers and nails to the hope that if I were patient and good—something I had not been before, but had wanted to be and failed—then he would forgive my indiscretions and, because he had once loved me, come back to me.

After all, he was my god.

assimilated / alien

exotic / emigrant

yong soon min

model / minority

objectified / other

<u>yong soon min</u> is a Korean artist/activist. This work is from a 1989 installation entitled *Make Me*.

la vida real

m i g u e l   b a r n e t

With my first month's salary I went to Houston Street to look for a second-hand refrigerator. The Bowery was in its heyday. Packs of drunks on each corner, drinking pure alcohol out of small bottles, panhandling and wiping windshields with dirty rags. They'd press the button for the red stoplight and descend on cars like a swarm of wasps. It's pretty much the same way today, although I noticed it more when I first arrived. They didn't work, they didn't eat, they slept on the street in the cold, covered by newspapers and old burlap rice bags. When I saw all those people on the Lower East Side I felt comforted. I said to myself: "Shit, they're worse off than me."

José went with me to buy the refrigerator. I got it cheap because it was used and didn't work. We rewired the motor, changed the fan belts and gave it a paint job. I couldn't get over having my own refrigerator. It solved a big problem for

miguel barnet was born in Havana, Cuba, in 1940, where he lives. He is a professor of ethnography and folklore. *La Vida Real*, from which this piece is excerpted, is the fourth in a series of testimonial novels (*Biografía de un Cimarrón*, *La Canción de Rachel*, and *Gallego*) which combine oral history, sociology and anthropology in fictional memoirs.

me. Before, I had to keep my milk and meat cool on the window sill. Another time, I went to the East Side and got a used mattress. I remember folding it and carrying it home on my back from the 60s and Lexington to 19th Street and 8th Avenue. I was so beat when I got home that I threw myself on the mattress and slept like a log until the next day.

My first snowfall. I kind of liked it. The first day the snow's very pretty, a blanket of coconut flakes sprinkled over awnings and cars. But then it gets all grimy and hardens to ice on curbs, in puddles, on stoops. Having had no experience with icy streets, I fell several times. It can be quite dangerous to fall on the ice—you can't keep yourself from sliding, you lose all control and you risk splitting your head or cracking your ribs.

When I got to the restaurant where I worked, the boss told me to shovel the snow out front and, since we hadn't spelled things out in a contract (or in any way, for that matter) I did it without bitching. My fingers became frozen stiff; I thought the tips would break off. The cold went right through my gloves, my bones rattled and my face got beet red. I picked up a pair of woolen long johns in a thrift shop which I took off only to wash. Even with them on, I still froze. Salt melts the snow but the slush has to be scraped up with shovels or rakes.

A busboy is nothing but a servant. Sometimes I had to even wash dishes or give the restaurant a good cleaning. I couldn't complain, since there were hordes of Puerto Ricans waiting in line for restaurant jobs. I saved my tips and bought a hand sink. Placido and I had become friends so he let me install it. He knew how clean we Cubans are. Every day I would give myself a towel bath, from head to toe, and he would chuckle: "I'm going to keep a tab on you for the next few months." But I never kicked the habit. When I put on some weight I even bought a bathtub and put it next to my bed. I no longer had to wash outside. It was a big relief, a real comfort.

Many people used to go the baths on 57th Street and 9th Avenue or in the Village. I never went because I had my own sink and bathtub. I did go with Puerto Rican, or as we call them, _boricua_, friends to the swimming pool quite often. It was in a hotel in Brooklyn and it was very cheap. I met many Latinos there and picked up some really good-looking women. It was a long indoor pool with deliciously warm water. One day it was filled with blood. Blacks from the barrio had begun to come. They had every right, of course, but the Italians didn't like that very much. There were violent protests but I kept a low profile to avoid quarrels.

"It's not your problem, Julian," a Dominican friend told me. No one ever asked me what I was doing there and I got no dirty looks like the others. But I was colored, too, though I wasn't from the neighborhood, nor was I coal black. As soon as a black guy would put one foot in the place, the war was on. Of course, the blacks didn't come singly; they came in groups, like Apaches, to protect themselves and to kick ass if they had to. One night, just around closing time, at nine o'clock, an Italian and a black from Harlem started cursing each other out. A beer bottle sailed through the air. The Italian drew a switchblade and threatened the black from the edge of the pool. Just then another black lunged and caught the Italian by the neck and stabbed him in the back as he was falling into the water. Since there were no security police, the pool turned into a blood bath. People screamed, some just for the hell of it, women ran from one side of the pool to the other, but no one went in to fish them out. Wounded, they hobbled up the stepladder, only to collapse and bleed along the edge. Everyone blamed the black; racism has always been strong here. When I was summoned as a witness, I limited myself to saying what I had seen. The Italian was to blame, but no one wanted to admit it. He had provoked the situation by showing off, just like a Cuban. The blacks took the case to court and won. Very few of them, however, ever returned to the pool.

My situation was very different. Even though my skin is dark, it's not black. I'm not trying to say that I can pass for white, but I am a light mulatto with wavy hair. Now that it's turned gray, my hair is even softer. It's all the same to me.

Placido and I saw little of each other. Work at Liborio's was very exhausting, running from here to there the whole day long without a chance to catch my breath, without a moment's rest until the next shift arrived. If the clientele was good, I was all set, they might even leave me tickets to

Broadway musicals. I wasn't a theater buff although I was known to take in a show from time to time. Sometimes the artists, mostly from the chorus lines, I think, would come into Liborio's. They were wild about Cuban food and drank rum in tall beer glasses. I gave them the red carpet treatment so they would ask: "When's your birthday, Julian?" and they'd have tickets ready for me. Naturally, I invented monthly birthdays. Then I would scalp the tickets for the orchestra or even standing room at the entrance to Schubert Alley or the Plymouth. I almost never went myself because I was sure I'd fall asleep in the plush seats. In those days Tallulah Bankhead, Mary Martin and Ann Miller were the stars on Broadway. At least they were all over the newspapers and commercials.

One night Placido showed up at my door with a copy of the Daily Worker, the communist newspaper in the U.S. He read me the headlines and said: "It's one of the few newspapers you can trust. Almost all the others are run by the Mafia." Nowadays, the Daily Worker is called the Daily World. It was founded in 1924. Every now and then, Placido would show up and read me the headlines. But since I didn't know English, I would buy La Prensa or El Imparcial whenever I wanted to find out the details of some crime. Saturday afternoons, before going to the restaurant, I would go to Central Park to catch a free ballgame. A lot of Hispanics would gather there. Baseball is the national sport of Cuba, and although I was not much of a fan, I did enjoy it and it didn't cost me a cent. I would bundle up because the cold is unbearable, although it is true that you can get accustomed to anything.

Placido helped me to get to know New York. He took me my first time to the movies on 42nd Street, theaters that now cost $5. Then, you could see two movies for thirty-five cents before six o'clock. At six the price would go up to seventy-five cents, and not only was it more expensive, it was also more dangerous. All kinds of brawls would break out in those movie houses at night. I remember seeing a white break a black man's jaw just because he sat next to his wife. The movies were much better in the afternoon; you paid less and you avoided all sorts of problems. But, speaking of money, I didn't get to enjoy myself much those first weeks. I didn't have the time nor the energy to go out in the snow in temperatures thirteen or fifteen degrees below zero.

I spoke to Placido about Miguelito and he gave me an idea. Since the restaurant's owner already knew me and knew how well I worked, Placido suggested that I recommend Miguelito to him. In those times, Cubans were sought out, not because we were liked but because we worked like mules, to tell the truth. So I went right up to the boss and told him what was on my mind: "Those who wait get the dregs."

"Tell him not to come yet," he told me.

I gave Miguelito reason to hope when I wrote him and he answered right away, thanking me. After a month, the boss told me to call him to substitute for me because I was being promoted to waiter. I had learned the names of the dishes in English and could even say "bread and butter." To tell the truth, you really didn't need English in Liborio's because almost all the diners, even the Americans, spoke Spanish. They liked to show off to their guests and it was an opportunity to practice. In any case, it was a popular neighborhood restaurant, and I didn't need to worry about any special requirements.

Placido gave me permission to let Miguelito stay in my room with me for a week. I thanked him very much because I didn't know if Miguelito had any money or would just stray in. But he did come with some money, so we found him a room to share a few blocks away with a Venezuelan who had arrived recently. It was more or less like my room, except for the heating.

"Hey, Julian, is it always this cold?"

"It is, but you can get accustomed to anything, Miguelito, you'll see."

Blacks turn white with the cold; their skin becomes chapped and chaffed. The blacker you are, the more you feel the cold.

"I won't make it here, Julian."

"Sure you will, compadre. Get another blanket and a cap that'll cover your ears and you'll be alright."

He got used to it like everyone else. He learned in a jiffy what it takes to be a busboy and earned more tips in a week than I had in three months. He was a whiz at the job, although he still had it in his head to sing and tap dance. But you don't become an artist just by living in New York: a water rat doesn't make a sailor. So he signed up for singing lessons with Bobby Cortés, a Puerto Rican who owned his own school in the Barrio. He bought theater clothing and patent leather shoes for dancing the *guaracha*. That's how he spent his money. He didn't drink, he didn't play the numbers, he didn't go to the movies. Instead, he was a fixture at Manhattan Center. He liked to go there and dance to Machito's Orchestra and the Afro Cuban Boys. Every day he made new friends, most of them from the neighborhood. He joined church choruses thinking that they were an avenue to stardom. He wanted to be a Cuban Eddie Cantor or Al Jolson, but language and color were big obstacles. You couldn't even sit in the boxes at Radio City Center—they were only for whites. A black there was a mirage. Miguelito was the only gray black in Manhattan. Not just because of the cold, but also because he would rub himself with whitening powders. But even that didn't work. The theater mafia controlled everything and in the end they would always choose an American black over a Cuban one.

Bobby Cortés would tell us how he was exploited as a singer. He'd compose a tune and take it, let's say, to a radio station or a Latin band. If it was good, the band played it and copyrighted it in Washington. But always in some other sonofabitch's name, never in Bobby's. That's how they stole so many of his songs, *guarachas* and *boleros*. They suckered him because he was honest and no crook.

I went to many Latin parties with Bobby and Miguelito in Jackson Heights, the Lower East Side and in the Barrio. I mixed with the *boricua* crowd, the largest group of Latins and the friendliest to us Cubans. Right away, Miguelito got tight with a Puerto Rican woman, although he continued to write to his wife, enclosing photos of the Empire State Building and the Statue of Liberty. This woman was very jealous and threatened to scratch his eyes out if she caught him writing to his wife in Havana. So he wrote the letters in my apartment and received those from his wife in my mailbox. But correspondence dwindled with time. Distance, at first, draws people together like a magnet; over time, though, the attraction peters out. The present takes precedence and you begin to live for the day. And because of one thing or another, with work, the subway and a new language, the immigrant has no time to think of his loved ones. It happened to me, too, although to tell the truth, the only person I ever wrote to at all was my sister Yara.

So, Miguelito eventually got into the swing of things here and he soon forgot his wife. The Puerto Rican woman had him coming and going, so *ajorado*, as they say, that he couldn't get a "but" in edgewise. She had thick eyebrows that met in the center, but she was pretty, although somewhat of a hick. When he went off with his *boricua* friends to sing at some party, she tagged along. If he had to work dancing and singing on weekends, she tagged along. She tailed him without ever taking her eyes off him. How could he help but forget his wife!

"Shit, she no longer writes to me!" he told me one day, when he found my mailbox was empty.

"How do you expect her to write to you if you never answer her letters!"

Carmencita had Miguelito around her pinky. They moved in together on the Lower East Side, where she got a job packing baby clothes. Every day she would try to make Miguelito jealous. "The foreman tried to grab me," or "The Ecuadorian woman's husband looked at me like this and like that."

"Look, Julian, I really like this woman, I love her, but she's nuts. When she's not jealous of me she tries to provoke me by flirting with other guys."

"Leave her and concentrate on your music."

But he was head over heels in love. Even with all that, he still worked very hard; I've never met a guy more on the ball. His good humor brought him tips that rained like manna from heaven. He would get to the restaurant after a night's carousing, singing his own songs in the haunts of the Barrio. He got away with it—everyone spoiled him.

"I dreamt this one up last night," he'd say as he pulled out a score. He wasn't a bad composer; on the contrary, he was really talented musically. I never did understand how he managed to do so many things at once. He wanted nothing more than to make music, but there was no money in it; a musician had to take on other kinds of work because music just doesn't pay the rent. He also had to pay for his music lessons and the furniture for the new apartment, which cost him an arm and a leg. Miguelito always moved among *boricuas*, and although he criticized them, he was always with them, so he almost never had to speak English. Besides, English classes cost a fortune in those days. In any case, you learn enough through osmosis in the street and from newspaper headlines.

Carmencita's sister had come from Ponce a few years back. She brought her six kids with her and got on Welfare. Her husband had to stay in Puerto Rico because there was a warrant out on him in New York. In those days, people were practically starving in Ponce. They arrived here like desert travellers dragging themselves to an oasis. Carmencita helped her find a room in the Bronx. She also tried to get me involved with her. She was honey colored and real saucy, but I was scared off by the six kids. We went dancing together at Manhattan Center, to Coney Island and we killed many hours at the little lake in Central Park.

She would say to me: "I'll leave my husband for you."

I tried to talk her out of it, for the sake of the children and my own peace of mind. "There's no need to rush."

But these *boricua* women have fire inside them; they're hotter than Cuban women. To tell the truth, she had me hooked, but I got loose just in time. Her husband wrote that he was coming in March with a safe-conduct permit. I imagine that he wanted to see the kids. Jeanette's mother never knew about me; we always managed to get out without her mother noticing. When her husband arrived he went to live with her. I kept away but he suspected something and he tracked me like a rabbit, though he never found me. Jeanette and her husband had a second honeymoon of sorts, but in the long run it ended in disaster. His dirty dealings followed him all the way to the Bronx, and when the cops showed up to arrest him they got into a gun fight and he wounded a cop. He ended up doing time in the Tombs, New York City's prison. After her mother and kids were asleep, Jeanette took two bottles of seconals and lay down in bed. She never got up again. Her funeral was the saddest thing I had ever seen. The kids couldn't understand what had happened and they cried inconsolably. It made Carmencita a bit crazy. Luckily, a lawyer from the Working Class Committee, Phil Dutch, helped the family with money and sent the kids to school. Miguelito and I gave the old lady forty dollars for the flowers and the phone calls to Ponce. Jeanette's parents weren't able to come to the burial and her husband wasn't let out for it. Her friends, Miguelito, old man José Diaz, Placido and I had to take care of everything.

Then Carmencita went religious. She began to pin sacred images on the walls of her apartment and she made offerings of water, flowers and miracles for the health of the kids. It was the saddest thing to see the kids walking all alone on the streets of the Bronx, with an addict father in the Tombs and a mother six feet below. For several months we had no parties. The bands found themselves another singer for the meantime. Carmencita made Miguelito go into mourning for the death of her sister, putting him in a bind since they needed the earnings from his singing.

When Jeanette's husband got out of jail, he got a job finishing furniture in the Bronx. Some have it that he quit drugs and the bad life. His kids were already teenagers and some of them had taken to the life of the street because the grandmother hadn't been able to keep them in line. I went to see him one day with Miguelito to ask a favor. He wouldn't shake my hand. Miguelito told him: "This guy's like my own brother," but that didn't make any difference. He had a stone face, like all defeated ex-cons. He snorted contemptuously: "You and I have to settle things first."

But I never saw him again. I've never stopped wondering if Carmencita didn't drop some hint to him about me and Jeanette. That's why the Abakua sects don't trust their women; sooner or later, they all set their tongues to wagging. If you don't believe me, there's the story of the woman whose tongue was cut out because she revealed the tribe's secrets. I heard that story on the docks in Havana from the Nanigo sea stevedores, and there's no greater truth than that. We didn't get along and we never saw each other again, as I told Miguelito.

"No, Julian, the man is content finishing furniture now. Leave him be."

But the wheel of fortune went round and round and a few months after getting out of the Tombs he was sent back again. Luckily, neither Miguelito nor his woman ever got wind of it. I've always lived on the up and up. I like to put my head on my pillow and be at peace with myself.

I continued working at Liborio's, but in May '52 Miguelito and I got a lucky break, unusual as it is in a city where all business is controlled by the Mafia and what they here call WASP's, well-off white Americans. We Latins are labelled and discredited as spics. A spic is a Hispanic, almost as low here as an Indian in loincloth. Some Latins think that just because they've made money or hit the jackpot that they are equal, but if they go into Lord and Taylor's or Bloomingdale's speaking Spanish, they get disdainful stares. Or the clerks go right up to them and ask: "Can I do something for you?" That'll make them stop sniffing around. Latins, you know, are curious types and they'll go into a large shopping center just to look around, to while away the time, to try on sample perfumes or to hold up a fabric and say at the top of their lungs: "Yoo hoo, look here Maria, isn't this color divine?" And the people don't like this kind of display, it's against the rules. Americans are dry and to the point. We Hispanics look things over this and that way and cause a ruckus wherever we go. _Boricuas_ invented rivalry; they're always bickering. Cubans invented showing off; you can spot a Cuban a thousand miles away with his flashy style. Today, education has toned things down a bit, but we're still recognizable. And yet there's something positive in all this. Cubans have big mouths and won't stand for anything. Americans are something else. As far as money is concerned, Americans like to move to the rhythm of the Conga. But if you mess with them, they'll smash you. That's why I admire Fidel. He's put them in their place.

translated by y. espínola

andy warhol's quarter
e d w a r d   l i m o n o v

A cartoon character with moonlight hair was walking on Madison Avenue, a purple rucksack on his back. One might say Tintin on promenade. "Look, another Andy Warhol impersonator!" my friend said. We were coming from uptown.

"No," I said, "that's him. Absolutely and positively him. I saw him a few times at Glickerman's parties."

Tintin stopped at the intersection of 63rd Street and picked up the receiver from a street telephone, then started to look in his pockets for a dime. "Christ, he needs a dime. Jesus, Andy Warhol looking for a dime! Should I give him one?" my friend asked. "I have one."

"If you wish," I said.

He went up to Tintin and tapped him on the shoulder. "Andy," he said. "Hey Andy, I have a dime!"

edward limonov was born in Russia, lived in New York City in the 70s, and currently lives in Paris. He is the author of several novels, including _It's Me, Eddie, My Butler's Tale_, and _Memoirs of a Russian Punk_.

I didn't hear what Tintin responded. I was standing near the mailbox on the north side of 63rd Street, with the November wind blowing from uptown. I saw them fumbling with change.

My friend came back with an idiotic smile. "Ha," he said, "he gave me a quarter."

"You can be proud," I said, "it's not easy to make a profit on Andy Warhol."

"No profit. I gave him two dimes and five pennies. One at a time, with him waiting."

"You gave it yourself, or did he ask for it?"

"He asked," my friend said. "He's a fucking billionaire, but he patiently waited for fifteen cents."

"That's why he is a billionaire. But tell me, why didn't you give him that miserable dime for free?"

"You see," my friend said, "I wanted to get something from him as a memory." He looked at the quarter in his palm.

"Scrape something on it," I said, "so you won't mix it up with ordinary quarters."

He took my proposition seriously and scraped the letter "W" on the face of George Washington with a key. "Unbelievable," he said. "The boys in Kharkov wouldn't believe us. What a story! We're walking down Madison and Warhol himself, just like us also walking along, the most important genius of our time! And his sneakers aren't even Adidas, just some insignificant model, and that rucksack of his, polyester shit." He grimaced in disgust.

"That's his principles," I said.

'What do you mean by that?"

"He wears polyesters on principle. He worships nylon shirts and all those non-natural products. He is the prophet of artificiality, the spiritual son of Picabia, moonlight Nazi Czech—The Killer of the old fat-assed culture. Waiting for fifteen cents is perfectly in accordance with his principles. Militantly anti-Romantic, he enjoys calculations and takes pleasure in talking about money."

"How do you know all that?" my friend asked.

"Because I read, unlike you," I said.

"I am an artist. I don't need books. Reading is important for writers."

"So, run after him and kiss his ass. He also claims that he doesn't read books. But he wrote one. *The Philosophy of Andy Warhol.* It so happens I learned English reading his book. Somebody gave it to me."

"What's it about? Interesting?"

We had reached 57th Street and stopped indecisively on the corner. Actually, we had no plans and plenty of time ahead. He had lost his job as a photographer at the New York University Hospital the week before. I didn't have a job at all—I was on welfare.

"I should've asked him about a job," my friend said. "He's from a family of emigrants, also. And Czech, you know, Slav. We have the same blood."

"I thought you were Jewish. And anyway, Andy Warhol has no blood, he's electric. I'm sure if you part his hair you'll see the wires, microchips and all that."

"Stop it," he said. "Who are you to laugh at him? He is the Superstar, and you are zero, welfare recipient that you are."

"It's still not night yet," I said. "I am only thirty. I have time."

"Sure you have." Suddenly he looked very sad. "What are we gonna do?"

"Let's go to Central Park. We can buy some hotdogs and a small bottle of brandy. And I have a pint."

"Again? Pleasures for the poor. We've gotten drunk in Central Park maybe a hundred times. Okay, let's go. What else can we do without money."

We turned to the right.

"I wonder," I said, "if he goes to Central Park sometimes? I mean Andy."

"What for? He goes to the Plaza for champagne with Liza Minelli. Unemployed scum, like us, go to the parks, to sit and wait for nothing. Fuck, I wanna be rich! Riiich and famous!" he screamed. The passersby on 57th looked at us suspiciously.

"Why didn't you kidnap Andy Warhol on Madison," I said. "You missed your chance, baby. It was easy to do. He was all alone, no bodyguards. Just snatch the genius and push him into the trunk of a car."

"Do you think he's worth a lot?"

"You doubt it? You could also force him to work in captivity. He'd produce the pictures and you could sell them. You'd have no problems with him. He'd be a model prisoner. I read his book closely, word by word, using a dictionary. I know he doesn't need much, Andy. A tape recorder would be enough."

"I'd feed him only Campbell's soup," my friend smiled maliciously.

"He might hate Campbell's soup."

"He'd eat it for the sake of his image. Also, I could use those photos of the corpses that I took for the hospital, you remember, I showed them to you. He could just drop some acrylic paint on them, a few drops here and there, and it would be worth tens of thousands! I'm sure I could produce better droppings myself, but his signature is important."

"Yes, I know, you're a genius also," I said.

He didn't respond to my sarcasm, he was following his own thoughts. "How do people manage to get so big, so symbolic, so unique, huh Edward? Fucking Czech. Did you notice, Edward, that they're ugly people, those Czechs?"

"Haven't seen many. Actually, I've known only one Czech woman, in Rome. She was hysterical, but rather of ordinary ugliness."

The autumn leaves were scratching asphalt on 57th Street. The wind suddenly whirled them up and threw them into our faces.

"What fucking weather," my friend said. "And he's walking around with only a light jacket on."

"Who?"

"Warhol."

"I told you, he's electric. And maybe his shirt is heated. He could easily put batteries in his rucksack and walk around as long as he wishes, you know, like he's wrapped in an electric blanket."

"I have one at my place, stolen from the hospital of course. I was supposed to talk to him instead of counting pennies. Shit! I was supposed to ask him, 'What's your secret?'"

"I can lend you his book. Apparently, as a boy he was sick and tired of all those Czechs around him talking a minority language, so he put all his strength together in order to get out. I believe that one day he got very angry, I mean seriously angry with the world. And that is the best thing that can happen to a man. Extremely rare as well, maybe nine in ten million might experience it. Then, angry as hell, you can get beyond the man. To get there once in life is enough, and you'll always remember that one time."

"What's beyond?" my friend asked. "Does he say?"

"He didn't say. Actually, he didn't even mention that he went beyond. But I have a strong conviction that he did."

"And what do you think is there?"

"Nothingness, I guess. Indifferent, non-hostile Nothingness. No need to worry, you just choose yourself as you wish to be. That's what Buddha discovered also. Another Superman, Buddha."

"Do you think Warhol is as big as Buddha?" My friend became suddenly sad.

"That's a good question," I laughed. "To put it shortly, our Czech discovered that if you don't help yourself, nobody is able to help you."

"You're talking like Madame Margo, the reader and advisor who lives under my apartment. Are we going to the liquor store, or not?"

We bought a bottle of brandy and four hotdogs. We scrounged around for the pennies to pay for the hotdogs, but finally we were obliged to give up the struggle. The hotdog man, a Yugoslav, took Andy Warhol's quarter and put it in the pocket of his apron.

"Anyway, I couldn't possibly spare his coin for long," my friend said when we placed ourselves on the bench. "That's against my principles."

My mother kept a detailed baby book for each of her five children. She wrote a brief description of anything interesting that happened in my life every week until I was one, then every month until I was eight. She hired a professional photographer, a Chinese man named Victor, who came to our house once a month to take pictures for the baby books. Sewn to my book is the green Parcheesi chip I swallowed when I was five months old. When I was five, I had so many nervous tics that my uncles would playfully mimic me. My mother took them all to Dr. Bode, the family doctor, who gave my uncles a stern lecture and asked them to ignore me, and it worked. Throughout the book, I'm always in a fattening program.

My Uncle Victor had ten children. In the 50s, after his seventh child, he and his wife, Elodia, had an audience with Pope Pius the XII, whose real name was Eugenio Pacelli. Victor complained to the Pope that his birth control method, the rhythm method, didn't work at all, witness his very large family. The Pope chuckled and replied that it was a good method, to keep trying it. His eighth child, conceived, according to Victor, while practicing the rhythm method in Rome, was named Pacelli Mendoza.

tony mendoza was born in Havana, Cuba. He has been an engineer, an art student, and an architect. His has two books of photographs, *Ernie: A Photographer's Memoir*, and *Stories*, from which these photographs are taken.

Ana Maria's party for Sergio and Enid was very animated. As a family we are hard of hearing, and almost everyone is a drinker. Family parties tend to be loud.

tangents

a d r i e n n e   t i e n

Nothing could keep me from my summer escape! And there I go right over the George Washington Bridge and baamm, I'm out. Hands on the wheel, head vibrating full of top forty songs from the summer of sixty-nine. The first New York man I dated couldn't drive. I couldn't believe it. Where my immigrant parents raised me up, birthplace of the American automobile, not being able to drive is like not being able to cook a fried egg! But lots of New Yorkers can't drive, maybe that's why they stay, maybe that's why they didn't feel like I did at the beginning of this summer—a fly on solar boil, caught between a screen and a window, the dead weight heat all around like fresh tar on a closed-off street, and no way to get quiet for sleep at night except by shutting the windows, and then the skin puffs up soggy like a rotten tomato, oozes yellow sweat like one giant pustule. If I hadn't found someway to get out of the city this summer, I would have thrown myself out of my apartment window and

landed on top of Tran Di Yuet.

adrienne tien is a New York City writer who works in film.

• • •

"Where do you live?" I'm often asked. "Chinatown," I say, and I want to add that it has nothing to do with the fact that I'm Chinese. I just chanced on a loft space that I could afford there. My father was deeply disturbed when I made my move. Only FOB's live in Chinatown, the immigrants, the one's who can't speak English, the ones who still have to make it. To him, his daughter living in Chinatown means she's not making it. He doesn't understand, I got a loft!

And my mother tries continually, desperately to save me from myself. Checking the mail—of all the ironic things, she sends me a review of the best-selling *Joy Luck Club*, as if to say, can you do this? Rhetorical question. Her answer arrives in the form of catalogs from law schools across the nation. She's been using my name and forging my signature on dozens of letters requesting applications. To date, I've gotten twelve application booklets! Her's is a vote of no confidence, my father's of incomprehension.

Why go on about their thoughts? I haven't lived with my parents for more than a decade. Instead of relatives, I have housemates. My portion of our loft is at the front, with big windows facing the Manhattan Bridge and a convergence of streets. An enviable space, but I'm oppressed by a sense of guilt that originates in my brain and refracts up from the sidewalks. Every day, the trucks fart their way in and belch out crates of green vegetables, fruits, cans of soda, whole pigs and plastic bags full of bean sprouts. Come to think of it, I've never seen hairties or hairbands delivered. Perhaps those bins of colored do-bobbies, the Kudzu of New York, appear through spontaneous generation. I often see bones tumbling off handtrucks onto the streets, I frequently pass the tourists sitting down to wonton soup, and I wonder do they taste the shoe leather?

I said I feel guilt. Yes, not only from the obvious source, but also when I compare my life to that of the immigrants around me. If I couldn't speak Chinese, perhaps I'd ignore them altogether and not feel anything, but when I buy milk, garlic, a bottle of oil or soya sauce, our lives touch like tangent circles. A few of the grocers and waiters now recognize and occasionally speak with me. Each one has asked and then keeps asking again and again, "What do you do?"

They see me on the street at all different hours of the day, all the days of the week. No pattern, no set schedule, no time put in at the shops, the stalls, the basement kitchens, no waiting tables, no baby strapped up in a red embroidered carrier on my back.

"Writer," I said once. The grocer's face lit up. "Ah, yes, you must be very smart." No, no, I thought, I'm half crazy, or is it lazy. If I was smart I would be a dentist, a doctor, a lawyer, an MBA, anything but the half-baked writer that I am. If I was smart, I'd be a publicist, but I'm nothing but an oyster on the half-shell. One of a million, *wasting away, leave me alone, Ma . . . I can't do anything but this . . . and someday maybe . . . for a hobby okay, but you need to think of the future, a career . . .* so many like me, dreams mixing and floating with the carbon monoxide rolling up from the streets like bundles of black insulation, bumping in poofs against my windows. I gotta get outta here. A truck roars, the subway runs past full blast like a meat grinder on wheels. Down there in all of that, in her place almost under the bridge, she sits

Tran Di Yuet.

• • •

One of my housemates, BB, a sculptor, noticed her first. "Have you seen the woman that's selling her stuff outside our door? God, what a face she has, what life! What beauty!"

One day after dropping my laundry off for someone else to wash, I stopped. She sat outside our door on a little stool next to a wooden tub. Her face was strong and bright from country mornings, her tiny eyes jet black, and her cheeks red as ripe apples. She smiled at me. She waved her hand and as I stepped over, she lifted the slatted lid covering the wooden thermos tub. Inside, fresh, homemade cubes of ivory-white Do Fu were floating in clear, cool water. She held up one finger, one dollar.

"Thank you," I said in Chinese, "But I'm not cooking tonight."

She loved that! I could speak Chinese! She didn't care that I had laminated postage stamps hanging from my earlobes and lived with four men who weren't even Chinese. I explained about learning the language in college and living for awhile in China. "You're so smart," she said. "Really smart." No, I thought, no, but because she thought so, I felt it might be. Maybe I wasn't so worthless? _You're so thin . . . can't gain weight because of the pollution . . . living in a place like that, no steady job, with your education . . . Ma! Have I ever asked you for money. . . ._

From then on, we always exchanged smiles. Sometimes, we'd chat for a few minutes. How many kids, how was life? I could only understand about 20 percent of what she said because of her dialect accent. As for what I said, I myself only understood 30 percent of that. What she understood, I don't know, but her enthusiasm in our conversation never flagged for a moment. She would call me over and cheerfully fire off some few sentences, nodding away at the elliptical phrases I returned. I found out she lived in a tiny apartment across from my loft with her husband and four children! After that I was careful to close my blinds at night. Had she seen me parading around in my lacy Macy's nightie (a Christmas gift, I swear), going from work area to phone area, to bedroom to sitting area—my space three times what she and her family had for their six braided lives.

• • •

Tran Di Yuet was out there every morning, every as in seven days a week. She stayed there with the trucks blaring, the buses exhaling, the people squeezing past on the sidewalk, and the cars sidling up to the curb, scraping her back. She was there until the sun went down. Then her husband or sometimes her fourteen-year-old son would come over and help her carry the tub across the street and up the five flights to their apartment. When did she make the Do Fu? In her sleep?

Money, money, how to make money? How to make the green stuff? Tran Di Yuet's dough was ground soybeans, fermented with gypsum, squeezed dry, compressed into protein cakes. My way was temporary typing assignments in corporate offices. And there are so many days when I can't do what Tran does, I can't bear to go out and bring home the bacon. And some days I can't write and I just sit reading a novel or yakking on the phone to my other unemployed friends. What a life! Great, until I'd start thinking I don't deserve to be so free. What if my mother saw me at home midday, midweek. What if Tran knew. Writer, whisper the grocers, writing stories. Do they believe it? Do I?

I stopped to talk to Tran Di Yuet. She told me she came from the south of China. I told her my family's old home was Hupei, North of the Lake as in the opposite of Hunan South of the Lake. Lake North, Lake South, Uptown, Downtown, Midtown, East Side, West Side, Wall Street? It's too damn hot to be hearing jackhammers! I commented on her hairdo. I didn't really like it but I said I did. She was losing some of her glow. Her cheeks were only a trace rosy, and now with this new haircut and tight perm, she looked like she was trying to look pretty when before she had been beautiful because she was without artifice. She admired my long hair and told me that back in China, she had worn her hair long to her waist and done it up in a bun. She smiled, a big smile, showing her square white teeth as she mimicked how she combed out that long shining black hair and looked at herself in the mirror.

"No time now. No time for combing long hair. Just one quick wash." She bent her head and mimed a one-two scrub. A waiting customer suppressed his impatience, eyes popping slightly. I said good bye and she lifted the lid of her wooden tub and placed two squares of Do Fu into a plastic bag.

One Tuesday morning around ten-thirty, I came down the stairs, heading to the library for some inspiration. I go there to see all the books and the people reading, and then I think: see, people read, people are reading, writers do something, you are meaningful, now go home and write. On this particular day, I came down and there was Tran Di Yuet, same happy face, but she was sitting behind a silver cart, with sliding glass windows, and a little gas tank attached on the side. I broke into a smile to match hers.

She grinned at me over a vat of bubbling grease. Sizzling away were pieces of green pepper and eggplant cut like little boats, holding some kind of stuffing.

"Come, I'm treating you."

With a wire mesh scooper, she lifted a couple of pepper and eggplant pieces from the pool of hot oil and set them on a paper tray. "Hot sauce?"

She stuck a plastic fork in the little fried pieces and handed them to me.

"*Hoa Chi.*" I nodded, raising a green pepper to my lips. The fried pieces were good, like potato chips only even more satisfying because they were thicker, fresh cooked, and in spite of all the grease, still part virtuous vegetable. A line was forming at her cart. Old customers back for the Do Fu, now sold on the side, new ones curious for a taste of the fried delights. She worked so damn hard, out on the street even when it rained and now she had saved up and gotten a vending cart! If I had an iota of her energy, I'd have written several novels of epic proportions.

She'd had the cart for about a year passing through the winter months, the quick spring ones, and then as I began to tell you, the summer arrived. I was going to explode, I couldn't hear anything inside my head except the phone ringing, cars honking, the subway wheels screeching, beeping from my answering machine, beeping from other people's beepers, and then bleep into my head came the idea to rent a car and drive the hell out of the city until I got into green country, and I'd do this whenever I felt like it.

So there I was busting up the West Side Highway listening to jazz greats and singing "Hallelujah, I'm a Bum." Three times I did it, picking up a little blue Sunbird from Sunshine Rent-A-Car, shooting out over the GW bridge and up to some nameless place, occasionally staying the night in a motel listening to the chirp of crickets. First time I rented the car, I decided to swing back to my house and take care of my laundry. The only space I could find to pull up in was right in back of Tran Di Yuet. She turned from her frying vat with surprise. She nodded at the car with interest and I blurted out, "This isn't mine, it's a friend's." I was so embarrassed, caught mid-week, not working and with a car. I hoped the grocers didn't see me. "I borrowed it for some errands," I added. Tran Di Yuet stared at my car. I realized she hadn't been looking so healthy lately. Her cheeks were gone white like the underside of a fish. Had she been ill? I wondered if something was wrong with her.

I ran upstairs and came back with my bags of laundry and hoisted them into the car. I wanted to get away before my shame at having a car and free time made me sign up for the Army. Tran seemed about to ask me something important when a customer came up, and I quick seized the chance to jump in my car and cut out of there.

Heavy hot summer air got swept upside down and blown back cool as I cruised ole Riverside Drive. I put on some sunglasses, took the curves smoothly and felt joy in my heart. I was born lucky. You dog, you lazy bitch. *Look Mom and Dad, one of these days . . . I'll make . . . I won't end up with nothing as nothing.* Stop it. You are different, going somewhere else, the place that you don't know you are going until you get there. Thoreau?

Yeah, right out of the city for now.

On my fourth trip out, I came down the stairs, thinking to buy one of Tran's treats for the road, but she wasn't there. Another guy was set up in her place selling butcher knives off the top of a cardboard box. In the last month, she'd been letting up on herself a little. I hoped her occasional absences meant her family circumstances were improving to the point that she could afford a day off now and then. I zipped on up the highway, going so fast and thinking about something so stupid that I ended up shooting past the bridge and found myself in Westchester County, flying along the green shady Sawmill River Parkway. What the hell! A different route. I decided to swing into one of the towns and see if there might be a cheap apartment for rent and maybe a part-time job posted up at the general store. I rode into Dobbs Ferry.

I came round and out near a path that led up from the commuter train station. Ahead, walking on the shoulder of the road, was a figure somehow familiar, yet impossible for me to take in as recognizable. I slowed my vehicle to a crawl as my mind constructed that, yes, it was

Tran!

What was she doing walking along the road in this small town so far from her spot next to the soot-sneezing bridge? I thought of speeding up and rushing past. I couldn't have her thinking I owned a car. She'd never understand that I was renting and out for a leisurely drive, no destination in mind, no deliveries to make. She'd think I was rich, she'd never realize that I was just like her in urban America, barely keeping my head above the bills flowing out of my mailbox each day. I wasn't a good-for-nothing, got-it-all-easy American-born-Chinese, a hollow bamboo tube. I was working, I was writing, dammit, that is work too. What was she doing here? Of all the weird things. I could make a quick right and avoid her completely, but something was wrong. She was walking slowly with her head bent down like the crook of a cane. I pulled up alongside her, but even with the car rolling right next to her, she wouldn't look up. Why would she imagine anybody but a crazy person stopping for her. She stared straight ahead with tears running down her cheeks. I pulled over and jumped out of the car.

"Tran!" I called. "Tran!"

For an instant she was horrified to see me, no doubt convinced I was a ghost, and then a wave a relief swept away her shocked disbelief. I pointed at the car. She nodded and followed me back and climbed in the front seat. She sat there like a child and didn't look at me. What had happened to her rain-or-shine smile? Cars whizzed past. I turned on my hazard flashers.

"What are you doing here?" I said in Chinese.

She shook her head and raised the back of her hand to each of her eyes.

I waited for her words to hit me like static from a radio, hoping there'd be one or two that rang clear. Nothing. No words.

"Where are you going?" I asked. "I'll take you there."

I looked at my sunglasses, discarded on the dashboard. I hoped Tran didn't think my shorts were underwear or notice that my top was a mere square of silk held up by straps that could better be described as strands. I didn't expect anyone to see me when I was wearing my wild, sexy driving attire. Tran Di Yuet had on her usual garb, blouse untucked, plain dark cotton pants, soft slip-on shoes.

"Where are you going?" I asked again.

She reached into her pocket and pulled out a neatly folded piece of paper. I unfolded it.

Our eyes met and she began to speak. "I already have four! I can't afford any more. We're working for the ones we have. Can't afford . . . not enough money."

"I understand," I said. I wondered why she was coming all the way out here, who referred her, what the insurance deal was, but then it would have been too complicated to ask, and she might have only understood my saying why, why, why, as if I questioned what she was doing.

I parked the car. We approached the clinic and then my head went dizzy with fear and anger. Protesters came at us like rabid bats, waving signs and shouting. Placards swiping all around us like giant fly swatters. *Murderers, killers!*

"What?" Tran asked me, horror scaling her face, twisting her mouth into a gaping expression.

Mine fell open. How to explain? Three men approached with a clipboard, momentarily thrown off by facing Asian women, our faces telling them of birth in yellow river basin, centuries of famine, toil, coaxing green sprouts from mud, filling hollow bellies with grains of rice, leaves of trees, no-names and footbinding. They faltered, then started in. "You're about to commit a sin. Come pray with us. We'll help you. The heartbeat of a fetus. . . ."

Tran hid her proud, worn face in her hands. One of the men was shaking his gory poster at her. I grabbed it. Different people kept blocking our path. I marched toward the doors of the clinic, scared, my heart pounding, Tran's arms linked with mine. I shouted back at those who shouted at me and nothing was heard but the noise of human bellowing. We got inside and there was one protester, handcuffed to one of the chairs in the waiting room, stretching her arm out to make us take a pamphlet, her smile twisting wretchedly like a figure from Dante's *Inferno.*

I handed Tran's appointment paper through the window to a tired-looking nurse. Outside the protesters had begun a chant: "Stop the murders, stop the murders."

"What are they saying," Tran asked.

I looked down at Tran's hands, one on top of the other on her lap. I'd never seen them still. They worked so ceaselessly, dipping the mesh-spoon into the frying grease, squirting the hot sauce on, folding the wax paper bags, handing over the plastic forks, taking the dollars, quarters, dimes, and in quiet moments, wiping the smooth steel of her cart with a damp, battered rag. I reached and squeezed her tanned, wrinkled hands. They began to shake as the chanting of the protesters grew louder, angrier, more vehement, and I thought, I hope they don't smash the car, we need it to get back to the city.

love

arthur   nersesian

She was hideous! It had always been easy for me to fall head over heels
for some bouncing blond from Texarkana, Texas, to sip her like a dry martini
and smash the crystal in the fireplace of fate. But it was only Budweiser that
my dear pal Helmsley was guzzling as he nestled his head in the folds of her
belly and looked up into her cavernous nostrils.

She rambled on stupidly above his silence. Could love wed her
boisterousness to his boyishness? Could love amputate the twenty years that
tossed her ahead of him? Could love repair so much? If so, then for the first
time in my life, sitting there, I realized how love was truly great.

For different reasons, we had all downed what would have measured out
to at least a keg of beer. Amanda, who had drunk twice as much as Helmsley,
was none the drunker. Suddenly, Amanda jumped to her feet, and yanking

arthur nersesian was the managing editor of the *Portable
Lower East Side* from 1990 to 1994. He is the author of
The Fuck-Up (a novel), *New York Complaints* (a collection
of poetry), and *East Village Writers Block* (a play). He
teaches at Hostos Community College.

up Helmsley she decided it was time to go. By way of farewell she let out a profound fart. I was too drunk to mind anything, though. I knew I wouldn't make it even as far as the door. I sat there and ordered another beer.

Alcohol corrodes one's dexterity and sense of proportion, but it also heightens one's emotions. Smelling that fart, I thought of Helmsley in love. Had I spent my whole life up until now confusing love with a series of erections. Love to Helmsley must have been an utter necessity, whereas for me it was always just a luxurious distraction. I wish I had the need to lust after some goiter-necked, tooth-decayed, leg-blistered old bag. If I could love like that it would be a pyramid of emotions, an Arc de Triomphe of affections.

When the time arrived for the bar to close, I had to be helped out. No sooner did I plop myself down on a neighboring stoop, my stomach reared up. Staring down at the pool of vomit that had fountained out of me, I made out the expensive Italian food I had eaten earlier that evening. The regurgitated pasta and cheese were little islands in a vast sea of beer.

I recall through that drunken stupor feeling a deep loss—it had been such a magnificent meal. Only the power of love could win back that meal. If I could love it enough, I would be able to eat it up all over again. It probably would taste just as good, once I got over the disgusting appearance. I knelt in the slop and gazed into it with as much devotion as I could muster. Dogs eat their regurgitations, I prompted myself. Slowly stretching my fingers out, I stroked along the meaty lumps and cheesy threads, and then brought my finger tips to my lips. I tried, but for some reason I just couldn't get beyond the bilious stench. True love was required, but all I had was counterfeit endearment.

"Hey," someone yelled, following it with a prodding kick to my ribs. A large guy with mountainous shoulders loomed above me. "What da fuck yo doin'?"

A gang of teenagers behind him were looking down at me grimly. They looked as if they knew when a good beating would be therapeutic. As I scrambled to my unsteady feet, I realized there was no chance of running away.

"Well, I was just eating, you know, a meatball hero, and I look at my hand here, and my high school graduation ring is gone, so I . . . uh, upchuck here, and I was just looking for it, you know, it had a diamond stone."

"Diamond?" the most brilliant of them queried. "What public school has a diamond for a graduation stone?"

"Who said public?" I countered. "It was parochial."

"Which one?" asked the guy with the twin-tower shoulders.

"Maternal Lamentations," I lied. "Over in Sheepshead Bay."

"Yea," one of the morons said to my relief. "We just beat them in basketball."

"Fuck it," I said, looking wistfully at the vomit. I slowly walked away. After I had staggered two blocks, I looked back and saw the bastards kicking through my poor puddle of vomit. As I turned away, I heard one of them yell to the others: "Gypsies steal gems that way."

absence makes the heart
l y n n e   t i l l m a n

The woman said don't leave me, then walked into a ballroom, the kind that is easily imagined. He saw her, she who had been left, in a purple gown. Her dress froze in the space she inhabited and it seemed to him it was by this lack of movement that she projected a singular state. The wine, musicians, perfume, dancing men and women, and the breath of lovers coming in quick, hot, uneven spurts was a tableau of such familiarity, unoriginality, she did not need to look. Separate from the others, she seemed to him a duchy, defined by borders both real and imaginary. No doubt those borders were in dispute, and she chose to stand alone. He did not think of her as stateless, bodiless. Such metaphors might occur with the absence of others. There was such a plenitude, so much given to the imagination.

Her hand touched a mouth whose very construction seemed to spell pleasure. What a mouth, he thought, a mouth to create hunger rather than

lynne tillman is the author of *Motion Sickness, Haunted Houses, Absence Makes the Heart, Cast in Doubt,* and *The Madame Realism Complex.* She is also the co-director and writer of *Committed,* an independent feature film.

satisfy it. His eyes lingered on the lips as if they too were eyes that could swallow his by their very reception. Her breasts rose and fell, and that she breathed, was alive, was to him a miracle. Such beauty could not be real. Her round breasts must be the mountains and valleys of that unimaginable state. Hadn't he once admitted that one could not imagine a mountainless valley, a linguistic impossibility. But she was flesh, and he was careful to conceive of her—her breasts, for instance—as possible. He thought, Unimaginable is not the state, not-yet-realized is better. He was drawn to her, as if drawn by her, her creation. She was a painting, a study in purple, she was a dangerous flower, she was a fountain bringing youth to those who drank her. He felt stupid, like a story that doesn't work.

It was a battle for her to think. It was pointless. She spoke to herself. I am the one who waits. I am the one who will be waited upon. I have the kiss that can change men's lives. I can awaken the dead. I can never die. I am empty. I am perfect. I am full. I am all things to all men. She shook her head violently. He watched everything. The shake of the head, a sign to him. A fire lit. Something was burning. He felt ill, he felt wonderful. She was sublime, and he wondered how words like that existed before her.

His approach across the floor was a dare, an affront, a move, as if the floor were a chessboard and he had made his opening. He approached and avoided, missing the hem of her dress by inches, causing her to move slightly, but just enough to let him know she could be moved. Her movement irritated him. When he looked back he saw that she had resumed her previous position. His irritation fled and fell into an unwanted past. Her position was irresistible and unknowable. He thought, If she turns out to be like pudding, sweet but thick, it will be easier to leave her.

Just then, as he was toying with flight, a woman hurried to her side. She cupped her hands to her mouth to speak words meant just for her. He imagined that someone had been slighted, her indifference to someone had been noted, or perhaps it was a practical matter, when she had to leave in order to be ready for an early morning rendezvous. With a married man. An important figure in the government. With whom, he wondered. The woman took her arm and the two walked out of the room, their shadows larger than life. Were her eyer full of tears? Was she that delicate, so easily hurt or affected, such an angel to feel for others? The crowded room emptied with her departure, and love that is despair led him to follow her, to find her.

Her father lay in state on a hospital bed. Nothing was attached to him anymore. His head was turned from her and frozen. Couldn't she give him life, she who loved him more than any man. His hand was ice. His ankles were swollen and purple like her dress. His eyes were fixed and dilated. He did not know she was there. This must be death. And as nothing is attached to you anymore, no tubes dripping colorless liquids, I must also become detached from your body. Now, what man will love me, and who will I be able to love.

He did not expect to arrive at this place, a hospital. He covered his mouth with a handkerchief, telling himself it was merely a precaution. Her purple dress disappeared down uninteresting white halls. The sterility hurt his eyes, yet he knew she would see his compassion, especially in this setting, and think well of a stranger so much in love with her as to appear in her hour of need. He would rescue her from grief, whatever it was, and she would be his.

Her face was ugly with crying, red eyes covered by eyelids that were swollen. The corners of her mouth turned down, her beautiful mouth framed by sad parentheses. The color had run from her cheeks and in its place was none. She had aged, suddenly. If she had seen herself in a mirror, she might have imagined it was because she was unattached. She startled him, he who was the mirror she could not look into to see herself. Her transformation was temporary, he reminded himself.

He told her he had come, even though she didn't know him, because he loved her. Would love her forever. He recognized, he said, the absurdity of his approach, but having seen her and felt what he did, could the ridiculousness of feelings be a reason not to act on them. Wasn't this all we had, inadequate as they were? He told her that he knew one day she would love him, too. He told her he could soothe her pain.

I cannot compare death to words. Death is too great a contrast to life. And love is an invention, but death is not. I was not able to give my father life, though I am unchanging and eternal. And you too will die and blame me. Blame me for having been born. Or you will leave me before you die, saying I have hurt you, shortened your life. Taken your best years. I do not want to take your breath away.

With these words he determined to have her. It was true, her voice was not as mellifluous as he might have wished. But what man could believe her words, words meant, he was sure, only to test him. He had waited forever to meet a woman who might challenge him to appreciate the brevity of life. Her reluctance must be read as mystery, a deception from one whose own creation was exampled in the stories he loved.

She turned from him, racing down the hall, her dress swinging around her legs, jumping at her ankles. Don't leave me he called. Don't leave me. She stopped abruptly and spoke to him from such a distance that he could not really see her face. And he could not hear what she said, her words strangled in a cry that is peculiarly like a laugh. Don't leave me, I too said, then walked into the ballroom.

the *aunt jemima method*
d a r i u s   j a m e s

I am sucking back a Bud in B7, scowling at my reflection in the mirror above the horseshoe bartop, when a buxom, ponylegged White Rasta babe snakes her way through the crowd, positions herself behind me and starts to finger my hair.

"May I feel your dreads?" she asked. Her face was clown white, highlighted by soft lavender pastels. Her eyes crinkled in flirtation.

I didn't even bother to turn around.

Reggae-addled white girls who took the liberty of tangling their sour-smelling fingers in my hair, usually followed the act by a request to buy some "herb"—a substance I neither smoked nor sold (being an outstanding student enrolled in the Alcohol And Hard Narcotics School of Get High). The assumption behind the request so annoyed me, I've been known to bite the person who asked it.

darius james grew up in New Haven and currently lives in New York City. He is the author of *Negrophobia* (St. Marten's Press, 1993).

My hair looked the way it did because I'd broken the teeth of one too many metal sponge-cake cutters in pursuit of the perfect Angela Davis-style afro (circa 1970s), and had vowed never to comb it again in life; not because I had realized while in a pot-induced stupor that the corpse of a former Ethiopian ruler was the one and true God.

Nappy, unkempt hair had its advantages, though. Like the Purple-Assed Baboon, who asserted its studliness by wearing its genitals on its face, I wore mine on my head.

And unless she had a precoital strategy better than her opening gambit, I was in no mood to play *Exotic Other* to her psyche's psychotic sexual mythologies.

Of course, if I *were* in the mood, I'd be more than willing to indulge my own shallow fascinations with "exoticism," and engage, by an implicit mutual consent, in a coupling rife with racist implications. And I'd know that going in (pun intended). Fuck "Jungle Fever" and its myopic, afrocentric idiot's babble.

My dick. My business.

But, as it was, I just wanted to get good and drunk. So without a glance in her direction, I told her she could fondle my hair on the precondition she bought me drinks.

After ordering a round of Buds, she rubbed my head, saying, as if she were Col. Tom Parker rattling a pair of dice in the back room of a Vegas casino, I'd bring her luck.

She told me her name was Maya; then, suddenly, in a conspiratorial whisper, she said she was a strawberry blonde.

I turned around for the first time.

"Who are you kidding? Your hair looks like matted broomstraw."

"No, really. I'll show you. Look."

And right there in the bar, she quickly wiggled her hips, rolling her daisy-patterned underwear down to her ankles. She kicked them under a bar stool and lifted her skirt.

The mound of her cunt was covered with a floss that looked as though it were spun of cotton candy. I smirked.

"_Pink_, huh?"

"Organically grown. None of that pseudo-punk coloring for me!"

"I c'n dig it."

After a few drinks, Maya confessed earlier in the evening she had fought her last fight with her Reggae-musician boyfriend on the Slimelight's dancefloor.

"I'm never going to see him again!" she insisted, pinching her lips. "_Ever!_"

She crossed her arms, pressing them against her bust, and tapped her foot in agitation.

"So what if he tours with Bob Marley!!"

I gently informed her Bob Marley was dead.

"That can't be!" she said. "How can he produce all those albums?!!"

Maya said she was new in town, a recent graduate of Yale. And now that she had broken with her boyfriend, she had nowhere to go.

By this time, it was last call. And B7 had turned into a frenzy of last-minute bedding arrangements. So I invited her to come back to my apartment.

Stumbling drunk, we left the bar.

Resting her head on my shoulder, Maya sang a love song made famous by Marlene Dietrich. She coiled her arm around my waist with her hand snuggled down the front of my pants. As she tugged my cock, her tongue whipped around the shell of my ear.

My hand cupped her ass. I fingered the downy crevice between the cheeks of her buttocks, my fingers working their way across her cotton-candy bush, inching towards the slick folds of her slit.

She squirmed on my finger like an impatient schoolgirl.

Back in my fourth floor walkup, I learned she had grown up in Hawaii and fucked with her tummy. She called them Hula Ummies. She'd plop on top and throttle my cock with her rigorously rotating ass.

This routine lasted less than a week before she was gone, her departure triggered by an episode involving my unpredictably fickle penis and sixteen ounces of flapjack flour.

It began when we dropped some acid I received from a biker who had climbed down from my roof during a rain storm. He'd been sleeping in the plywood penthouse occupied by the neighborhood gluehead during the day.

The biker said the abandoned building where he squatted next door was infested with junkies and he was too tired to fight them off. I offered him warmth and shelter. In exchange, he gave me five hits of four-way blotter acid.

Maya and I dropped the acid.

Swooning in a vibrant daze of Peter-Max psychedelia, we fucked back to back and slid belly-to-belly with a dollop of Vaseline smeared in between. We humped like dogs against the wall and the neighbors heard us howling in the hall. Eventually, Maya climbed on top, my battered penis popped and her ass slowly rolled to a stop.

My cock was still lodged in her cunt. I was pinned beneath her bulk. She wiggled her ass and my cock fell out: *wet, wilted and disinterested.*

She examined my flaccid member in the palm of her hand.

"Dis' muthafuckee am out o' poke an' beans!"

"Excuse me?" I said. "I don't understand white girl negro talk."

Her eyes narrowed into thin slits.

"Well, let me break it down for you then, brutha—*yo' shit is spent!*"

Suddenly, a lightbulb burst into one-hundred watt brilliance above her matted blonde hair. She pressed her hands against my heart with all her weight.

"I'm going to transform you with my magick!" she said. "I'm going to drain off all your fears and free the lusty Dionysian within!"

I was flattened against the mattress, unable to breath. She smelled of sour sweat and bed-grit.

"The Dionysian?" I rasped.

Maya grinned and leapt from the bed.

She took a worn paperback copy of Nietzsche's *The Birth of Tragedy* from my bookcase, skipped into the kitchen and returned with an open box of Aunt Jemima pancake mix.

Pouring the box of pancake powder into a small pile on the floor, she began to stomp her feet like a drunken Flamenco dancer, bellowing like a sick cow. Her feet thudded on the floor with the thunderous rapidity of a drum roll, raising cyclonic swirls of off-white dust.

The acid had reduced my brain to soap suds. I didn't know what was happening. I saw one big titty flip this way and another bigger titty flop that way. Both big titties spun around and around and swung from side to side, all in a gritty cloud of Aunt Jemima pancake mix.

My dick said, *Fuck this crazy-ass bitch*, then shriveled up and disappeared inside my scrotum.

Then Maya started in with Nietzsche.

She took a crystal pendant from around her neck and swung it before my eyes. She read dramatically from the book.

"Under the influence of the narcotic draught," she began, "the slave is a free man."

Her eyes gleamed. Her face twitched lasciviously.

"He feels himself a god, he himself now walks about in enchanted ecstasy, like the gods he saw walking in his dreams!"

Maya tossed the book aside, falling to her knees. She lifted my rumpled cock.

"I want something to put in my mouth."

And wrapped her distinctly negroid-looking lips around the bulb of my penis. She hummed and growled. My cock felt like a wad of bubble gum.

As my cum dribbled on her tongue, I hallucinated thick black waves with gilded edges. Her face fragmented into black squares and shimmering triangles, blowing away in a cloud of pancake mix.

Maya looked up. My cock was limp in her fist.

"It's useless," she concluded. "No mo' poke an' beans."

Two hits of acid and four low-pressure ejaculations later, she was gone.

"sex series (bridge)", *1989-90, by david wojnarowicz. photo courtesy: ppow gallery*

between the inside and the outside

d a v i d   w o j n a r o w i c z

"If I had a dollar to spend for healthcare I'd rather spend it on a baby or innocent person with some defect or illness not of their own responsibility; not some person with aids . . ." says the healthcare official on national television and this is in the middle of an hour-long video of people dying on camera because they can't afford the limited drugs available that might extend their lives and I can't even remember what this official looked like because I reached in through the tv screen and ripped his face in half and I was diagnosed with arc recently and this was after the last few years of losing count of the friends and neighbors who have been dying slow vicious and unnecessary deaths because fags and dykes and junkies are expendable in this country "If you want to stop aids shoot the queers . . ." says the governor

david wojnarowicz, writer, artist, photographer, filmmaker, performance artist and AIDS activist, died of AIDS in 1992. He is the author of *Close to the Knives* and *The Smell of Gasoline*. This text is reprinted with permission of the estate of David Wojnarowicz, and the photograph appears courtesty of PPOW.

of texas on the radio and his press secretary later claims that the governor was only joking and didn't know the microphone was turned on and besides they didn't think it would hurt his chances for re-election anyways and I wake up every morning in this killing machine called america and I'm carrying this rage like a blood-filled egg and there's a thin line between the inside and the outside a thin line between thought and action and that line is simply made up of blood and muscle and bone and I'm waking up more and more from daydreams of tipping amazonian blowdarts in "infected blood" and spitting them at the exposed necklines of certain politicians or government healthcare officials or those thinly disguised walking swastikas that wear religious garments over their murderous intentions or those rabid strangers parading against aids clinics in the nightly news suburbs there's a thin line a very thin line between the inside and the outside and I've been looking all my life at the signs surrounding us in the media or on peoples' lips; the religious types outside st. patricks cathedral shouting to men and women in the gay parade: "you won't be here next year—you'll get aids and die ha ha . . ." and the areas of the u.s.a. where it is possible to murder a man and when brought to trial one only has to say that the victim was a queer and that he tried to touch you and the courts will set you free and the difficulties that a bunch of republican senators have in albany with supporting an anti-violence bill that includes "sexual orientation" as a category of crime victims there's a thin line a very thin line and as each t-cell disappears from my body it's replaced by ten pounds of pressure ten pounds of rage and I focus that rage into non-violent resistance but that focus is starting to slip my hands are beginning to move independent of self-restraint and the egg is starting to crack america seems to understand and accept murder as self-defense against those who would murder other people and it's been murder on a daily basis for eight count them eight long years and we're expected to pay taxes to support this public and social murder and we're expected to quietly and politely make house in this windstorm of murder but I say there's certain politicians that had better increase their security forces and there's religious leaders and healthcare officials that had better get bigger dogs and higher fences and more complex security alarms for their homes and queer-bashers better start doing their work from inside howitzer tanks because the thin line between the inside and the outside is beginning to erode and at the moment I'm a thirty-seven-foot tall one-thousand-one-hundred-and-seventy-two pound man inside this six-foot frame and all I can feel is the pressure all I can feel is the pressure and the need for release.

no matter how much you promise to cook or pay the rent you blew it cauze bill bailey ain't never coming home again

e d v e g a

In the not so merry month of May, when her studies had completely evolved into a drag, and in spite of ample evidence of her love of knowledge and her eventual metamorphosis into a scholar of consequence, Vidamia Farrell, finishing her junior year of high school, once again became as restless as she had for the past five years since her father and mother, but mostly her mother, had finally come to some understanding of how important they each were in her development and agreed it was ethnically beneficial for Vidamia to spend part of the summer with him.

As she stood rigidly inside a quadratic equation and stared at a sky full of nimbusian elephants, she thought again of her father, Billy (The Kid) Farrell. She did not meet her sire, The Kid, William Bailey Farrell, until the age of

ed vega is the pen name of Edgardo Vega Yunqué. Born in Puerto Rico and a resident of New York City, he teaches writing at the New School for Social Reasearch and is the author of *The Comeback, Mendoza's Dreams,* and *Casualty Report.* This piece is adapted from the novel of the same name, to be published by Ballantine Books in 1995.

twelve when she learned that once upon a time he'd sat in the middle of a Vietnamese rice paddy, under a shower of steel, cradling the broken and forever useless body of Vidamia's uncle, Joey Santiago of Rivington Street on the Lower East Side, whom she would never meet since time and space did not allow for such prestidigitation. Billy had cried while he held the eviscerated corpse of his ace, his homeboy, his reefer smoking main man, but did not notice that the drizzle of steel, while it had barely touched his own head, had meticulously erased, by means of a slow leak of what must have been a carefully blended mixture of blood and brain fluid, forever his catalogue of the musical techniques of Thelonius Monk, Bud Powell, Oscar Peterson and other pianists of jazz note; and, which had that aspersion of steel not removed from consciousness the complex knowledge of flatted fifths and improvisational virtuosity which Vidamia's father, Billy Farrell, had, he would have been unable to perform adequately his own rendition of such standards as "Moonlight in Vermont," "April in Paris," "Back Home Again in Indiana," and "Autumn in New York," not because he lacked a geographical metronome, but because that baptismal of steel had neatly severed at the root the middle and pinky fingers of his right hand, rendering him immediately an eight-fingered jazz pianist, a thing more rare than an arctic orchid.

On that occasion, after about an hour, when things calmed down and the shooting became intermittent, as if they were talking about weather, the medics came. Fighting their way through the sticky heat and the soupy stirfry of growing rice, detached limbs and involuntary bowel movements, plus the flies which had come to pay their respects to the dead, they removed Joey from Billy's eight-fingered shock-induced clutch and saw his head not to mention the empty places in his hand and immediately whisked him off in a medivac helicopter.

Back at the hospital while they shaved his skull as prep, they stretched the epidermis of the palm of his right hand over the fist knuckles of the aforementioned AWOL middle and pinky fingers and as if they were doing needlepoint the medical team stitched finely this digital disaster. Not a minute elapsed before they went into his cranium, sealed the brain drain and sewed him up as best they could but not before inserting, where the hole had been, a minute steel plate, which on certain ionospherically hospitable nights, mostly while he was asleep, picked up a country music station in West Virginia, so that at times his battlefield nightmares were accompanied by music more suitable as the soundtrack for moonshiner and revenuer films starring people like Robert Mitchum and his sons. But having failed to scoop up from that rice paddy all the spilled McCoy Tyner, Horace Silver, Dave Brubeck et al., plus the repository of blues, ragtime, dixieland, swing, bop, westcoast and progressive solos of a thousand and one musicians ranging from Blind Lemon Jefferson to Ornette Coleman, they were left wondering why Billy Farrell had nothing to say and simply stared dumbly at the ceiling, every once in a while holding up his right hand, now securely bandaged against infection, and within that mitt of gauze attempted to wiggle those absent digits which at one time, together with the other perfectly matched trio of his gifted right hand, surrounded beautifully intricate melodies as would the hand of a child a delicate and frail spring butterfly, holding it, admiring it briefly and then letting it go and watching it dance lepidopterally away.

For eight months, first there and then back in the States, he sat and stared ahead, seeing but totally blind, looking at his crab hand and not recognizing it. Doctors and counselors and chaplains came to him but none of them apologized for their failure to scoop up the music from that rice paddy and of course having lost, along with the spilled music, temperament, inventiveness and technique. Billy Farrell had only love left and eventually told everyone he was fine and said thank you very much and God bless you and they asked where they should send his full disability check and he told them please send it care of my Grandpa Buck Sanderson in Yonkers, New York, the chaplain has the address.

● ● ●

When Vidamia grew up and found out that other girls were called Gloria, Carmen, Maria, Teresa and not Vidamia, and that if they looked as she did they had last names like Rivera, Rodriguez, Vasquez and Lopez and not Farrell, she demanded to know everything about her father. When her mother resisted by saying it wasn't important she went to her grandmother, Ursula Santiago, who had raised Joey and her mother and no less than one hundred brothers and sisters, it seemed. All Ursula could say was that her father had been in the war with her uncle Joey, that his name was Billy Farrell and he had blond hair and used to live in Yonkers.

"How did they meet? He and my mother, huh?"

"You have to ask your mother that."

"She won't tell me."

"She must have her reasons."

So in the summer of her twelfth year Vidamia set out to find her father by going to Yonkers and looking for every Farrell in the town and by chance running into a policeman by the name of Arnold Tyson who had been in high school with Billy Farrell and in his patrol car drove her to see Maud Farrell, Billy's mother, who was also known as the big, good-looking blonde who tends bar at O'Hanlon's in Mount Vernon.

"Mrs. Farrell, this little girl's looking for Billy," Officer Tyson said, urging her up on a barstool. "Says Billy's her father."

"You wanna ginger ale, honey?" Maud Farrell had said.

"No, thank you," Vidamia had replied.

"What's your name, darling?" Maud Farrell then said, scooping up ice cubes with a glass.

"Vidamia Farrell," said the little Spanish wisp with freckles on her nose as Maud described Vidamia to her friend, Ruby Broadway, also known as the good-looking Negro woman who ran the house, where the firemen went when they grew tired of listening to wives talking about green stamps, color TV's and new skin-care products.

"And you know my son?" Maud said as she set the glass on the gleaming surface of the not yet set up bar.

"No, but I know he's my father. He and my uncle were in the war. My uncle died."

"Could be," Maud Farrell said, looking at Officer Tyson and pouring ginger ale in the glass. "As Irish a face as you'd want. Same shape mouth as Billy. Drink up, honey."

"No, thank you," Vidamia said.

"Look, if I'm gonna be your grandmother, you better do as you're told," Maud said, depositing her formidable bosom on the bar and squinting her eyes like I Love Lucy so that Vidamia was charmed into smiling. "It's free and it'll make your nose tickle."

"Okay," said Vidamia and drank from the glass in little sips, letting the bubbles strike her lips.

And so Maud Farrell became a grandmother to Vidamia and on Saturday afternoons when she was off from O'Hanlon's she fed Vidamia bologna sandwiches and ice cold root beer and slowly brought her carefully in touch with her lineage, explaining through family anecdote, fable and myth that Billy Farrell had indeed been in the war and had suffered a life threatening injury which had left him incapacitated. The Kid, she called him, telling Vidamia he had been so christened in his Yonkers-Mount Vernon boyhood for no apparent reason by his maternal grandfather, Buck Sanderson of banjo playing fame who, it was told, mostly by himself, played on Mississippi River boats and knew a thousand and one tunes which he taught the boy from the time he was one and a half years.

It turned out, Vidamia learned, that Billy had flown from California to New York, staying with his momma's parents, listening to the two of them bickering about everything as he always had in his childhood, but knowing the two were inseparable, the one New York Irish and the other one pure Tennessee mountain with his ever-present banjo which it seemed was the only way he could communicate. He allowed Grandpa Buck to teach him the guitar, letting the big old man hold him while he cried and when he couldn't form a B7, knowing that at one time the chords flowed into his mind complexly, going directly to his left hand, that wonderful rambling and walking left hand, chording and chording, laying it down as if it were a road filled with beautiful landscape, knowing that if he should suddenly die then he would do so with the awareness that he had lived fully; so that after a while when he knew twelve or so chords and could play and sing folk songs such as "The Fox" and "John Henry" and things like that, together with some simple Leadbelly like "Easy Rider," he called his mother Maud, and told her he was going into the city, meaning New York City, and his mother Maud, with the concern only a mother could have, said he should be careful and that if he was starting to get horny there were plenty of girls right in the neighborhood willing to douse his ardor, especially Margie Biancalana, the little Italian girl whose father owned the barber shop and who just last Saturday had said Hi, Mrs. Farrell, how's Billy, or maybe Judy Botnick, who was studying to be a doctor but always liked jazz music and was asking for him, or even Pauline Fitzgerald, although with her you had to worry about catching something because it was rumored that she was handing it out to everyone, and that he was welcome to use her apartment while she was at O'Hanlon's during the day as long as he changed the sheets and straightened up after he was finished because she sometimes got the same way and had men friends because she was still a relatively young woman and that she hoped that he didn't think it was because she hadn't loved his father, may he rest in peace, because she had and still did, or that he wasn't angry now because she was discussing adult matters with him.

"Naw, Ma," he said. "It's nothing like that. Thanks, anyway. I'll be all right. Don't worry."

"That's what you told me last time, you big jerk" big, good-looking Maud said, acting like a mother. "I'll be all right you said, and they shot you full of holes, like they did your father in Harlem, the spic bastards." "I'll be okay, really."

"Billy?" Maud said, her voice starting to break on the phone. "Don't, Ma." "You got enough money?" "Yeah, I'll be back tonight. I'll call you." "I love you, you big son of a bitch."

And like he always did he reminded her of what that made her if he was an s.o.b. and she laughed and said, that's right and don't forget it and then they said good bye and he said good bye to Grandpa Buck and Grandma Maureen and dressed in jeans and a green fatigue jacket and walked down the road across into the Bronx with his long blond hair and beard and took the subway train to Manhattan.

Because what Ursula Santiago hadn't wanted to tell her granddaughter, Vidamia Farrell, was that her father had somehow managed to get himself down to the Lower East Side and over a period of a week, sleeping in parks and in the subway but always calling Maud at O'Hanlon's or at home and telling her that he was fine, utilizing every spare moment in asking one person after the other until he found the Santiagos and came up to their apartment and looking like some lost soul, pale and thin and like the life had been drawn out of his eyes, said he'd been with Joey when he died. Viet Cong grenade, he'd said. Telling them that he and Joey were best friends and Elsa, just fifteen years of age, who had brought him into the house, watching him worshipfully and Ursula knowing that the girl was smitten and the first time she got a chance, she'd go off like a bitch in heat. And that's exactly what had happened.

The Lower East Side had reminded him of Saigon with people talking and he not understanding and the smells so foreign that he had numerous flashbacks of explosions, rapid fire shooting, whining mortars and whirring helicopters but did not run for cover and calmly kept telling people he was looking for Joey Santiago's family, going up and down the street from Houston to Grand Street, talking to junkies and housewives alike, to little kids and Jewish peddlers, pleading with them and showing them a picture of Joey in a green undershirt and his dog tags around his neck until he found Vidamia's mother, Elsa, on her way home from Seward Park High School and she remembered a letter she had received from Joey and a picture he'd sent with him and Billy in it and it was like a dream come true because back then she had fallen in love with the handsome boy and could recognize him even with his beard and the sadness which he now wore and she said you're Billy Farrell, ain't ya and knew that someday she would marry him so went her fantasy so that before they had spoken ten words or taken ten steps there had been an enormous outpouring from Elsa's primed bartholin glands which caused the nylon and cotton fabric which covered her virgin loins to become soaked and fragrant with love.

• • •

Vidamia Farrell sat staring out the window of the Tarrytown prison to which she had been confined by her mother, the one-time Elsa Santiago of Rivington Street in the Warsaw ghetto of Latin America, from which she had emerged victorious through effort and travail to obtain a Ph.D. in psychology; establishing a private practice of psychotherapy cum counseling of marital irregularities and discords and when Vidamia was six years old wed Barry Perez Ferrer, a CPA of considerable art, of whom it was said in big business he could balance and make dance any number of accounts on the head of a financial pin provided you gave him enough musica for tax write-offs; the two of them making money faster than it could be printed and taking this inky currency and investing it every which way in mutual funds, real estate, stocks and municipal bonds so that in twelve years this hyphenated conglomerate of Puerto Rican ingenuity, without much beating around the pubic area, was worth one million cool dollars and affected the life-style of the rich and famous complete with numerous, meaning muchos, Mercedes, not of the Santiago or Perez or Ferrer but of the Benz variety, together with cabin cruisers, multiple homes as well as orgasms, trips to Europe, membership in private clubs and enough plastic pecuniarities to rebuild a small underdeveloped country or even the South Bronx if they so wished which they did not, wishing instead to do good deeds in their own community of Westchester County where it could be more appreciated since it is a well-known fact that truly poor ghetto folks have, among their many flaws, a horrid sense of appreciation. And in any case if the Puerto Ricans which were left behind were going to make anything of themselves they had better do it as Elsa and Barry had, by pulling up on their own bootstraps.

Forgetting, as if culturally lobotomized, that at one time she was a Latin from Manhattan, who with her mother Ursula Santiago shopped on Orchard Street for clothing bargains and on Saturdays accompanied her down to Delancey Street to shop in the market for chicken and chops, listening to her mother say shiken and shops and not being ashamed of her like some people because back then she was proud to be a Puerto Rican like they said and ready to throw down if anyone black, white or oriental got it into their head to be fucking with you; girl, what's wrong with you that you be coming around with your bad self selling tickets; you better dig yourself, homegirl, and don't be sniffing round my man like some stray *perra puta*, know what I mean; cauze if you don't am a teach somethings you ain't never gonna learn in school.

Going to school with Sonia Escobar, Mandy Lugo, Denise Aguayo, Baby Contreras, Daisy Marrero, Carmen Texidor, Hilda Pantoja and Josie Villegas, who became a cop and who would've thought it since she was the baddest of the homegirls and the one who, when they were eleven or twelve, introduced them all to erf, all of them playing hooky one afternoon and lighting up the joint in Carmen Texidor's basement apartment while Carmen's mother, who was the super, was in the hospital giving birth to the twins and all of them getting high and giggling at the slightest little thing and talking about boys and getting hungry and cleaning out the entire kitchen of anything that had the slightest resemblance to food.

And now this little spic-mick making her recall how painful that existence had been and how far she had come from that wretched childhood and how stupid she had been, how utterly romantic she had been, about Billy Farrell and his frayed psyche; how desolate everything had been knowing she would never see her brother Joey again and in later years, when she had the opportunity to be psychoanalyzed, learned how badly she had felt that she did not at all miss Joey or care what had happened to him in Vietnam; that her only concern had been this animal hunger which she felt deep inside of her tiny womb, that void crying out to be filled with this Billy Farrell and who knew, Freud or anybody, what the hell that was about since it could've been that somewhere along the line she'd had sexual designs on her own dead brother.

But back then at fifteen latching on to that fatigued arm as if it were the most natural thing for a girl to do in the middle of Division Street and walking with him, unconcerned by time until they had hit the number streets and the alphabet avenues and found themselves down by the river watching the cars going over the bridges into Brooklyn and her life crying out for him to possess her, to be inside of her and not knowing what the hell that was about since all her homegirls did was talk and none of them had done it yet, not even Mandy Lugo who was a year older than all of them, but feeling all the knowledge inside of her and knowing that she was going to have a child by him and instinctively setting up a nest at Sonia Escobar's apartment in the projects on Avenue D while Sonia's mother was in P.R. and Sonia was supposed to be staying there but didn't want to because she was afraid her stepfather, who was in the merchant marine, was going to come home and try to mess with her like he had tried to do with Sonia's sister, Migdalia, except that Migdalia told him if he kept it up she was going to tell her mother and he said if she did he'd beat the shit out of her.

Migdalia, whose boyfriend was Li'l Louie Puente, who at sixteen already had three bodies, said bet; if he laid a hand on her in anyway she'd wait until he was asleep and she'd take a knife and plunge it into his heart and his stepfather believed her but Sonia wasn't sure she could carry that off and went and stayed at Migdalia's mother-in-law's apartment over in Chelsea and did some baby sitting of Migdalia's two kids from Li'l Louie who was doing a bit in Attica for drugs; going back carefully to the projects each day to water the plants until Elsa came to her with a story about a friend of her dead brother's who had been messed up by the war, and not being from New York had no place to stay and he couldn't stay at our house because you know how mothers are about boys; yeah, a gringo whiteboy, who was all lost and whatnot, not wanting to admit to Sonia how much she had been affected by him and wanting no matter what, to keep him around and Sonia giving her the keys and telling her that if anyone asked she was a cousin, watering the plants.

And then instinctively going up there and setting up house early in the morning when she was supposed to be going to school and one thing leading to another and she couldn't believe she was doing this thing on that big huge bed and feeling like she did, so open and it didn't even hurt much like it was supposed to and after the third day liking the full feeling inside of her and it all came out, the feeling and the words that went with it, crazy stuff that she wasn't sure whether she'd heard on a novella or it was part of the genetic arsenal of being a Latin woman, which she realized later on when she had been educated, was insane; but saying those things with all her heart in English and in Spanish and punctuating it all with *si, si, Vida mia, si.* And after a while he asked her what she was saying and she said nothing, but he insisted and said it sounded like a sweet rose or something like that, she couldn't recall now and she relented and said what? *Vida mia*, what does it mean? And she said it means my life. Like I'm your life or my life belongs to you, or something like that? he asked and she said, not hearing the words anymore, but listening to the life growing inside of her, yes, something like that. And she held him while he cried and said thank you and God bless you, that's the most beautiful thing I ever heard.

By Friday, her mother knew what was going on because all the baby fat and innocence had vanished from Elsa's body and her hips were wider and her breasts fuller and she talked with the confidence of *una mujer en cinta*, which she was, pregnant as a pause from that first emission of love which Billy Farrell shot into her virgin womb. So her mother said what was she going to do with a child to raise at such an early age and of course Elsa denied everything and cried, but her mother knew and they made the best of it and even tried having Billy live with them and that was okay because he contributed mightily to the household income from his disability check and even got a job handing out flyers for an exercise studio down on Wall Street to bring in extra money, but it didn't work and the more pregnant Elsa became the sorrier she was; she cried and carried on and had to drop out of Seward Park High School and was used as an example by wary mothers and overzealous guidance counsellors; so that after a while, she drove Billy away and in front of Ursula Santiago, who knew genuine pain when she encountered it, he apologized for letting Joey die and said whatever they did, if it was a boy please name him Joey.

"And if it's a girl?" Ursula Santiago said.

"Vidamia," Billy Farrell said, looking longingly at Elsa.

"Yeah?' Ursula said, looking at Elsa.

"Yeah, sure," Elsa said looking at the linoleum in the kitchen.

"Here's my number," Billy said. "If you and the baby ever need anything."

And he went out the door back to Grandpa Buck Sanderson's in Yonkers and stayed in his room for five months until Christmas, not talking or playing the guitar, just thinking about life and trying to remember who he was and where he'd been which is all that every customer at O'Hanlon's in Mount Vernon ever heard come out of the big, good-looking blonde who tends bar, about how Vietnam had totally screwed her boy's life, damn the Communist sons of bitches.

One time he snuck down to Grand Street and in the park saw Elsa big as a house, beautiful and happy, talking to some girls with baby strollers and his heart broke some more but he knew it was no use and he couldn't bother her and he just kept walking knowing he might as well have remained with Joey in Nam; not blaming anyone but wishing the hell he was back before the whole thing started. He saw again Miles bringing the horn to his mouth and then back down and saying, through the haze of cigarettes, reefer and whiskey in the club, What you lookin' at! And don't you I'm a pianist, Mr. Davis me. He a pianist, Ball. Ain't that a bitch. How old are you, sixteen? Fourteen? Ooh-whee! Sit down and let me see what you can do. Red, get up for a minute and let this boy stretch. Green Dolphin Street? Yes sir, Mr. Davis.

And when the baby was born and it was a girl, Elsa told her mother she wanted to name her Katherine and her mother asked her what kind of people did she think they were promising the father what the child would be called and then going back on their word like some backstabbing, conniving sneak. Vidamia, just like the father asked and make sure you spell his last name right to the nurse for the birth certificate, because he's a veteran and the government checks things like that for benefits.

"Vidamia? That ain't no name, *Mami*," Elsa said.

"It is now," Ursula Santiago, her mother, said.

skinny takes a walk

k u r t   h o l l a n d e r

The D train rumbles across the bridge. Brooklyn spreads itself on either side, then disappears behind the tunnel. I'm alone in the subway car, with nothing to do but translate the pain-relief and abortion ads from Spanish. Even after that I'm still twelve stops from Coney Island.

When my father took me, my brothers and sister out to Coney Island on our divorced-Sunday trips almost a decade and a half ago, abortion was illegal, there were no ads in Spanish, and the fare was a tenth of what it is now.

I've changed a little, too. Not in height or weight, perhaps, but in subtle, more important ways. For instance, on the ride out I had always been excited and antsy, picking fights with my brothers or swinging from the hanging straps, while coming home I'd nod out of exhaustion. Now, in my maturity,

kurt hollander was the founder and editor of the *Portable Lower East Side* from 1983 to 1994. He is a writer of fiction, art criticism, film scripts and is a literary translator. He is also the editor of *Poliester*, a contemporary art magazine of the Americas. He divides his time between Mexico City and New York City.

I can sit still throughout the whole trip, even though I'm both tired and anxious.

I am always tired these days, even though I sleep almost twelve hours a night, plus the occasional afternoon nap. People tell me it's sick to sleep that much, and they tell me I must be depressed. I've always slept that much and I don't believe that I have always been depressed. Sleep is something I like, something I'm good at, and it only makes me anxious when people keep telling me it's unhealthy.

This morning, because I wanted to prove that my sleeping habits don't automatically spell depression, or that early risers can also be depressed, I got up at eight o'clock after only seven hours of sleep. Once awake, however, I realized that I had nothing to do, nothing that required my presence. I decided to take a trip.

The subway pulls into the Brighton Beach stop and I get off, into the wintery wind of February. I walk down Warbash Walk, grey housing projects flanking me on all sides. Apart from the monolithic buildings, the whole controlled community seems so toy-like. Toy plots of grass, toy playgrounds, toy-sized old people walking hurriedly, nervously past.

My grandparents had lived in these co-op projects for the last quarter of their years. They liked living here, they felt secure being surrounded by people exactly like themselves—old, Jewish, tiny. After they completely shrunk away from the land of the living, my father had moved into their apartment. My father is still big and brawny, but, if he stays here long enough, he's sure to start shrinking away, too.

My father will be glad to see me. We haven't seen each other in months. I stand in front of his door. I picture sitting there for an hour or two, listening to my father lecture on the infinite possibilities of life. Infinite possibilities within the confines of a controlled community.

I get back in the elevator and return to the street, dispirited. I walk toward the beach, just three blocks away. Few people are on the street at this hour, and only a couple of couples are promenading on the boardwalk.

Passing beneath the boardwalk, I notice shadows cast from people behind me. They are close behind, also walking toward the water, but I don't turn around to see who they are. If I turned around they might think I was going to try something—the people out here, especially the senior citizens, are paranoid. I don't want to scare anyone more than is necessary.

If these aren't senior citizens behind me, but are actually the kind of people the senior citizens are afraid of, then I don't want them to think I'm nervous or afraid. That would only incite them further. Although, if they are those kind of people. . . .

Walking through these logical possibilities, I'm startled by loud, human-generated squawks coming from behind me. I stiffen but keep walking, the sand slowing my steps. I am almost out from under the boardwalk when the squawks sound again, closer this time. And then, as if in answer, more squawks come from in front of me. I'm surrounded.

The second set of squawks had come from the other side of the bathhouse. I round the corner. There are five of them, wearing only bathing suits and swimming caps on this cold day, all old enough to be my grandparents. They're a little taken aback when they see me, shivering within my six layers of clothes, turn the corner, but then the squawkers behind me, two more senior citizens, come around the beach house and join them. They slap each other on the back and laugh deeply and with great gusto. I'm impressed by their energy and vitality, neither of which I, in the thick of my young years, possess. As I make my way away, unnoticed, I realize who they must be—the Seagull Club, Coney Island's answer to the Waspish Polar Bears.

Halfway to the water I turn around and look back. Behind the beach house is the boardwalk, dividing the sand from the land, and rising above that, the amusement park. The parachute drop is still there, tall, skinny, neglected, closed down for as long as I can remember. The Cyclone has been shut down again, but the smaller rides that have no worldwide reputation and are cheaper to insure are still running.

In its present state, with its mix of Russians, Puerto Ricans, tourists, old-timers, the poor and poorer, its crumbling facades and expensive rides, its forgotten glory as America's number two seaside resort, Coney Island is just right for my wintery entertainment.

But lately I've begun to feel that I'm not worth entertaining. I've lived with myself now for twenty-eight years and I'm getting very bored. I no longer keep up a running interior dialogue, and the whiny voices in my head irritate the fuck out of me with their recriminations and litanies of defeat.

I turn away and walk to the ocean's edge, watching the water do what it does—forwards, backwards, up, down, sluggishly. A snippet of someone's poem surfaces:

My old boat goes round on a crutch
And doesn't get underway.
It's the time of the year
And the time of the day.

I walk along the scummy edge of the sea, avoiding the hypodermics and plastic tampon cartridges, mumbling again and again, "It's the time of the year/And the time of the day."

When the lines slur into an indistinguishable mumble, I close my eyes and begin to count my steps. In the city, on relatively narrow sidewalks, I've managed to take twenty-five steps with my eyes closed. Breaking a rib against a parking meter put me off of this kind of sensory deprivation experiment for a while, but out here on the beach there aren't any meters or other obstacles.

7. 8. 9. Louder than any rush-hour traffic, the crash and hiss of the waves and the wind fills my ears. 13. 14. I've lost all sense of direction. I might be just about to step into the water, but I wouldn't care if I got my dirty sneakers wet.

17. 18. 19. It's usually around twenty steps with my eyes closed that the sense of forward motion falls away. In my temporary blindness I begin to feel as if I'm not moving, as if walking is no longer locomotion and my steps aren't adding up to distance traveled. Time, not space, is elapsing.

25. 26. 27. My sole tie to reality are the numbers spoken aloud, they're my only destination.

30. 31. These are more steps than I had ever taken. I'm walking into virgin territory. I can go on forever.

"This is a rip-off!"

I stumble, opening my eyes and throwing out my arms. I had been heading toward the boardwalk. With a few more steps I could have been sure of walking right into one of the supporting beams.

There is no one near me.

"If you come to Coney Island you're going to get ripped off, it's that simple."

The voice, loud and metallic, is coming from on top of the boardwalk, almost directly above me. I jump up, grab onto the boardwalk and pull my head over the edge. A young white guy with a bright red bowtie is standing a few feet away, a megaphone in his hand.

"This ain't no exception—we're going to rip you off, too. But it's only a $3 rip-off. And for that measley bit of money you get to see the wonders of The Two-Faced Man, of Cyrano, the man who can hammer nails up his nose, and of Sheena the Shark Lady, all this and more, right here in the Coney Island Fun House."

This young kid ain't a real barker. He's too clean cut, too peppy. He even seems to be enjoying himself. Real barkers are misanthropic, slimy old crooks who wear ostentatious suits to hide their poverty and their flask of rotgut.

I didn't like this kid's casual allusion to getting ripped off here, either. He was using the poverty and violence of this neighborhood as a tourist advertisement. Sure, everything out here was and continues to be a swindle, a seaside sham. But there's always been real life going on here, too.

As a kid growing up in Williamsburg, my father had come out here every weekend. It was his stomping ground. He knew the local characters, the old barkers and even some of the freaks—real genetic freaks, not like the freak-impersonators this kid was trying to palm off on the tourists.

My father had befriended the pinhead girls, taking them for rides on the roller coasters. And while the pinheads were being thrown around the turns and squashed against the back of their seats, screaming and moaning, my father would reach across and squeeze their breasts.

I was always impressed with my father for having done such an unfatherly thing. Although older now than my father was then, I haven't yet squeezed the tip of a pinhead's breast. Nor is it likely that I ever will. In fact, the number of things like that that I will not do in my lifetime far outweighs the number of things I will.

It seems as if all the adventures had been used up by the time I came on the scene, and what's left is always already insignificant when seen against all that has been. This outing won't change anything. I realize that, I see it all too well, and so I take my leave of the Fun House, the boardwalk, and of Coney Island herself.